CITY OF GOLD

'My Lord Brouckner and Sir Edmund Pooly carried me down into the hold of the India ship, and there did show me the greatest wealth lie in confusion that a man can see in the world. Pepper scattered through every chink, you trod upon it; and in cloves and nutmegs I walked above the knees; whole rooms full. And silk in bales . . . as noble a sight as ever I saw in my life.'

Pepys' *Diary*

' . . . that common receptacle of all abandoned and undone men, the East Indies.'

William Hickey

'The man who has left behind him a great number of works, in temples, bridges, reservoirs and caravanserais, for the public good, does not die.'

Sheik Sadee

CITY OF GOLD

The Biography of Bombay

GILLIAN TINDALL

faber and faber

This edition first published in 2010
by Faber and Faber Ltd
Bloomsbury House, 74–77 Great Russell Street
London WC1B 3DA

A CIP record for this book is available from the British Library

ISBN 978-0-571-25897-0

Contents

Acknowledgements

The study of Bombay would have been impossible for me were it not that copious documentation is available in this country. My thanks in this respect are due first and foremost to the staff of the India Office Library, especially to Dr Brigid Allen for some research assistance and to Mrs Pauline Rohatki for her help with pictorial material. Also to the staff of the London Library, especially to Douglas Matthews, and to Ms Mary Thatcher and her staff of the Centre for South Asian Studies in Cambridge.

Other academic help and advice have been provided by Professor Peter Marshall of Kings College, London, Professor John Carey of Merton College, Oxford, and Professor Donald J. Olsen of Vassar, Dr George Michell, Dr Robert Skelton and by Dr Gavin Stamp. To all these, my thanks – and also and especially to Dr V.S. Pramar of the MS University, Baroda, whose unique work on the houses of Gujerat provided me with some important markers in an otherwise uncharted field.

Many thanks, also, for incidental help and the generous loan of books, to the following former inhabitants of Bombay: Mr and Mrs W. Olins, Mr and Mrs John Hewitt, Mr and Mrs V. Grenfell, and to Christopher Taylor for his invaluable street maps. To Mrs P.A. Pank also, for her help in the production of map-work for the book, and to T.R. Fyvel and the *Jewish Chronicle* Library for information on Indian Jewry.

So many people in Bombay have been generous to me with their time, advice and interest that their names read like a roll-call of the many different communities within that city. I am wary of the traditional writer's acknowledgement to the person 'without whom this book would not have been written', but it is literally true that I would have found research in Bombay far more difficult without Fr. John Correa-Afonso SJ of St Xavier's College, who so kindly made available to me the resources of the Heras Institute, including material unavailable anywhere else, and who was also generous with his personal support and interest. My especial thanks also to Professor and Mrs Rustum Choksi and their family, Mr and Mrs H.M. Servai and their family, to Rafique Baghdadi, and to Foy Nissen of the British Council who, among many other kindnesses and the taking of many photographs, read this book for me in manuscript and corrected a number of errors.

My gratitude, then, to these and to all the other people who told me things I needed to know or arranged for me to see places I needed to see or introduced me to others I needed to meet and in general, by introducing me to present-day Bombay, helped to illuminate its past. To Admiral R. Gandhi of the Indian Navy and his staff at the headquarters of the Bombay Marine, and to Mr K.J. Taraporewalla of the Bombay Port Trust. To Dr M.D. David of Wilson College, Dr N.S. Gorekhar of the Ajuman-e-Islam, Dr S.C. Misra the MS University, of Baroda, and his staff, Dr Kumud Mehta, Dr Cynthia Deshmukh, Mr S. Rege of Siddharth College, D.B. Kamble of the Scottish Mission Schools. To Minoo Chhoi, his cousin Mr Jamshed Jeejeebhoy and to Mrs Perin Jeejeebhoy; to Mr S.K.J. Mody and Mr J.K.J. Mody, Mr K.H. Madon and Mr R.A. Davierwala; to John A. Soloman of the Shaare Rason Synagogue, the Director and staff of the Haffkine Institute, Mr A.C. Eapen of the Bhabha Atomic Research Centre and his family, Vijay Merchant of the Hindoostan Mills, Mr A. Rogay and family, Mr B.J. Munsiff, Miss Jer Jussawalla. Also to friends of my husband and myself who took an interest in my work, particularly to Mr Govind Advani and his family, Dr Vashu Mehta and her family, Mr and Mrs G. da Cunha, Mr and Mrs A. Gore, Mr and Mrs Sument Patel, Dr V.C. Talwalker and his family and to Noella Pinto and her family.

I should also like to thank Nissim Ezekiel, of the Indian PEN Club, for his permission to quote from his poem *Island*, and K.D. Katrak for permission to quote from his poem *Malabar Hill*.

And final thanks, as always, to my husband, Dr R.G. Lansown, who took a number of the photos reproduced in this book. He also introduced me to India in the first place.

Picture Acknowledgements

I am indebted to Fr. John Correa-Afonso of the Heras Institute for permission to reproduce nos. 1, 2, 3, 5, 9, 13 and 19; to the India Office Library for nos. 10, 20, 29, 35 and the jacket material; Mr S.K.J. Mody for nos. 8, 21, 26, 30, 36 and 39; to the Dr Bhau Daji Lad Museum (Victoria and Albert Museum, Bombay) for nos. 6, 15 and 18, and to Mr Pheroz Madon who made the copies for me; to Mr S.S. Rege for no.37 and Mr Gerald Cobbe for no.11.

Photos nos. 7, 16, 17, 27, 31, 32, 33 and 41 were taken by Mr Foy Nissen. Nos. 4, 12, 14, 25, 34, 38 and 40 were taken by Dr R.G. Lansdown. Nos. 22, 23 and 24 were taken by myself.

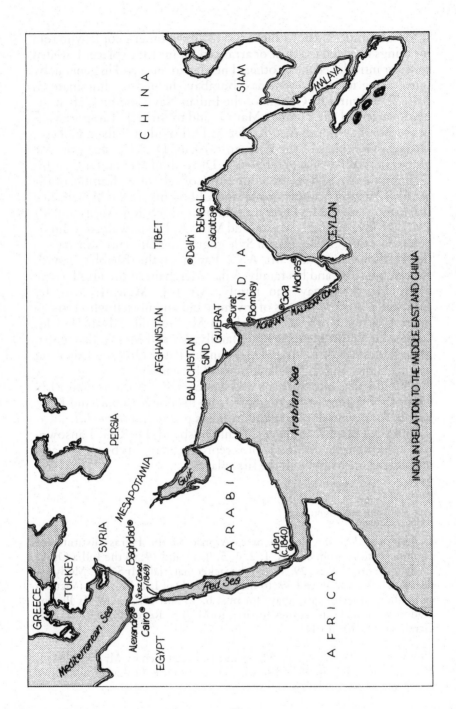

INDIA IN RELATION TO THE MIDDLE EAST AND CHINA

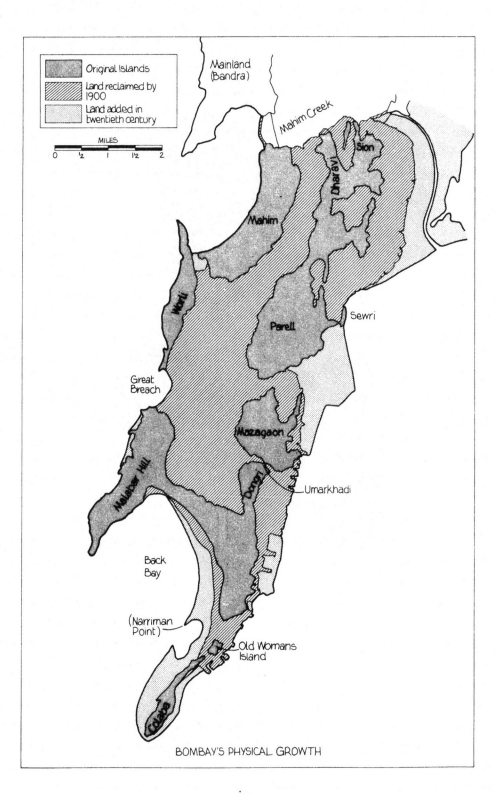

MILES

Original Islands
Land reclaimed by 1900
Land added in twentieth century

Mainland (Bandra)

Mahim Creek

Sion

Dharavi

Mahim

Worli

Parell

Sewri

Great Breach

Malabar Hill

Mazagaon

Dongri

Umarkhadi

Back Bay

(Narriman Point)

Old Womans Island

Colaba

BOMBAY'S PHYSICAL GROWTH

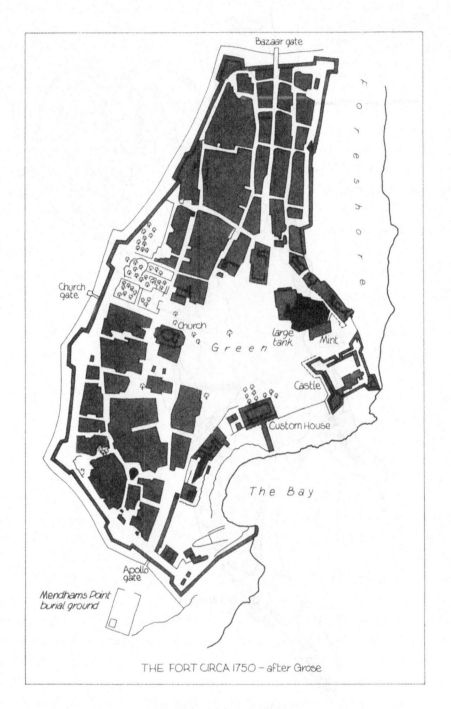

Bazaar gate

F o r e s h o r e

Church gate

Church

Green

large tank

Mint

Castle

Custom House

The Bay

Apollo gate

Mendhams Point burial ground

THE FORT CIRCA 1750 – after Grose

x

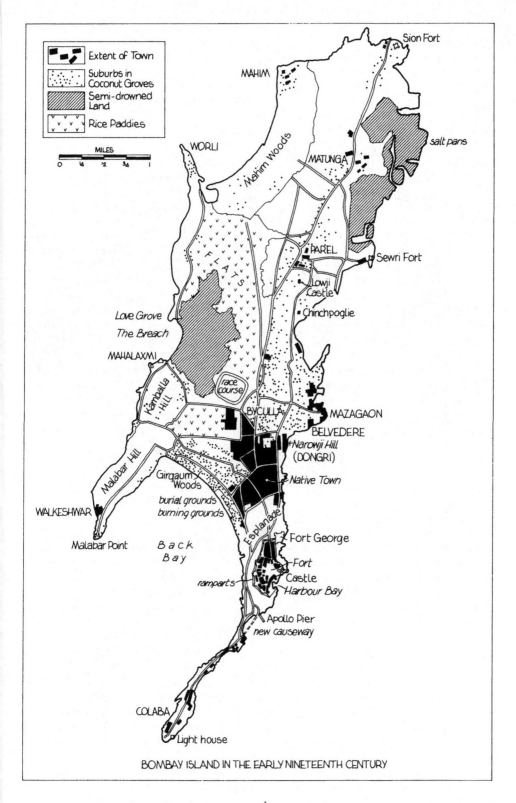

Extent of Town
Suburbs in Coconut Groves
Semi-drowned Land
Rice Paddies

MILES
0   ¼   ½   ¾   1

Sion Fort

MAHIM

salt pans

WORLI

Mahim Woods

MATUNGA

PAREL

Sewri Fort

Lowji Castle

Chinchpoglie

Love Grove
The Breach

MAHALAXMI

FLATS

race course

Kamballa Hill

BYCULLA

MAZAGAON

BELVEDERE

Narowji Hill
(DONGRI)

Native Town

Malabar Hill

Girgaum Woods

burial grounds
burning grounds

WALKESHWAR

Esplanade

Malabar Point

Back Bay

Fort George

Fort
Castle
Harbour Bay

ramparts

Apollo Pier
new causeway

COLABA

Light house

BOMBAY ISLAND IN THE EARLY NINETEENTH CENTURY

xi

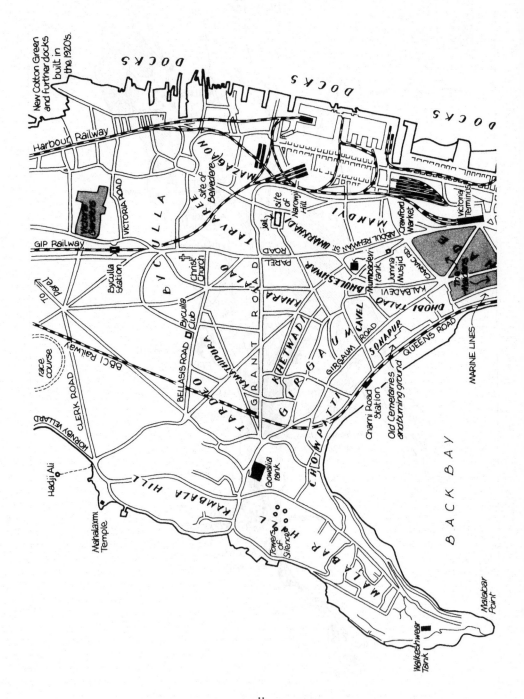

New Cotton Green and further docks built in the 1920s.

DOCKS

DOCKS

DOCKS

Harbour Railway

MAZAGON

Site of Belvedere

GIP Railway

Victoria Gardens

VICTORIA ROAD

BYCULLA

Byculla Station

TARWADI

Christ Church

Byculla Club

Narowji Hill

jail

site of

MANDVI

Crawford Market

Victoria Terminus

ABDUL REHMAN ST UMBRKHADI

PAREL ROAD

KHARA TALAO

Mumbadevi tank

Kalbadevi

Junna Musjid

KALBADEVI

Mumbadevi

BHULESHWAR

DHOBI TALAO

to Parel

BELLASIS ROAD

TARDEO

MATUNGHA

GRANT ROAD

KHETWADI

GIRGAUM

CAVEL

Girgaum Road

SONAPUR

Charni Road Station

Old Cemetaries and burning ground

QUEENS ROAD

MARINE LINES

race course

CLERK ROAD

BBCI Railway

HORNBY VELLARD

Hadji Ali

Mahalaxmi Temple

KAMBALA HILL

Gowalia tank

CHOWPATTY

MALABAR HILL

Tower of Silence

BACK BAY

Walkeshwar Tank

Malabar Point

xii

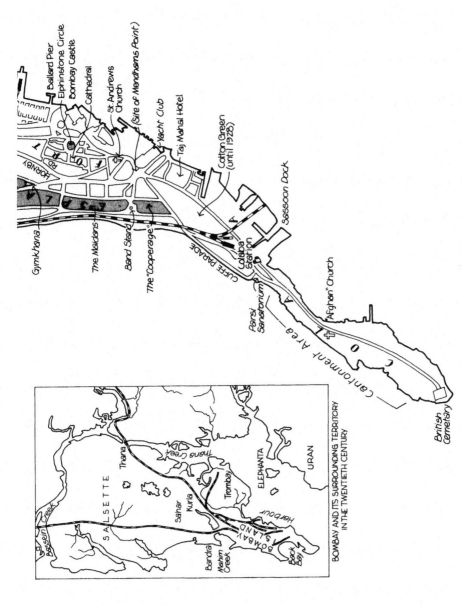

Ballard Pier
Elphinstone Circle
Bombay Castle
Cathedral
St. Andrews Church
(Site of Mendhams Point)
Yacht Club
Taj Mahal Hotel
Cotton Green (until 1926)
Sassoon Dock
HORNBY RD.
Gymkhana
The Maidans
Band Stand
The "Cooperage"
CUFFE PARADE
Colaba Station
Parsi Sanatorium
"Afghan" Church
Cantonment Area
British Cemetery

CENTRAL AND SOUTHERN BOMBAY IN THE EARLY TWENTIETH CENTURY

Bassein Creek
SALSETTE
Thana
Thana Creek
Sahar
Kurla
Trombay
ELEPHANTA
URAN
Bandra
Mahim Creek
BOMBAY ISLAND
Back Bay
HARBOUR

BOMBAY AND ITS SURROUNDING TERRITORY IN THE TWENTIETH CENTURY

Preface

'The City of Gold' is two places. It is, firstly, the city to which people come hoping to make their fortune, and have been coming with that in mind for three hundred years. Great fortunes have, indeed, been made there. But in the search for gold ('the great Indian lottery' as it was known to early British settlers) many have died. For a hundred years, from 1766 to 1866, their bodies were laid in a place known as Sonapur, which also means 'the city of gold' since, according to an Indian saying, to die is to be turned into gold.

This book is about those who sought gold, and those who found it in one form or another, and about the physical creation they left behind them.

Gillian Tindall

I *Arrivals*

Unsuitable for song as well as sense
the island flowers into slums
and skyscrapers....
> Nissim Ezekiel, *Island*

Thus Bombay, in the mind of one of its eight million inhabitants. An inhabitant who, by the very fact of belonging to a special, 'untypical' minority, is typical of a city which has been, from the start, one of the meeting points of the world.

Like London, like Paris or New York or pre-war Alexandria, Bombay contains not just many different social worlds but whole solar systems of different societies moving separately and intricately over the same territory. Ever since its insignificant and hesitant beginnings it has acted as a draw for people of so many races and languages, Indian, Middle Eastern and European, that there is no one tongue in general use there. For a while the largest city east of Suez till you came to Tokyo, and the largest in the British Empire after London, Bombay has always just missed being a world capital. Today it is, like all Indian cities in western eyes, ramshackle, disorganised, apparently in need of urgent social first aid. Yet in comparison with Bombay many more illustrious western national or federal capitals seem like small towns expressed in a grandiose manner – self-regarding, provincial, fossilised in one particular period or rôle; and others seem to have passed their prime and are losing their *raison d'être*, like old hedgerows growing out, hollowing at the centre. But Bombay lives.

Bombay, the capital of the state of Maharastra and the chief city of western India, is essentially a market place and counting house. A minor trading post four centuries ago under the Portuguese, it has retained that character throughout its other metamorphoses; still, today, it has the largest cloth market in the world, and over 40 per cent of India's maritime trade passes through its docks. For it owed its original development as a trading place partly to its quality as a natural harbour, and though its one original sheltered bay has long been swallowed in vast dockyards its character as a world port has been retained – in a period when the London docks, on which those of Bombay were modelled, are grass-grown relics; and those of New York, that Other Island which Bombay also resembles physically, are a pathetic vestige of their former selves. Tonnage through the port of Bombay is, by contrast, on the increase, and more refitting is done there now than anywhere else in the world. Currently a new container-port is being built on the far side of the bay. In Bombay – and this is a theme to which one returns again and again in this city – the past continues not only to be but also to thrive, co-existing chaotically but apparently profitably with more recent developments.

The same pattern is found in its rôle as a manufacturing city. For just as nineteenth-century Bombay came to mirror London in its banking-and-office function, so at the same time, and unlike London, it developed as a manufacturing city in its own right. By the 1880s the clear, hot skies of Bombay were being polluted with a smoke that might have been imported from Bradford or Oldham, issuing from tall chimneys that in some cases *had* been brought, brick by ochre brick, from Home. Today, when the chimneys of Manchester's satellite cotton towns are going or gone, and the mills stand empty, part of the silent process of Britain's decline as an industrial power, the mills of Bombay work on round the clock. 'We don't actually need to have mills within the city any more,' a Bombay manufacturer said to me in the late 1970s. 'Modern transport methods make this unnecessary: it's unhealthy, and it brings more and more people flooding into the city for work with all the problems that creates. But the mills are here: they stay. India is like that. Nothing is ever changed; we just add something else to what is there already.'

In its present population density and growth rate Bombay thus recalls the past of European cities rather than their present. (The population has nearly quadrupled in the last four decades, and the density, at over 100,000 per square mile, is one of the highest in the world.) The population of London has been falling slightly for decades; even her suburban growth was largely completed before the Second World War. Paris and other continental cities are still undergoing considerable suburban expansion, but this is to a very large extent a matter of reducing population density within the town by displacing the people from the centre to the outskirts. Such are the patterns of twentieth-century western affluence and concepts of town planning. But in India the general affluence is absent, and though some of the concepts of town planning are there they tend to be borrowed western concepts which have little reference to the realities of Indian life. There is, in any case, not much of a social mechanism for putting such ideas into practice effectively. Thus the unrestricted growth of Bombay continues and continues; it develops organically, by a monstrous yet natural means, as London and Manchester did in the past but do no longer. The urban stain spreads and spreads, engulfing older villages and suburban settlements, driving back the palm trees, smothering once-pleasant bungalows with the fumes from chemical works, scattering the shores of creeks with shanty-towns and polluting their waters with human existence at its poorest. It makes you think of Cobbett's 'Great Wen' and the anarchic evils of early industrialisation, which in the West have been abolished or assimilated. And yet to see it in these terms is already to fall into a sentimental and peculiarly British trap – that of thinking of industry and its concomitant urban growth as something inherently bad, something that menaces 'natural living'. On the contrary, industry is the life-blood of a city or a country, and urban growth is an index – if a crude one – of a kind of essential health and vigour.

Calcutta grows also and, like Bombay, its population is continually swollen by the addition of the rural poor seeking work in the city, but the pressure on Calcutta is in some respects less because the city is less prosperous. Calcutta, the one-time imperial capital, is today the economically depressed capital of a state, Bengal, whose fertility and prosperity have been declining for decades and are still declining. In contrast, many of the problems of present-day Bombay are directly attributable to her economic strength; this is a simple but fundamental point usually overlooked by urban commentators raised in the enduring William Morris-cum-Fabian tradition of social observation. If Bombay had not continued commercially prosperous, if engineering works and petrochemical plants had not been added in this century to its older textile industry, if it did not have its own off-coast oil-field ('Bombay High') and newly built refineries on adjacent coastal sites, then it would not have remained such a mecca for in-coming peoples, seeking work, seeking money, seeking life itself in an escape from the grinding, near-static poverty of India's rural heartlands. And this 'flood' has been coming, and swelling the town, for a hundred years already: even the image of it has remained

19

constant – that of a potentially dangerous 'encroaching tide' of humanity, 'swamping' the city and its amenities. The true point, that growth has been the essential characteristic of the city from its beginning, is persistently missed. As one modern commentator more astute than most has written,

> The image used [is] of a great, irrational movement that was beyond control, even though it was precisely the growth of income in the city which promoted its population expansion . . . Attempts to look at Bombay as an instrument for the economic development of India are rarely made at all. More often – despite its many relative advantages in comparison with other Indian cities – it is seen as an appalling welfare problem for which the only remedies are, if not the dissolution of the city, then its radical curtailment . . . The paradox remains – India is too poor to become richer; the more dynamic and growth orientated the economy of Greater Bombay becomes, the worse its condition.
> (Nigel Harris, *Economic Development, Cities and Planning: Bombay*)

Such indeed was the traditional paradox and problem of the European commercial meccas of the nineteenth century: that squalor and prosperity seemed to increase in direct proportion to one another. However justified the present-day critics of Bombay may be in some respects, they seem, like their counterparts in nineteenth-century Britain, to lack a basic awareness of how a town functions. They are imbued with a general anti-urbanism which hardly makes them the most perceptive of commentators. In contrast, many of the less-educated citizens of Bombay, not having been brought up on the received opinion that the City is Evil, think it a fine place, where a lot goes on and there are chances for all and one can put up with dirt and overcrowding for a stake in the place. 'Ah, Bombay!' said one businessman yearningly to me: 'You can almost smell the money in the streets there.' To him it really was a city of gold. And even if not much of this gold comes directly the way of most of the people who actually live in the streets, the general prosperity of the place holds over them a kind of minimal economic umbrella which, in a rural area, is simply lacking. In the countryside, if your crops fail you are likely to die. In the metropolis, if one dodge for scraping a living fails, at least there are many others to be explored, including lucrative begging. There is wretched poverty in Bombay: but it is not hopeless poverty.

Other present-day observers, wanting to convey to the

unimpressed outsider the glamour which Bombay holds for many incomers, speak in tones of bemused admiration of its thriving film industry: it is the centre of Hindi film-making, an extraordinary insulated eastern Hollywood populated by stars still more legendary than those of California in the thirties and forties. As you trundle your push-barrow or banana cart, or hawk your vegetables or cigarettes or peanuts from some noisy street-corner, it is nice to know you are living almost next-door to such immortals: you even see them sometimes, getting in or out of cars and throwing their weight about in the proper manner.

> Bright and tempting breezes
> flow across the island,
> separating past from future . . .
> (Island)

But perhaps it is time to leave this subject for the moment and take a walk across this island, in search of the slums and skyscrapers and all the other flowers of urban compost, the stratified deposit of history.

Today, most visitors arrive in Bombay for the first time through its back entry – the long, desultory road in from both the brand new international Sahar airport and the older, ramshackle one in the northern suburb of Santa Cruz, the 'Sacred Cross' of Portuguese days. All Bombay's suburbs lie to the north, for on the west, the south and the east the island-city is surrounded by sea: it is only the northern reaches, therefore, that stretch out and out, mile after mile of sordid but living sprawl. Inward-bound from the airport there are at first scattered palm trees, and glimpses of blue mountains, and patches of low-lying field in a suspiciously virulent green, but these are already interspersed with cement apartment blocks, built only a few years back but stained and crumbling in the remorseless climate. The unwary western visitor, with his eyes adjusted to European or North American standards, wonders if these are some of the Indian slums he has read about – until suddenly the blocks are replaced by a patch of waste ground on which has been spawned an indescribable agglomeration of mud-huts, black against the sun, built one upon another, roofed with rush matting, rags, beaten out tin-cans, sheets of dirty plastic or anything else that has come to hand, and pullulating with human and animal life. *These* are the true slums, the first sight of which is an unforgettable experience. The traveller, recoiling, hastily adjusts his sights, and realises that the

21

dreary blocks, with their fungus stains and their festooned washing, are on the contrary decent lower-middle-class housing.

In recent years official attempts have been made to remove the shanties from the actual verge of the main road, but perpetual vigilance is required: shanty-towns grow of their own volition, seemingly overnight, on any unguarded scrap of land. Sometimes they remain there for many years, acquiring the patina, the character and even the tiled roofs of the villages that they really are. They cling to the blackened shores of polluted creeks, the occupants using the waters as their only domestic supply and contributing their sewage to the shoreline slime. Sometimes the shacks cluster like a vegetable growth against some more solid building or focal point. For a number of years a colony in full sight of the road from the airport nestled beneath the legs of an enormous hoarding which declared: 'Your Income Tax Inspector is your Friend – Trust and Confide in him'. Another suppurated peacefully in the shadow of a huge film-poster, from which a changing but constant repertoire of celluloid gods and goddesses gazed outwards, almond-eyed and swollen-breasted, at the passing cars, as uninterested in the humble life at their feet as temple gods are in the crowds before their shrines. When the cars stop at traffic lights, the small, almost naked children of the shanties come skipping and hopping dangerously between them to beg insistently at the windows. By the time he reaches Mahim Causeway, where the road curves over a substantial and permanently odorous creek before entering the dusty, booth-lined main road of Bombay itself, the visitor is apt to be feeling queasy, intimidated and culture-shocked.

How much better to arrive, as travellers did in every era before our own, at the other, southern end of the island. Here, at Apollo Bunder,* with the original deep harbour on the right, settlers for Bombay have been landing since Portuguese days and indeed long before: the Island, or rather cluster of islands (see Chapter II), is thought to have been the 'Heptanesia' of the Greek cosmographer Ptolemy, though the name Apollo Bunder is nothing to do with the Greeks who explored this far into the unknown lands of the sun. It is a corruption of *palav*, misheard by British ears with a classical education, and relates rather to native fishing grounds or to local vegetation. But the name of the sun-god is a good one for that point, for it remains today a fine place to stand in the evening breeze when the light ebbs minute by minute from the sky, while the dubious

---

* Bunder, or Bandar: jetty, landing place.

fudge-coloured waters wash at the steps below where fishing boats are still moored.

The other name for Apollo Bunder is 'The Gateway to India', since in 1927 a rather grand archway, something between the Arc de Triomphe in Paris and a segment of a Moorish palace, was erected on the sea-front at this point to commemorate the visit to India of George V and his Queen in 1911. This last and indeed belated imperial monument, which is often assumed to be much older, has spent much of the time since Independence wired across – not to prevent kings and other Britishers returning through it, but to stop the street dwellers of Bombay from selecting it as a suitable camping place.

Today's few passenger liners tie up at Ballard Pier, half a mile to the north, but for hundreds of years Apollo Pier, or the succession of jetties at that place which preceded it, was the spot where passengers were brought in Bunder boats to disembark while the ships that had carried them rode at anchor in the bay. What did these travellers see?

Eighteenth-century views of Bombay show a fine vista of mountains apparently right on top of the shore: surveying the same terrain today, attempting to perceive its natural contours under the urban mass that now covers it, one does not know how much to allow for eighteenth-century picturesque licence (the same that described the Lake District in terms of the Alps) and how much for the fact that some at least of Bombay's hills have been physically removed. The travellers of the eighteenth and early nineteenth centuries, before the major part of the transformation took place, commented enthusiastically, for the most part, on the shoreline of low, white buildings set amid palm trees which met their sea-wearied eyes (extremely sea-wearied, in the days when the voyage from Europe round the Cape still took over six months). But not all were as ravished by the sight as the anonymous writer in the *Asiatic Journal* for summer 1838 – the very year, by chance or otherwise, when the first steamships made the journey to Bombay via the Mediterranean, Suez and Aden:

> Bombay harbour presents one of the most splendid landscapes imaginable. The voyager visiting India for the first time, on nearing the superb amphitheatre, whose wood-crowned heights and rocky terraces, bright promontaries and gem-like islands, are reflected in the broad blue sea, experiences none of the disappointment which is felt by all lovers of the picturesque on approaching the low, flat coast of Bengal with its stunted

jungle. A heavy line of hills forms a beautiful outline upon the bright and sunny sky; foliage of the richest hues clothes the sides and summits of these towering eminences, while below, the fortress intermingled with fine trees and wharves running out into the sea present altogether an imposing spectacle on which the eye delights to dwell.

Leaving aside the wharves, with their suggestion of mundanity and the defiling presence of Trade, that major ambiguous fact of Victorian existence, it might be Paradise itself that is so described. Even more enthusiastic was Mrs Postans, writing the following year. For her, 'the pale purple Ghauts, towering higher and higher, in pikes of varied form, their lofty summits dim in the misty distance, blending with the soft haze of a tropic sky, form a picture which fascinates the eye, and spell-binds the imagination as completely as it baffles the power of language to portray'. One should add that Mrs Postans was a keen observer who, though prone to flights of poetry, was not often at a loss for words.

But not all visitors were so impressed; there were many who regarded the approach to Calcutta, in Bengal, as much more imposing. (The rivalry between these two great outposts of England is another of those themes which crop up again and again in Bombay's story.) Here is Emma Roberts, another of the intrepid Victorian lady travellers, and one of the first to take advantage of the new steamship route:

> The bunder, or pier, where passengers disembark upon their arrival in Bombay, though well-built and convenient, offers a strong contrast to the splendours of Chandpaul Ghaut in Calcutta . . . There is nothing to indicate the wealth or the importance of the Presidency to be seen at a glance; the Scottish Church, a white-washed building of no pretentions, being the most striking object from the sea. Landward, a range of handsome houses flank so dense a mass of buildings, occupying the interior of the Fort, as to make the whole appear more like a fortified town than a place of arms, as the name would denote. The tower of the Cathedral, rising in the centre, is the only feature of the scene which boasts any architectural charm; and the Esplanade, a wide plain stretching from the ramparts to the sea, is totally destitute of picturesque beauty.

But even she had to admit that the hills behind the city were wooded and beautiful.

Such was the city in pre-industrial days, before its walls were demolished and when it must have had very much the character and appearance of a European medieval city dislodged in place and time. But within a generation this William Morris dream-city, 'small and white and clean' – so long as you did not look at it too closely – had been transformed by a process of accelerated change into the archetypal Victorian townscape, august monument to material and moral progress or terrible incarnation of Modern Babylon according to taste. Another traveller, arriving in the early twentieth century when the place looked set to become the imperial capital, regretted the fact that 'there is, in place of the palms, a line of factory chimneys: while a quite common row of quays meets the sea in place of the coral strand . . . the buildings appear, at the distance, to differ but little from those at Limehouse. Of elephants there are none.' This traveller's book is called *The Other Side of the Lantern*: by that period the mass-produced myth of India, the Brightest Jewel in the Imperial Crown, home of elephants, tigers, immensely rich princes and excitingly wicked heathen, had created general expectations which certainly were not satisfied by factory chimneys and quays.

A better idea of what happened to Bombay in its great period of expansion and change post-1850 is conveyed by the author of *India Revisited* (1886):

> The transformation effected in this great and populous capital of Western India during the last twenty years does not very plainly manifest itself until the traveller has landed . . . He who has long been absent from India and returns here to visit her sees strange and beautiful buildings towering above the well-remembered yellow and white houses, but misses the old line of ramparts, and the wide expanse of the Maidan behind Back Bay . . . And the first drive which he takes from the Apollo Bunder – now styled the Wellington Pier – reveals a series of really splendid edifices, which have completely altered the previous aspect of Bombay.
>
> Close to the landing-place the pretty façade of the Yacht Club – one of the latest additions to the city – is the first to attract attention, designed in a pleasing mixture of Swiss and Hindu styles . . .

Elsewhere he describes the new large buildings of Bombay as 'conceived for the most part with a happy inspiration, which blends the Gothic and the Indian schools of architecture'. No subsequent commentator has failed to remark on this same remarkable inspiration, but not all have found it such a happy one. This writer – Sir Edwin Arnold – also seems to have been the originator of the much-plagiarised remark, 'I left Bombay a town of warehouses and offices; I find her a city of parks and palaces'. 'Palaces' echoes, by implication, the traditional appellation 'city of palaces' for Calcutta, where the great, white, pillared mansions of the indigo and jute wallahs had for long been such an irritant to the self-esteem of Bombay. Bombay in the 1880s, one is meant to infer, could hold its own with any place on earth. But in fact the offices and warehouses, which were Bombay's *raison d'être* then and for always, had not really given way to palaces; they had merely disguised themselves in palatial garb: palaces for railway companies and courts for tax-inspectors. The city had not really changed its character. It had simply come into its own, after a long apprenticeship, in the full flowering of nineteenth-century capitalism and imperialism.

It is that same city which is visible today, battered, over-populated but still essentially *there*. Nineteenth-century Manchester, Bombay's twin-sister in cotton, has been substantially destroyed; so have Liverpool, Birmingham, Leeds, Halifax, Southampton and many other places; London itself has been altered in many parts beyond recognition – though it was London that was the model for cities like Calcutta and Bombay. In the words of an astute Indian commentator, Nirad Chaudhuri, 'It was only after seeing London that I discovered the true lineage [of these cities . . . They were] half-caste offspring of London, whereas the northern Indian cities were descended from the Islamic and pre-Islamic cities of the Middle East . . . London is the first and archetypal city of our age, created by modern government, bureaucracy, finance, world empire, international commerce and industrialism . . . It is the Mother Megalopolis of our era . . . '

Today, many of the London buildings which set the pattern (sometimes literally) for similar ones in Bombay have been reduced to rubble, brick dust and a great muddy void to be filled with the glass and concrete of a different way of thought. Paradoxically, it is now only in places like Bombay that the quintessential British nineteenth-century city exists. Let us enter it.

Facing the Gateway is the Taj Hotel; it was built in 1903 on the Yacht Club's pleasure basin, and was the cherished project of the legendary Jamshetji Nusserwanji Tata, one of the many Parsis of Bombay of whom much will be heard. There is a persistent story that several decades earlier J. N. Tata suffered the humiliation of being asked to leave the then-best hotel in Bombay, Watson's on the

Esplanade, on the grounds that he was a native. He swore then that he would one day build a hotel of his own which would far outdo Watson's in splendour and convenience: his Taj was designed regardless of expense, with its own electric laundry, turkish baths, post-office, chemist and resident doctor – 'We must try to do what we think our customers would like', J. N. Tata wrote to his son, in decisive veto of the latter's suggestion that William Morris 'aesthetic' wallpapers would be tasteful; the father's taste ran on more solid and philistine lines. Doubtless he did in fact know what his customers would like, for the hotel is still the best in Bombay eighty years later. Watson's has long ceased to function.

Many of le tout Bombay who today use the Taj as a general meeting place, bar, lunch-room, powder room and place-to-be-seen, like to recount that it has actually been built back-to-front, and that when the architect belatedly visited the site and discovered what was happening he was so distressed he committed suicide. There is, however, no truth in this pretty folk-myth with its hint of blood sacrifice. The hotel was designed by one Chambers, of a local European firm of architects, who knew quite well what he was doing. By siting the gardens in a patio behind the hotel rather than in front he was simply conforming to an oriental tradition. This was fortunate, for had the gardens and the widest flight of steps been in front, where European visitors may have expected them to be, they would today have been ruined by the fumes and noise of the Bombay traffic, which has now, c.1980, reached much that stage of reckless, undisciplined, hooting crisis that the traffic of Paris reached c.1930.

Next door to the original Taj is a recent annex-block, best described as a Moorish skyscraper but in fact one of the rare successful modern buildings in Bombay. It is said that Arabs visiting from the Gulf are accommodated here by the management rather than in the original block, however much they can pay, or indeed are excluded altogether: the British racism that once excluded Tata from Watson's Hotel may be defunct in India, but modern India has her own racism, flourishing along with caste and class. What is undoubtedly true is that many western visitors, once accommodated at the Taj, never move far from it. Occasionally they emerge to buy an expensive postcard of the Gateway, or a stuffed mongoose-and-cobra from one of a string of stalls near the sea which always seem to be over-stocked with this commodity. They retreat back into their air-conditioned palace again, slightly impeded in the process by a colony of particularly dirty street-dwellers who have made the pavement by the Taj their begging pitch. After a few days of this, the Taj-guest flies back to London, Washington or Milwaukee and tells his or her friends about the horrible poverty in India.

If Bombay is, as some think, an Indian city with a western façade, then the Gateway and the Taj are this façade in spite of their determinedly oriental opulence. But perhaps, on the contrary, Bombay is really a British city which has been occupied, like post-imperial Rome, by an alien people and culture? Perhaps we shall find out.

For the moment, let us walk up the road that rests on the skeleton of the old Apollo Pier, past the one-time Yacht Club whose 'mixture of the Swiss and Hindu styles' now conceals the Indian Atomic Energy Commission who have occupied it since Independence; past the erstwhile Yacht Club Chambers on the opposite side of the road where the Club itself leads an attenuated existence amid white wickerwork chairs and steel engravings of sailing clippers in Bombay harbour. The kitchens are said to cater for the homesick palates of British residents reared on middle-class nursery fare, but how many of these still remain in Bombay seems doubtful. The men who could write of the Yacht Club in the evening, with the wistful courage that was the perpetual note of the voluntarily exiled Englishman, 'Tone it all down and in the dim light the view might be that from Plymouth Hoe' (J A Spender, *The Indian Scene*, 1912) – these men have long returned to Plymouth and other homes in the west, and gone under the damp green grass.

Up to the corner, where the Council Hall (a one-time Sailors' Home, designed by F. W. Stevens in a style sometimes described as Byzantine) sits solidly on the dust of Bombay's founders. Before the dockyards were built this was Mendham's Point, site of the earliest British cemetery in Bombay, now shared by a busy road-junction with a fountain, an Anglo-Indian dressmakers called Salomé, an old-established dealers in antiques and ivory (Phillips), and the Regal Cinema. We shall return later to that dust beneath, poor stripes in the reddish soil of a labourer's trench.

By taking a half-turn right round the back of the Prince of Wales Museum (fine 1900s Moorish domes and a garden) we would find ourselves walking through a ghostly rampart gate into the Fort area, past the neo-classical Scottish church, built 1820, and still 'a white-washed building of no pretentions' but not now visible from the sea. But we will leave the Fort for another chapter, and continue northwards instead on the very line of the walls themselves. You

may think you are walking up the busy main road called Mahatma
Gandhi Road as far as the Flora Fountain, and then up Dr
Dadabhoi Naoroji Road to the celestial vaults of Victoria Terminus
(Stevens again – St Pancras Station splendidly crossed with Moghul
Mausoleum). Or, if you have grown up in Bombay, you may know
that you are walking up Esplanade Road and then up Hornby Road,
names which hold more historical meaning for Bombay than the
newer, Indianised ones. But actually you are walking on the very
land which, from the early eighteenth to the mid-nineteenth
century, was occupied by a complex erection of walls, bastions and
ravelins: when these were demolished in the 1860s the modern roads
were laid out on the site just as, in Paris at the same period, the
boulevards extérieurs were laid out on the demolished fortifications
of the Fermiers Généraux. Even today these roads outline the Fort
clearly, preserving its identity, its name and its internal street-
pattern. For it was not just a fort in the usual sense of the term but, as
Emma Roberts remarked, a fortified town, densely packed with
houses. The actual fort, its nucleus, Bombay Castle, guarded the
seaward side of it.

So, up the main road where run the red, double-decker
London buses of antiquated design, so that the visiting Londoner
feels their destinations should be the London suburbs, not of today
but of his own childhood. The scene is, in any case, unnervingly
familiar and yet different, as one's childhood would be if one were to
revisit it. There in a row on the left sit, first, an unmistakable
educational establishment in the grand tradition (the Elphinstone
College, in a galleried style usually referred to as 'Venetian Gothic');
then next to it, imitating a Romanesque church, the little Sassoon
Mechanics Institute, unchanged since the day it was opened for the
edification of the modest man in the late 1860s; next to that is the
vaguely neo-classical Army and Navy Building, now no longer a
department store but once a branch of that same enterprise in
Victoria Street, London SW, which equipped generations of
Empire-builders with tropical outfits, zinc-lined chests and red-
flannel cholera belts. Next again comes Watson's Building, long
defunct as a hotel but otherwise much as it ever was; its cast-iron
pillars and tiers of wrought-iron galleries are reminiscent of French
nineteenth-century colonial architecture, but its true genesis is
probably the many-tiered wooden Gujerati house of which Bombay
can still provide examples. It was the first iron-framed building
constructed in Bombay, and when it was going up in 1867 on the
otherwise empty Esplanade a traveller remarked on it as being

'something like a huge birdcage . . . risen like an exhalation from the earth'. It has been pointed out to me as 'one of the oldest buildings in Bombay'. Of course it is not. It is, rather, like the Flat-Iron building in New York, one of the oldest examples of a type of architecture that was once aggressively 'new'. In terms of sheer age, there are far, far older buildings hidden away in the Fort and in the bazaar district.

This brings me to a fact which I have encountered again and again in attempting to study Bombay, and which has to be recognised by anyone from the West with a feeling for history or architecture who visits India. It is that the ability, relatively common in England, to date a building roughly by eye, is much rarer in India. With honourable exceptions, most of the inhabitants of Bombay, including some very well-educated and knowledgeable people, seem less capable of assessing buildings in their own city than is the western visitor. Perhaps this is understandable. The visitor finds, in this area of Bombay, a type of architecture which is instantly familiar to him. 'Hallo, fancy seeing *you* here. I thought you were in London' – or Birmingham, or Leeds – is his feeling on encountering many of the larger public buildings, and he brings to them all his background knowledge of styles, dates and the evolution of British society which bred these particular buildings, or their prototypes. By contrast, the Indian observer, even if he was born and brought up in Bombay, is inhabiting a townscape much of which is, in the deepest sense, alien to the country and its culture: it is much harder for him to classify buildings or to place them in a general context.

But, this said, it is also true, and inescapable, that a working general knowledge of the past, and an overall sense of chronology, which is a common and indeed expected attribute in educated people in the western world, does not seem to be nearly as common among Indians even at the highest socio-cultural level. You may meet an Indian scholar who is a mine of information on some particular aspect of local life or architecture – the docks, say, or mosque carving – and be disconcerted to find that he does not appear to site his knowledge in a perspective of time in the way that his European or American counterpart would. Not infrequently, his chrono-logical perception of Bombay's past seems to be limited to a rudimentary division into Now and Then – Then, usually known as 'Old Bombay'. 'Old Bombay' is a sort of catch-all era, in which late-nineteenth-century Gothic railway stations are jumbled together with early-eighteenth-century ramparts, with Edwardian bungalows and with Bombay Castle, all co-existing in a timeless Then.

A full analysis of this Indian peculiarity is outside the scope of this book. But it is perhaps worth mentioning that in ancient India, before the British began to impose their concepts of historical reality in establishments like Elphinstone College, history was seen as cyclic rather than linear, and that Indian 'Histories' consisted largely of predictions about a hypothetical future as if that were the main function of the past – to provide fodder for this guesswork. Without going further into the subject here, it seems not unreasonable to suppose that whatever historical perspective Indian scholars do possess, it is one inaccessible to the western commentator – that some degree of reciprocal ignorance and confusion is in operation here. This is a book written by a westerner; it can be nothing else. One cannot see through others' eyes, and, like all views, mine is a partial one. But since Bombay, that 'half-caste offspring of London', was so largely constructed by westerners, looking through western eyes themselves, any other view than mine would be still more partial and perhaps less appropriate. Unlike old Delhi, unlike Ahmedabad or Jaipur or indeed Poona, western India's principal hill-station, Bombay has no ancient Indian past.

Up the road to the brightly painted Flora Fountain, which is never known as Hutatma Chowk, its official modern name. It was designed by a committee that included R. Norman Shaw, though it doesn't look like it, and was erected in honour of Bartle Frere, the Governor responsible for laying out much of the post-1860 'new Bombay' which is now so thoroughly ensconced in the public mind as Old Bombay with the patina of time lying on its Gothic surfaces. Once, before the traffic got the better of it, the Flora Fountain had a grass plot and palm trees as a surround. Facing it, commanding a fork, stands Oriental Buildings, an unoriental block (Stevens again) with a pitched roof vaguely filched from a French chateau. Up Hornby Road on the right stands Fort House, now disguised behind an enormous sign saying 'Handloom House' and 'Everett Shipping Agents' – the businesses that occupy its ground floor – but, if you look carefully at it, clearly a one-time private house, with a neo-classical pediment and a verandah that was surely meant to look out across something other than the buildings opposite. It was the mid-nineteenth-century town-house of Sir Jamshetji Jeejeebhoy, the first Parsi baronet, of whom much more presently. On the left, a little nearer the Flora Fountain, next to a grand domed building that once housed a branch of Macmillan, the British publishers, is an equally British department store – now

31

'Khadi' but once Whiteaway and Laidlow, the place where every new subaltern was sent to kit himself out. It was cheaper than the Army and Navy, but you could not have an account there. Still, today, with its bales of silk and cotton on wooden shelves, its separate cash and parcels desks and its superfluity of assistants gazing trancelike across their counters, Khadi distinctly resembles a large, provincial English drapers, c.1930.

Higher up Hornby Road come arcades under which boys and men sell stationery and leather bags with a freelance assiduousness that is absent from Khadi's state-employed staff. There are bookshops here and, as you near the great mecca of Victoria Terminus, two of the city's old-fashioned Irani tea-shops, the Empire and the Regal, with marble tables and spotty mirrors and reassuringly dull-looking cakes lying like museum specimens in glass cases. Quintessential, unassuming catering, poised between East and West, the Irani tea-shops are peculiar to Bombay; they are the legacy of a late-nineteeth-century immigration into the city, oases of musty tranquillity in the city's frenetic life.

At Nagar Chowk, by Victoria Terminus, a pause to admire the railway station gargoyles, its turrets, and the delicate peacocks sculptured beneath its many eaves. On the far side of the road, and almost as splendid, is the domed and minaretted Municipal Corporation Building. This is British Bombay at its exuberant best, the Saracenic-Gothic 'palaces' admired by turn-of-the-century visitors, then despised and even hated between the wars and now, tentatively, admired again. I speak, of course, of informed taste. Uninformed taste, as typified by the man driving the creaking victoria or rattling taxi or plodding bullock gharry, has never wavered in its appreciation of these massive edifices, which are admired just as much as if they were ancient Moghul palaces and perhaps, for all he knows, were. Whoever you are, you can see the point of architecture like that.

The precarious, littered circle of greenery in front of the Terminus was once the northernmost gate out of the Fort, the Bazaar Gate, and from here the road divides. We could follow it straight ahead, past the *Times of India* offices and along to the School of Art, where Rudyard Kipling was born in 1865 in a bungalow at the back of the tree-hung compound*: his father, John

---

* Compound: the enclosure surrounding a building, meaning anything from a courtyard to large garden.

Lockwood Kipling, ran the School in its modest early days; both School and bungalow have since been rebuilt. All his life Kipling appreciated Bombay, the Eden of infancy from which, like so many other children of the British Raj, he was sent home at an early age to a colder, sadder place misleadingly called 'Home':

> *Surely in toil or fray*
> *Under an alien sky,*
> *Comfort it is to say:*
> *'Of no mean city am I!'*
>
> *Neither by service nor fee*
> *Come I to mine estate –*
> *Mother of cities to me,*
> *For I was born in her gate,*
> *Between the palms and the sea,*
> *Where the world-end steamers wait.*

It may seem as if poetic licence is at work here, but in fact even today the sea lies nearer to that point than you realise, not far to the east of Victoria Terminus itself. The docks run right up the eastern side of Bombay island, an unseen but essential presence hidden behind dockyard gates and the harbour railway. The Port Trust owns, in all, some 1,800 acres of land and wet dock, or about one-eighth of the whole of the island of Bombay, nearly all of it land originally taken from the sea. But when Kipling was born that phase of land-reclamation was only beginning, and Mody Bay, beyond the railway lines, was not yet filled up by the Alexandra Docks (now called Indira Docks). The railway itself was a newcomer, and Victoria Terminus was not yet built: instead there was only a small station known as Bori Bunder after an old wharf that occupied a promontory at that point. So the Kiplings' bungalow, with the trees of the *maidan* behind it, could literally have been described as 'between the palms and the sea'. Today, there are more buildings and the *maidan* has many fewer trees than appear on nineteenth-century photographs.

'*Maidan*' is one of those untranslatable and indispensable Anglo-Indian words. It means a large, flat open space – a 'green' in English terms, except that it is only green for two or three months a year in the wake of the monsoon. For the rest of the time, except where sprinklers are put on it to create cricket pitches, it is a brownish, dusty, balding expanse. There are a chain of *maidans* in this part of Bombay, linked to one another but crossed by main roads: they constitute together the remains of the one-time open

33

Esplanade outside the fort walls, that 'wide plain stretching from the ramparts to the sea' that Emma Roberts noted about 1840. The *maidans* no longer reach anywhere near the sea (Back Bay, on the west of the island, that is): they are surrounded by buildings, but they still form a huge open space, there in the centre of one of the most densely packed cities on earth. Let us therefore, instead of taking the road straight up from Victoria Terminus, branch off to the left on the other side of the Municipal Building, since that will carry us along one side of this great space. Here, the long-distance coaches stop to carry passengers overnight to Goa and Aurangebad and other greener places; here there are soft-drink stands and fruit stalls and, still, a straggling fringe of pipal trees, the survivors of more luxuriant vegetation. It seems probable that most of the Esplanade trees have, over the course of a century, disappeared stealthily, bit by bit, into the tiny braziers of street dwellers and peanut sellers: they are still disappearing . . . Here, among the eccentric aerial roots of the pipal trees, families camp permanently, in a gipsylike litter of string beds and washing lines. Some keep chickens; several have hollowed out hard, smooth mud-ovens in the long-suffering ground. At night, seen from the other side of the open space, these miniature ovens glow like eyes. Most respectable people avoid walking across the *maidan* at night; it is perceived then as alien territory, but elsewhere at night and almost everywhere by day Bombay is a relatively safe city. Unlike Calcutta, it does not breathe out violence, its police do not flourish weapons, its poorer quarters have none of the desperate hostility of up-town New York. In spite of the horrors it harbours, it is a cheerful place, and its inhabitants do not obsessively warn visitors about rape, murder or even pickpockets. By day, crossing this biggest *maidan*, you need fear nothing but sunstroke, a cricket ball on the head, the sight of men relieving themselves in the peaceful air and, at certain seasons, a white bull (incarnation of Nandi, the sacred bull of Shiva) being led round and round for the edification of a changing audience of people and cows.

Far away at one end of the *maidan* is the green, fenced-in area that belongs to the Bombay Gymkhana, much tended by men who haul between them a giant roller, their bare feet squelching on the wet green turf: the members watch them from their wicker chairs. The word 'Gymkhana', so redolent of British India, indicates there, not an event connected with ponies but any form of club with open-air facilities – even the sporting connotation has more or less dropped away. The word, however, derives from 'ball-house' = a place where balls are kept; it was coined in the Bombay presidency.

But we are coming to the main road, Carnac Road, that runs across the northernmost end of the *maidans* and indeed across the narrow width of Bombay. Now renamed Lokmanya Tilak, after a dead nationalist figure, this road is one of the few cross-routes, and it is a real dividing point, a very old one. South of it, where we have been walking, lies British Bombay,. Imperial, Municipal, Big Business and still today Governmental Bombay, the Bombay of the banks and the Stock Exchange and the other prestigious giant buildings, new and old, the Bombay of western road systems. But north of Carnac Road you pass, abruptly, into another Bombay, and one which is immediately recognisable as such: the Bombay of the bazaar, the small workshops, the stalls, the rag-trade, the temples, the mosques: the Bombay of the people.

Historically there is a good reason for this split. What we have done is walk from the ramparts of the one-time fortified town, out across the parade ground that was deliberately cleared by the British in the mid-eighteenth century to create a free field of fire, out to the point beyond this field where the 'Black Town' of those days was officially allowed to begin. Comparable patterns exist in both Calcutta and Madras. A country can overthrow its rulers, declare Independence; a municipality can re-name the streets after national heroes, cart away the statues of kings and emperors – but the bones of a place, once formed, are not to be obliterated. It is the skeleton of eighteenth-century, pre-industrial Bombay, with its neat, separate sections, its wide open spaces, its creeks and promontories, that is still visible here, beneath the exhausted flesh of the modern city.

There are a number of routes we could take into the heart of Bombay. We could go up Kalba Devi Road or Abdul Rehman Street, in each case passing close by the Great Mosque in the heart of the cloth market district, the Moslem heartlands of the Bhendi Bazaar, where two-thirds of the street signs are in the cursive Urdu lettering, delicate as insect tracks. Or we could go up Jagannath Shankershet road towards the Hindu quarters of Girgaum and Khetwadi and Bhuleshwar, with their mixture of ponderously decrepit mansion flats and airy, galleried wooden tenements. (The names of the ancient settlements that the city has swallowed still cling to their territory. Girgaum means a hill-village, Khetwadi the place of fields.) That way, we would eventually reach Grant and Falkland Roads and Kamatipura, where the teenage prostitutes of Bombay stand in their so-called 'cages' – in reality, tiny, lit, barred shops in the Gujerati style, standing right on the pavement like any

35

other bazaar booths. This has been the *lal bazaar*, the red light district, for generations, but then everything is for sale, somewhere in the labyrinthine markets here in the central bowl of Bombay: leather, rubber, old iron, ivory, cane furniture, diamonds, sandal wood, birds . . . In the *chor bazaar*, the 'thieves market' whose centre is Mutton Street, purloined mosque lamps and jewelled sweetmeat boxes stand side by side with the jetsam of the Raj: Staffordshire pottery figures, damp-speckled sporting prints of Newmarket and the Pytchley, creakingly humorous framed cartoons from *Punch*, spoon-backed Victorian chairs made by local craftsmen in local woods and now pitted by worms, calf-bound volumes of sermons similarly eroded, Mabel Lucy Atwell ornaments, alphabet plates and brown Windsor teapots, horned gramophones faintly churning out 'Night and Day' or 'Tea for Two' above the shouts and rumbles of the bazaar.

To the east lies Mazagaon, an ancient Portuguese township now half-buried in dockland, but still a stronghold of native Roman Catholicism. To the west lie the smarter residential quarters culminating in Malabar Hill, the leafy eyrie of the wealthy. Further north again, in the districts that were once themselves leafy suburbs, lie the vegetable, hay and timber markets, a race course, the big Club and its gardens, acres of railway lines, hospitals, cemeteries, schools, film studios, mills, yet more mills and the industrial tenements that are known as *chawls*, sad as their name. Here too lies a one-time Governor's House, on the foundations of a still older Jesuit building: we shall return here later. Here in the Botanical Gardens, appropriately flanked by the animals of a small zoo, are congregated the statues of former British worthies, who have been removed from their street locations in the last thirty years by a nationalist municipality: they stand in a self-conscious row in a concealed side alley, like deposed maharajahs now living in straitened circumstances. Leaf shadows and bird droppings decorate their winged collars, fake Roman togas and queenly marble lace.

In the side streets the occasional ancient dwelling still hides its rococo pilasters behind high garden walls, or rears its sagging tiled roof and broken fretworked balconies above a row of shacks selling anything from hub-caps to herbal remedies for white patches on the skin. English lessons can be had at one door, sex-counselling at another, improbable treatment for 'incurable diseases' at a third. Here, the past does not exist: this is an eternal Indian present. Only fugitive place names that mean 'Fig tree creek' or 'House by the mangoes' speak here of a lost landscape.

Aching and interminable, mile after mile, the suburbs of today stretch to the north, swallowing rice paddies and coconut plantations, vaulting creeks and scaling wooded hummocks, planting a fertiliser works here, an outcrop of hutments there, and new cement towers where the herons used to stand and the bullocks used to graze. Greater Bombay now extends far beyond the original island, on and on to the airports and beyond, past bosky residential colonies and modern beach developments, fishing villages, orphanages, agglomerations of cowsheds and salt-pan grounds – all the ancillary services to a great town which have edged Bombay for two hundred years already, but which have been continually displaced outwards, and yet again outwards, in each generation by the relentless pressures of the town expanding from within.

There is much talk of New Bombay, the 'Twin-sister City' supposedly being built on the mainland, at Vashi, a location which bears something of the same relation to the island of Bombay as New Jersey does to Manhattan. There has been talk about it for twenty-five years already. Several variant plans, complete with bridge-schemes across Bombay harbour, have been put forward to induce the governmental world of Bombay to forsake its nineteenth-century Gothic buildings in favour of new glass and steel palaces on the new location. No such scheme has so far found general acceptance: those in positions of power cling to the island, and what is actually being built on the mainland is new factories with housing colonies for their workers. This, in the circumstances, must be considered a blessing. In Europe itself there has been a massive shift of opinion, in the last dozen years, away from the grand comprehensive plan to a more pragmatic approach, and indeed away from the 'garden city' model of town planning and back to a more conventional townscape. As it is, though New Bombay promises to be less of a white elephant than it would have been had the 'Twin City' delusion been pursued, the architectural thinking behind it still embodies that 1930s futurism which has been one of Europe's most unfortunate exports. Tall, western-style blocks (with no open galleries or courtyards to dry the washing) and air-conditioned shopping centres with inevitable high rates are inappropriate to traditional Indian living; as for the 'green spaces' which have been an obsession with western-trained architects for the last two generations, these, in India, are more likely to be covered with shanties than with grass.

In India, the complex question of how far you can provide

37

people with modern amenities and yet allow them to live and build in their own ways, is one that has yet to be solved theoretically, let alone in practical terms. In recent years some progress has been made with 'planned settlement areas': that is, locations on which incomers to the metropolitan area are provided with basic services (water, drain-ditches, latrines, paved roads) but are left to build their own homes according to their taste and means. But frequently these locations are in inaccessible places, far from the jobs, factories and markets which have attracted the people to the city in the first place.

It cannot be stated too often: the growth of the town – any town – is not just an unfortunate mishap, to be rectified or ameliorated by the application of 'welfare', grandiose planning and free contraceptives. Whatever the disadvantage of this growth, it is also a positive trend with economic and human reasons behind it. Urban sprawl, in spite of its pejorative name, is not a social sickness. Nor is the existence of the town itself, contrary to a deeply-rooted British myth, a sign of man's decline from some mythical state of pre-urban Grace. On the contrary, a strong case can be made out for the town as *the* vitalising, generative agent for the countryside, since it is the town that is the cradle of the technology and social organisation from which the countryside ultimately benefits. A flourishing agriculture is itself as dependent upon the existence of towns as it is upon the existence of arable lands. Cobbett was quite wrong, with his emotive metaphor of London as the Great Wen, for in the long run London, far from 'sucking goodness' from adjacent rural areas, brought prosperity to them. At worst, the town's meaning and effect is ambiguous. Charles Booth, the social scientist, knew this in the late nineteenth century when he wrote (of New York), 'There seems to be something subtle, an essence pervading giant metropolitan cities and altering everything, so that life seems more lively, busier, larger, the individual less, the community more. I like it. It does me good. But I know it has another aspect, and I am not surprised when people feel crushed by the wickedness of it, the ruthlessness, heartlessness of its grinding mill . . . '

Today Bombay, with a density of population about four times that of modern New York, probably resembles more nearly, in social and economic ethos, the New York of a hundred years ago. Certainly it contains grinding mills, both metaphorical and actual; it contains wickedness, ruthlessness and heartlessness. But it is also for many people, including some of the poorest, a place of

38

endeavour, activity, chances, succour, a place to seek your fortune and even find it. Battered, dirty, over-crowded and choked with exhaust fumes it may be, but it is also a city of dreams.

Late in the afternoon of the long, hot day, a breeze rises over the ocean to the west. It is a wind which once used to set all the tops of the palms on the island waving, and which now blows like a benediction over smart apartments and government offices, bazaar blocks and shanties, *chawls* and bungalows, carefully tended gardens and rancid gullies and over some eight million people. Bombay is still, for many of them, the place where they most want to be. For some, even, it is home, the inescapable zero-place however much assaulted and changed. The poem by Nissim Ezekiel quoted at the beginning of this chapter ends:

> *I cannot leave the island*
> *I was born here and belong.*

II *A Pattern of Islands*

It has been said that all towns are buried countryside, concealed earth whose natural contours and waterways continue to shape the settlement's history long after the hills have been diminished by quarrying, the valleys silted with the rubble of successive buildings and the once-clear fishing streams encased in iron sewer-pipes many feet below the level of the modern streets. In most towns, and even in cities, this basic material of landscape is still readily perceptible to the interested eye, moderated and disguised rather than totally transformed. It is still possible to see the lineaments of the eighteenth-century town that lie concealed beneath the twentieth-century one, and, beneath that again, the earlier rural settlement from which the eighteenth-century townscape grew.

But in some idiosyncratic cases the transformation has been far greater, the obliteration of Nature far more complete. Moreover, what the historian-detective may have in front of him is not one transformation but successive ones. The classic progression, what one distinguished urban historian (H.J. Dyos) has called 'the full declension – meadow-land to slum', may be replaced by several separate waves of transformation, like separate scenic arrangements in a theatre, each creating as much as it destroys. Moreover, this construction may consist not merely of what is contributed to the land's surface, but in sweeping and audacious changes in the very structure of the land. Both ancient and modern morality emphasise man's negative rôle as the Destroyer, despoiling Nature, laying waste her bounty, corrupting innocence, losing Eden, using up – to switch to twentieth-century terminology – her ecological resources, polluting streams, replacing fertile earth with sterile industrial blight. Yet in some cases, of which Bombay is one, man has created far more than he has obliterated; nor has the original habitat been meadowland. For from 'burying' landscape he has in fact assembled new landscape, by a series of prestidigitatory tricks, over the course of time, inventing it and inventing it from the very slight original material – from marshes, salt flats, isolated islands, open sea, seemingly from the air itself. The physical history of Bombay is the history of what one commentator (in *The Times*) called in the 1930s 'the great epic of reclamation which has been in process for two-and-a-half centuries and of which the end is not yet in sight'. Today, the best part of half a century later, it is still merrily – or contentiously – continuing.

Twentieth-century maps of Bombay show a tongue of land, about twelve miles long (or fourteen, taking in the thinner promontory of Colaba at its tip) and about three miles wide for most of its extent: it projects alongside the mainland, to which it is linked at its northern end by causeways, like a bizarre copy of New York's Long Island. But the earliest maps of the area tell a different story. When the English received the place, variously described as 'the Fort', 'the islands' and 'the Island', from the Portuguese in the 1660s, there was not one main island but seven, plus other islets in the harbour and certain bits of watery, semi-detached mainland which still, today, are not part of Bombay proper but are within the area currently administered as Greater Bombay. However, each of the surviving seventeenth-century maps demarks the islands in a slightly different way, almost as if, like Prospero's Isle, they had been insubstantial, assuming different forms for different visitors, and in a sense this was true. At high tides, the seas rushed through great 'breaches' or creeks between the seven patches of higher ground, isolating them one from another, but when the tides retreated much of this intervening land was a passable though swampy territory later known as 'the Flats'. It is these Flats which today form much of central Bombay. As you walk through bazaars, your eyes and ears assailed by words, written as well as spoken, in three or four main languages and many others, your nostrils filled with the compounded scent of hot dust and spice and diesel fumes, woodsmoke from charcoal braziers and a persistent trace-element of dried urine, you are walking much of the time through the very sea itself.

Till efforts were made to drain the Flats, little would grow on them but samphire and, round the edges, coconuts. It was in fact the coconut palm which helped form these salt swamps in the first place, and so raise Bombay out of the waters. Long ago, before the British or the Portuguese before them came, the palms were the main vegetation of the islands, and by a constant shedding of their great leaves into the shallow sea they gradually surrounded themselves with layers of decayed vegetable matter into which their roots could in turn burrow further. This humus was further thickened and extended, after men began to interest themselves in the palms, with hundreds of years of fish-manure. Central London is built on a terrace of river gravel, New York on rock, Leningrad on a marsh, Calcutta – notoriously – on the shifting black mud of a tidal estuary, but Bombay can claim the eccentric distinction of being largely based on rotten fish and the leaves of the coconut palm.

The seven original islands, the rocky skeleton of the one island into which they have been fused, account for well under half the present land surface. The most central island – and one which, perhaps for that very reason, has no name beyond 'Bombay' – included the Fort area and the land behind it stretching to Back Bay: it had a tongue of land to the north, on the eastern (harbour) side, then called Dongri, Dongaree or Dungharry, and a far more important promontory on the western side forming the curve of Back Bay and consisting of Malabar Hill and its smaller neighbour Kamballa (Cumballa) Hill. The other central island, considerably smaller, was Mazagaon, reached from Dongri across a creek called Umarkhadi (Oombarkhadi, Oomerkharee, etc.*) which still gives its name to a district of the city, and which means either 'Fig tree creek' or 'Salt water creek'. There is, on the edge of this district today, a road junction still known by the name of Pydhoni (Paidoni, Paydonee, etc.) which means 'the foot-wash', though it is thought that this creek was the earliest one to be filled in and it is probably the best part of three hundred years since anyone had the opportunity to wash his feet freely at this dusty cross-roads. Still, there is a tank near by (today covered over) belonging to Mumba Devi temple, the home of Bombay's presiding goddess, and also a municipal water trough at which the oxen who still pull carts in Bombay are watered: as if in folk-memory of Pydhoni's past, the carters bring them there and park them in groups to eat their lunch-time hay.

* Inevitably the spelling of many place names in English is an arbitrary decision. Not only has transliteration never been standardised, eighteenth- and nineteenth-century writers often preferring a different form to the one usual today, but pronunciation itself is variable according to which of the main languages current in Bombay the speaker is accustomed to use.

42

South of these two central islands, and part of a chain of rocks running out into the sea that today forms the long, curved tip of the city, were originally two more islands. The larger, Colaba, was at the end of the chain, but has today given its name to the whole promontory. The smaller, Old Woman's Island, formed a stepping stone in the middle; today it has long been absorbed into Colaba Causeway, the main road which runs where once ferries plied or the incoming tide washed unwary waders and their horses onto the rocks. (The picturesque name Old Woman's Island is thought to have been a British corruption of Al Omani's Island, or the Island of the Arabian sea-people.) Colaba and Old Woman's Island were for a long time the first sight that greeted the traveller on his way into Bombay Harbour. Nelson, for instance, arriving in India as a midshipman of eighteen, first saw 'the light of Old Woman's Island near Bombay' at two in the morning on 17 August 1774. His ship had left England before the end of 1773, and had taken the long, wearisome and hazardous route round the Cape that was then habitual.

North of Mazagaon, stretching right up to the creek of the Mahim river, which still cuts between Bombay proper and the mainland, was a long, irregular shaped island roughly divisible into four sections, known as Parell, Matunga, Dharavi and Sion. This land-mass, described by different commentators under all or any of these four names, and by other names in addition, was the one most vaguely and variously delineated by the old map-makers, and from the start of the British period formed a considerable bone of contention: was it or was it not to be considered a natural part of 'Bombay'? Today, it and the ex-salt marshes on its western side form what may be described as 'up-town Bombay', a long, weary haul of densely packed human habitation and activity all the way to Sion Fort, which is a seventeenth-century structure still surviving on its miniature mountain overlooking the salt-pans in the creek beyond. Well within living memory this area was still open land sprinkled with trees, a pleasant spot for a Sunday picnic.

On the northwestern side the island of Mahim, taking its name from the river estuary, still raised its coconut plantation well into the present century. Because it has a shore-line on the open sea and receives the blessed afternoon breeze, it remains today a relatively agreeable, leafy, suburban district, and so does Worli to the south of it, the seventh and last of the original islands. Between Worli and Kamballa Hill till late in the eighteenth century was the weak point, known as the Great Breach or Breach Candy, through which the tides seeped or poured according to the season, drowning all the land in the centre – the Flats. Longer ago, it seems probable, the waters of this breach virtually met those of Umarkhadi on the other side: hence the 'foot-wash'.

Such was Bombay when the British of the Restoration first came to claim it. Not, of course, that they were the first people there, though it was to fall to them to create the town. Centuries earlier had lived there a Dravidian fishing people called the Kolis: their name still survives, not only in 'Colaba' and in the various 'Koliwadis' in the city and in the district today called 'Cavel', but also in the word 'coolie', the western Indian term for any labourer. If Bombay can be said to have any aboriginal or indigenous population, it is these Kolis. A few of their fishing settlements still survive around the island today, including one half-way down Colaba. Permanently threatened by reclamation schemes, and towered over today by the large glass blocks of a modern development at Narriman Point on Back Bay, this remnant of the past goes on existing,* with huts of woven matting and bright-sailed boats, in a stench of ageing fish. It forms a remarkable example of the Indian capacity, apparently possessed by all classes, for pursuing a way of life tenaciously without reference to other ways of life being just as tenaciously pursued all round them. It is rather as if a prehistoric encampment were existing self-sufficiently on a corner of Hampstead Heath in London, or a Red Indian tribe in Central Park.

It is not really here, in such eccentric survivals as the fishing village on Colaba, that the historically-minded visitor or inhabitant can seek the lost pattern of islands that the British took over in the 1660s. If he wants to see a brief vision of this past he should rather take the hour's boat trip from the Gateway to off-shore Elephanta Island – in the vernacular *Gharapuri*, the 'place of idols'; this is famous for its rock temples† which were hewn out of the hill itself

---

* But this location does not seem to be its original one. Long-term occupants of smart Cuffe Parade say it was not there in their childhood.

† There are literally hundreds of such rock temples in western India, including some at Kennari, near Bombay, and the more famous ones at Ajanta and Ellora. Their characteristic oddity lies in the way in which pillars carved out of the rock to resemble architectural columns apparently 'support' the roof of the caverns – an imitative illusion designed to give Nature the air of architecture, since what these pillars would really be supporting, were they load-bearing, would be the whole weight of the mountain above.

some time towards the end of the Buddhist period in India, probably in the eighth century AD, and filled with the sort of carvings of which Christian visitors have traditionally disapproved. Today, Elephanta sits there in the sea much as it always has, with its primitive wooden jetty, its dark-skinned inhabitants, its monkeys and its groves of trees standing deep in the shoreline and with a few water buffalo similarly immersed: three centuries ago Bombay itself must have looked much like this. The Portuguese called here, named the place from the stone elephant they found in the caves, and used the other carvings for target practice, but otherwise neither they nor subsequent visitors have done much to alter the place. The late Victorians, in a burst of typically officious zeal, mended the elephant, by then in pieces, and removed it to the gardens of the Victoria and Albert Museum (Bombay, not London) – where it remains.

Bombay, although one of a number of places down that stretch of the western coast of India that were known as ports from ancient times, has no early history apart from the history of the whole region. Since this book is a biography of a town, I am not concerned with eras before that town had its beginnings. It is sufficient to note that various Aryan Hindu invaders, the ancestors of the Mahrattas, held sway in this part of India from the third century for the next thousand years or so, that there were scattered settlements on the Bombay islands, and that power passed into the hands of Moslem invaders from Gujerat in the north at roughly the same time as the Middle Ages were ending in Europe. The Moslem domination lasted about two centuries, or until the period of the Reformation in Europe, and it was during this time that the first beginnings of a Moslem community from the adjacent Konkan began to establish itself among the Bombay islands. (Today Bombay's population is still about one-third Moslem, though the community lost to Pakistan at Independence in 1947 many of its wealthier and more influential members, including that famous Khoja Moslem son of Bombay, Mohammed Ali Jinnah.) But nobody built a town on the islands.

Nor, when they came, did the Portuguese. The first man to discover the direct sea-route to India in the late fifteenth century was the Portuguese Vasco de Gama, but his ambition for the sub-continent apparently extended no further than his avowed aim, *buscar Christaos e especiaria* – to seek Christians and spices. The first Portuguese landing in Bombay, in 1509, was a rapacious foray, not untypical – 'Our men captured many cows and some blacks who were hiding among the bushes, and of whom the good were kept and the rest were killed.' Bombay was at that time the property of the Moslem ruler Sultan Muhamed Shah Begada, who initially repulsed the foreign invaders; but gradually, by repeated assaults, the Portuguese consolidated their holdings on the west coast. The Sultan's grandson, Bahadur Shah, was finally persuaded in 1534 to make over to the King of Portugal the seven islands plus Bassein, which was a chunk of mainland territory north of Bombay also known as Salsette. Here at Bassein the Portuguese built themselves a walled city overlooking the sea, which remains to this day. Its complex of churches stand roofless with trees growing through their chancels, creepers smother the gravestones of the earliest colonialists: it seems to have remained untouched, like a Sleeping Beauty's citadel, since the day in 1739 when the Portuguese were forced to vacate it rather hastily by a local Mahratta army. It is a poignant reminder of what was, and of what Bombay itself might have been today had history taken a different turn.

In theory, Bahadur Shah had traded Bombay and Bassein in return for Portuguese help against the power of the Moghul emperors. Such arrangements have frequently been made by imperialist powers in India, and in practice they have usually proved to be the thin end of a powerful wedge. It was the Viceroy of Goa, Nuna da Cunha – whose surname many present-day Bombay citizens carry – who made the arrangements with Bahadur Shah. He reported back to Portugal in cheerful tones: 'The land of the island [Bombay] is very low and covered with great and beautiful groves of trees. There is much game and abundance of meat and rice and there is no remembrance of any scarcity.' Other writers of the same period have left similar descriptions. Heitor da Silveira, who raided there several times before da Cunha's decisive campaign, proclaimed it to be *a ilha da boa vida* – the island of the good life. Evidently at this stage the lack of suitable grazing for cattle, and the lack of local market gardening, which were to create problems for the British on the island from the late seventeenth century till the coming of the railway era, had not yet become apparent. Perhaps this was because the Portuguese did not envisage any large-scale settlement on Bombay, or indeed its use as anything more than an occasional naval base.

The story of Portuguese settlement is largely the story of Jesuit settlement, and what they left behind when they were persuaded, in turn, to relinquish Bombay to the British 130 years later, was monasteries and churches and little else. In the course of this period

46

they, or the Franciscans, had built a huge church at Mahim, others at Dadar and Parell on the northern island and another at Mazagaon. All these church locations survive today, but the original churches have been destroyed in favour of newer buildings, some of them several times over. There seems traditionally to have been little perception in Bombay that a building may be valuable in itself, not in spite of being old but because of it.

Apart from assiduously abolishing temples and converting the local citizens, sometimes forcibly under threat of death (*buscar Christaos* . . .) the Portuguese did not interfere with the time-honoured local occupations of coconut and rice-growing, fishing and salt-panning, nor did they do much to develop trade with the outside world. Bombay's destiny as a world port still lay, at this time, hidden, and the seas lapped the roots of the palm and brab trees largely undisturbed.

Yet her principal sixteenth-century citizen, who rented the main island from the King of Portugal from 1554 for about £85 per annum, was in his way typical of the kind of cosmopolitan peoples who were later to make Bombay their home, and in so doing make Bombay. Garcia da Orta was a Marrano, which is to say that he was either a convert from Judaism or the descendant of those Portuguese Jews who had been forcibly converted in the preceding century under the Inquisition. He was a noted botanist and honorary Court physician – his name, whether by coincidence or in consequence, means 'of the garden'. His book on drugs and herbs was written in Latin, but afterwards translated into Portuguese and published in that language in Goa, which was the major Portuguese colony down the coast from Bombay. He died in Goa in 1570, and after him other prominent Portuguese rented Bombay on the same terms, but it was probably da Orta himself who was responsible for building the *Quinta* or Manor House on the Castle site in the Fort area, behind the present-day Town Hall.

Today this site is inaccessible to the public; it requires special permission to see the much-altered building there, which has been variously known as 'the Arsenal' and 'the Pattern Room' from the intermediary uses to which it has been put, and which today houses naval stores. Before it was put to military and naval uses it was the original residence of the British Governors. The lower part of its walls almost certainly pre-date the bastion wall round it, which is intact but is now embedded in the buildings of the Indian naval headquarters, and is not therefore generally visible either. (The only detailed street map of Bombay at present on sale obscures these

47

historic relics still further by labelling the site 'Fort George', which was a British construction situated a good half-mile to the north near the site of the present Victoria Terminus.) Yet this core building within the Castle walls may in fact be a precious remnant of the pre-British time, for the oldest parts of it are very probably what remains of da Orta's house. Nearby a sundial and coat of arms survive, of obviously Portuguese design, and the main gate through the bastion wall is surmounted by an engraving of soldiers in Portuguese pantaloons. There is considerable circumstantial evidence that the British, when they took possession of Bombay, simply used the Island's existing chief building – what was left of it – and fortified it, rather than building themselves a castle from scratch. The only surviving description of da Orta's Manor House as it was in Portuguese days is retrospective and nostalgic, but suggests that the place was not subsequently destroyed by the British, only transformed. John Fryer, surgeon to the East India Company, wrote in 1675 that when the British had first arrived a decade previously they had found 'a pretty well-situated but ill-fortified house . . . four brass guns being the whole defence of the island'. He continued:

> About the house was a delicate garden, voiced to be the pleasantest in India, intended rather for wanton dalliance, Love's artillery, than to make resistence against an invading foe. This garden of Eden or place of terrestrial happiness would put the searchers upon as hard an inquest as the other has done in its posterity . . . The walks which before were covered with nature's verdant awning, and lightly pressed by soft delights, are now open to the sun and loaded with harder cannon. The bowers dedicated to rest and ease are turned into bold rampires for the watchful sentinel to look out on. Every tree that the airy choristers made their charming choir trembles at the rebounding echo of the alarming drum; and those slender fences, only designed to oppose the sylvan herd, are thrown down to erect others of more warlike force.

It is logical to suppose that the 'delicate garden' was initially laid out by da Orta and stocked with medicinal plants and other botanical treasures. This curiously erotic passage (how had Fryer spent his earlier visit to the Island?) carries a strong suggestion that Bombay in pre-British days was Eden before the Fall and is often quoted as such, but this in fact is somewhat misleading. The island of Bombay was attacked on a number of occasions by the Malabars,* a warlike tribe who went in for piracy along the western

48

coast, and at least once, in 1626, by the Dutch and English, who formed a temporary alliance and raided the place. They 'left the Great House *which was both a warehouse, a priory and a fort*, all afire, burning with other good houses' (the account of David Davies, the English navigator). In addition, the Manor House was attacked again by Arab marauders in 1661 just before the British claimed it, and they left, according to a subsequent Governor (Aungier), 'little more than the walls'. It was hardly surprising that the British, when they came, should set to work to turn the shell of the much-abused house into a more strongly fortified place.

From the foregoing, it will be realised that the English nursed designs on Bombay some long time before they actually acquired it. The East India Company, which had been formed as a trading corporation in 1599 and was awarded its charter by Queen Elizabeth the following year, had had its eye on the place from the beginning, even though it early acquired a toe-hold up the coast at Surat. There was the abortive and disgraceful Anglo-Dutch attempt to claim it by force in 1626, and the general desirability of it as a naval base was discussed from time to time in England as the seventeenth century continued. By the middle of the century the growing power of the Dutch in India, and the signs of declining Moghul power that followed on the death of Shah Jehan, made the Company particularly anxious to have a second station on the western coast, and they petitioned Cromwell to this effect. But it was the ending of the Commonwealth and the Restoration of Charles II which provided the opportunity to get hold of Bombay: it was one of the possessions that came to Charles as part of his marriage contract with the Portuguese princess, Catherine of Braganza. As the poor woman was never to bear a child, it was the sole enduring advantage to accrue to Britain from the marriage. But what an advantage!

Not that many of the British were particularly impressed by their prize: there was a general feeling that the Portuguese had exaggerated the amenities of the place. Pepys, wearing his Admiralty hat, called it 'a poor little island'. Among those, like Pepys, with some factual knowledge of Bombay there would appear to have been confusion as to whether it was its present assets, then

---

* From the Malabar coast some 500 miles south of Bombay, not to be confused with Malabar Hill in Bombay. The hill may possibly, however, have taken its name from the tribe and their visitations there to worship at a shrine.

few, or its military and naval potential, which ought to be taken into account. Others who joined in the discussion displayed a remarkable vagueness as to detail. Lord Clarendon wrote of 'the Island of Bombay with the towns and castles therein which are a very little distance from Brazil'. Lord Clarendon was a man of the seventeenth century, when the entire world was being mapped, yet one can see in his mind the concentrated, toy-like, medieval world picture, making as few allowances for cultural and physical differences as it did for distance: if Bombay was worth having it would have towns and castles, would it not, as France and Italy and other central places did? And anyway all those regions on the outer edges of the earth were much of a muchness, their *raison d'être* being to supply the main countries of the world with the commodities they needed. Lord Clarendon may have been singularly weak on geography for a man in his position – he was in the King's confidence, and knew of a secret agreement that Britain should help the Portuguese against the Dutch. But his attitude was simply an extreme version of that combination of vagueness and opportunism which led a nineteenth-century observer (Sir John Seeley, Professor of Modern History at Cambridge) to comment that 'the British acquired their Empire in a fit of absent-mindedness'. At any rate they certainly did not, at this stage, realise what they might be acquiring.

The marriage was solemnised in 1662, and the young Duke of Marlborough (then Earl) was sent out to stake Britain's claim on Bombay, accompanied by the man designated by the Crown as Governor, but the Portuguese inhabiting the place stalled and quibbled about handing it over. These would have included not only the current Lady of the Manor, Donna Inez de Miranda and her retinue, but eleven other Portuguese households then recorded as having been living on the main island, doubtless backed up by the inhabitants of the more northerly islands where Portuguese occupation and hence Jesuit power was more firmly ensconced. Three years elapsed, during which the Governor-designate died of sickness, the first of many; it was his Secretary, Humphrey Cooke, who eventually received the territory from the reluctant Portuguese in 1665. Even then it was not known what the exact area of the new possession was to be. There was genuine doubt about how far 'Bombay' extended – how many islands, that is to say, it logically comprised. It is not clear in any case, at this distance of time, to what extent under Portuguese rule certain creeks had already been bridged, or even dammed and thus areas of swamp rendered more habitable – or at any rate more mappable. Some commentators of those very early years refer firmly to the place as The Island, but this may have reflected a point of view rather than a current reality. It is perhaps significant that the map John Fryer drew ten years after the British had come, which is still in existence, shows all the principal islands already united into one and somehow contracted into a solid lump, as if he had mentally squeezed the excess liquid out of the central Flats as out of a sponge, and in doing so had reduced the whole place to a more manageable size. In reality, we know that the Flats at any rate, and the Great Breach through which the seas rushed onto them, were to remain an intractable problem for another century and more.

Since the whole place had been governed, up to then, from Bassein on the mainland, it was possible to make out that all seven islands formed one entity. In practice, however, the more northern tracts of solid land were still sufficiently separate one from another and from the principal one to be claimed by the Portuguese as distinct territories. Cooke was finally told that he could take the principal island, with Malabar Hill (which *de facto* gave him the rocky outcrops of Colaba and Old Woman's Island as well), Mazagaon, and also the part of the long northern island which was called Parell, but not the bits of the same island which were almost separated from it and went by the names of Matunga, Dharavi and Sion. He could have Worli, north of Malabar Hill and facing the ocean, but not Mahim beyond it. There seems no doubt that the Portuguese had been deliberately dragging their feet, hoping to get away with ceding as little as possible. A month before they were finally forced, by order from Portugal, to do so, the Viceroy of Goa, Antonio de Mello de Castro – one of whose predecessors had been responsible for acquiring Bombay in the first place – wrote to his King: 'I confess at the feet of your majesty that only the obediance I owe to your majesty as a vassal could have forced me to this deed . . . I forsee the great trouble that from this neighbourhood will result to the Portuguese and that India will be lost on the same day on which the English nation is settled in Bombay.' Given the apparently rural insignificance of Bombay at this date, it was an amazingly prophetic statement.

No description survives of exactly the view that met Cooke when he landed. By the time Fryer wrote, ten years later, the British had already begun to leave their stamp on the place; they erected walls, further houses and a Customs House, rebuilt a Portuguese fort on

51

Dongri hill and erected another on Worli. The Customs House was an optimistically large building: it was subsequently a barracks and, much altered, survives vestigially today; but, like da Orta's house, it is now buried in a prohibited site – the dockyard. When the British first came, that stretch of open land west of the Manor House, which was later to form the Esplanade and today forms the Bombay *maidans*, was not yet cleared. The coconut palms which then provided the sole export crop of the place would have come right up to the foot of the raised mound on which the House and its garden stood. These plantations were called *oarts* – the word was long current, deriving from the Portuguese *orta* or *horta* from the Latin *hortus*: they stretched northwards across the main island to where the Flats began. Dotted among them were a Portuguese church, a few houses belonging to Portuguese, and the palm-thatched cabins of local Bhandris; these people had served as soldiers under the Portuguese and were to do so under the British, but otherwise occupied themselves in cultivating the coconuts, in particular in tapping the trees for their sap which was then fermented into toddy – a Bombay commodity of which we shall hear again. Towards the Great Breach the tree groves merged into batty-grounds (rice paddies), with a Koli fishing settlement on a hillock at Girgaum, near Back Bay, and another at Dongri. Then, on the Dongri side, came Fig-tree Creek, then Mazagaon, a much more important village. (*Machcha-grama* = fish-village.) This was a place of Portuguese settlement and had long been known for its mango trees. The mangoes of Mazagaon were celebrated: they appear in various native records and stories, and in Thomas Moore's *Lallah Rookh*, written in 1817 when India was beginning to catch the Romantic imagination. They fruited twice a year, once at about Christmas (the cool season) and once in May during the pre-monsoon heat. In the early years of the twentieth century two mango trees with this agreeable habit were still standing in private gardens in Mazagaon, oases in what had otherwise become a dusty dockland area.

Yet even today the unfashionable but pleasant streets of Mazagaon retain a strong whiff of its past; not just the eighteenth- and early nineteenth-century past when prosperous British and Parsis built their out-of-town houses on its wooded slopes, but the still older past of Portuguese days. Although it is becoming increasingly a Moslem area, parts of it have remained Roman Catholic* enclaves: you can walk along rather clean and quiet lanes between solid, old-fashioned stone houses where crosses mark the intersections, and almost believe, particularly at night, that you are in some corner of a provincial town in southern Europe. In Belvedere Road, which encircles the one remaining rocky outcrop in central Bombay, the old wooden bungalows have the delicately fretworked eaves and verandahs of traditional Indian craftsmanship, but between the lattice-work of the windows you glimpse Madonnas, Crucifixions and Sacred Hearts, surrounded by the lace and candles of the western world's cult. Look up, and, rising above the small public garden which tops the rocky hill, are tad-palms, the original toddy-producing trees of the Island. Here, in this corner, so near the docks and railways yet sheltered from them, is a brief vision of a Bombay that has vanished. The hill was once more extensive, and ended in a cliff with the ancient Mazagaon harbour curving round to the north of it. Today it hangs abruptly above the central yards of the Electricity Board; where the sea once washed its foot the harbour railway line runs, and beyond that the great Victorian dockland that was reclaimed from the waters.

When the part of the hill where the Electricity Board now are was scooped out to make a railway line and a fish market and cast into the sea, there disappeared along with it an ancient house that had been variously known as the Belvedere or Belvidere, Mazagaon House or the Mark House: the latter name was due to the eighteenth-century practice of white-washing it regularly so that it should be a landmark for vessels making their way into the harbour. It was lived in at different times by several locally distinguished people, and at one time by a lady who eloped from it into the night by means of a rope let from her window down the cliff and into a small boat in the water beneath. (See Chapter VI.) It ended its long life as the P. & O. Club. Drawings of it show a square, plain building reminiscent of a chapel rather than a dwelling house, and it is possible that this is what it once was. The Jesuits had been the first Portuguese in Mazagaon, and are thought to have built a chapel and monastery on the hill, but in 1572 the district was granted by the

---

* Native RCs, usually known as 'Goans', are sometimes of mixed Portuguese-Indian descent and are light skinned, but are more commonly the full descendants of Hindus who were converted by the Portuguese. Since the Portuguese also employed imported Negro slaves, known as 'coffrees', their blood as well was added to the ethnic mix, with the result that some of Bombay's RC community are rather darker than their Hindu neighbours, and have curly hair.

King of Portugal in perpetuity to the de Souza e Lima family. The Bombay *Gazetteer* of 1909 records 'the island of Mazagaon was one of the few places that escaped absorption by the priesthood', and indeed the family managed to retain a tenacious hold on the place from father to son or son-in-law, legitimate or otherwise, for the best part of two hundred years, keeping at bay not only the priests but also, till the mid-eighteenth century, the East India Company. The surname de Souza (da Souza, d'Souza, de Souze) is still common in the district. At one time the estate was considered to extend across to the Charni *oart* on the opposite side of the complex of islands (the name survives today in Charni Road railway station) and also to include Narowji, alias Dongri, Hill on the south side of Fig-tree Creek. The de Souza house on Mazagaon Hill was said to have 'belonged before to the Jesuits', and it was this same house that later became known as the Mark House. No doubt the railway engineers who briskly removed it and a large chunk of its hillside in 1864 neither knew nor cared that they were removing a rare relic of Portuguese times: it was then just known as 'an old and haunted house'.

A still greater and less excusable loss is the Nossa Senhora de Gloria church at the foot of the hill; the de Souza family endowed this Franciscan church in 1632 on the understanding that its management would remain vested in their family. Its Church Street, leading from the sea, was bisected by the harbour railway in the late nineteenth century, but the church survived this upheaval – only to be demolished in 1911. Today its site, after standing empty for many years marked by a cross, is being filled with new housing, and if you ask for the Gloria church you will be proudly directed to a structure in standard North Oxford Gothic, built half a mile away and opened in 1913, and now spoiled by the erection of a fly-over directly in front of it.

The northernmost section to which the British, when they came, were able to lay claim was Parell (it was usually spelt thus up to the nineteenth century and subsequently with one 'l'). Here were more coconut groves, mangoes and tamarinds, a Brahmin village and also a Jesuit monastery and church; it is another of those key sites, like the Mark House, to which historical accounts of Bombay keep returning. That, with Worli (or Varli, as it was then called), completed the British possessions – together with the 4,000 acres of Flats in the middle, the 'drowned land' on which, at that date, very little could be grown. Across these were the ruins of a stone causeway, whose origins are obscure but which seem to have pre-dated Portuguese occupation.

On the edge of the Flats, on a rocky outcrop by the Great Breach, there had anciently been an important temple to Mahalaxmi, the goddess of wealth. This had been destroyed, possibly by the Portuguese (the popular theory) but perhaps by the Moslems who came before them, and there was no trace of it when the British arrived; today, however, Mahalaxmi flourishes again on that spot, and even has a railway station named after her. The Portuguese or others had also virtually destroyed the shrine to Walkeshwar, the Sand Lord, which stood on Malabar Point, breaking down the great stone *lingam* which had once been an object of veneration for the marauding Malabars. However, this cult could not be entirely suppressed, for Fryer records there in 1675 'the remains of a stupendous Pagoda near a tank of fresh water'. Under the British (who, to their credit, were far more tolerant than their predecessors or perhaps simply did not care as much) a new temple was donated in 1715 by a wealthy Hindu,* and a Brahmin village regrouped itself here. It was recorded by many visitors through the generations as a 'picturesque spot' and some of the old houses and temples remain today. The tank too is there, a great stone construction with flights of steps and dubiously blue-green water, just as it was when it reminded eighteenth-century European travellers of an open-air Roman bath: such visitors, reared in an exclusively classical tradition, tended to see the influence of Alexander the Great everywhere. Once, almost to within living memory, Bombay had many such tanks scattered about its districts, the chief source of water for many of its citizens. A few are still there, covered over, but Walkeshwar is the last to survive anywhere near the centre in its original state, and it is another of those places which offer a sudden view of a lost way of life.

The word 'pagoda', which later became attached to Chinese temples only, was the term in common use for heathen worshipping places in the early British days in Bombay. Its origins are disputed, but it seems to have been borrowed from the Portuguese who, in turn, may have got it from the Moslems, for one theory is that it is a corruption of *but-khana* or 'idol-house'. In coping with the Hindu

---

* Rama Kamathi. He also built a temple in the Fort. He was in some way connected with the command of native troops under the British, although he possibly had connections with the pirate Angria. In 1720 he was tried for conspiracy against the Government, was tortured, and died in prison. It was subsequently discovered that the most important piece of evidence against him had been forged, and reparations were paid to his son.

pagodas and their attendant cults, of which they heartily disapproved, the Jesuits seem sometimes to have followed a practice commonplace in Europe a thousand years earlier, that of attempting to substitute one cult for another. For instance, just as St Paul's in London was built on the site of a temple of Mercury, so the monastery at Parell was constructed on a site already in use for heathen worship – the name of the place comes from *paroli*, a shrine. So too was the Portuguese church on the main island; its first site was just beyond the Fort where Victoria Terminus now stands and which place was already occupied by the temple to Mumba Devi: however, they managed to co-exist. The church itself was moved by the British during the eighteenth century to the far end of the *maidans* during one of their periodic fits of clearance, and that second church too was swept away later: a stone cross marks its site, and that *maidan* is called Cross Maidan to this day. Mumba Devi, who was displaced at the same time as the first church, went northwards to wet her feet at Pydhoni, but the sacred tank remained on the original site; its sacredness was gradually forgotten and a hundred years later it was in use as a washermen's tank. It was by then called Phansi Talao, the 'gibbet pond', for nearby stood the public gallows and pillory. These were removed shortly after India came under the direct power of the Crown in 1858, but the pond stayed, an odd and little-regarded survival, till it was filled in when the grand railway terminus building was begun in 1878.

Mumba or Mombai is a goddess without a mouth – ironically, she is the Mother Goddess of Bombay, the city with no one common language but many. An early eighteenth-century commentator (Burnell) describes her as 'seated in a poor hovel upon a small altar decked with flowers, her head being three times bigger in proportion than her body'. (The British of the period were routinely shocked by Hindu devotions, since they seem to have been unable to understand that the rather grotesque figures of the gods and goddesses might possess for their devotees a symbolic rather than a physical importance, and in any case they considered the figures to be devils.) Though an obscure local deity, an aboriginal personification of the Earth Mother, Maha-Amba-Aiee or 'Mumba Devi' has turned out durable. The very name 'Bombay' almost certainly comes from hers, for the city is called 'Mumbai' in the vernacular. The British settlers assumed the name to come from 'Buan Bahia', the Good Bay in Portuguese, and this theory was reiterated in most nineteenth-century books about the place, but it is now discredited: it cannot be right, since the earliest Portuguese settlers already called the place Bombaim.

In recent years it has been persistently suggested that the name of the city should be Indianised, and that Bombay should become Mumbai for the whole world. In June 1981 this has, in theory, come to pass. The mouthless goddess must be laughing.

III 'The City, which by God's assistance is intended to be built'

> *. . . cities simply cannot be 'explained' by their locations or other given sources. Their existence as cities and the sources of their growth lie within themselves, in the processes and growth systems that go on within them. Cities are not ordained, they are wholly existential.*
>
> Jane Jacobs, *The Economy of Cities*, 1970

Any account of the early decades of Bombay's British history leaves the reader wondering how it was that the whole enterprise did not flounder. How, amongst frequent deaths, internal disputes, shortage of funds, mutinies, a revolt, and attacks or threats of attacks from without from four separate but intermittently collusive enemies, did the town get founded at all? Yet it did. Perhaps it is important to remember, in view of the dominating image of the high-minded Indian Civil Servant that we have inherited from the more recent past, that the early settlers in Bombay, as in the other two presidencies of Calcutta and Madras, were men of a very different cast. Whatever they lacked in integrity and moral fervour, and most of them lacked a great deal, they were at least courageous and determined in their self-seeking. The early name for the East India Company was 'The Company of Merchant Adventurers to the East Indies' and that indeed was what they were – traders, bent on making personal fortunes. Some of their activities were frankly piratical, and all were carried out in a time when India was many months away from England so that neither immediate censure nor ready help could be expected from the Company servants at home.

When Bombay became a Crown colony in 1665 it was obvious that its governance must be carried out with some semblance of order and decency. But this was not easy to arrange.

Sir Humphrey Cooke arrived to find 'neither Government nor Justice' in the place. The Portuguese had already made themselves difficult toward the British and he paid them back in the same coin. He annexed Mahim, one of the northern islands which had not been included in the final agreement, and attempted to confiscate Roman Catholic (i.e. Portuguese) plantations when the incumbents refused to renounce the Pope. (The amount of Bombay Island that actually *belonged* to the Crown, as distinct from just being in its sovereignty, consisted mainly of rock, drowned land and shoreline – a shoreline which, two hundred years later in the days of the great dock-building, was to become immensely valuable.) Cooke also got on the wrong side of the Moghul overlords of western India, and this in turn annoyed the East India Company servants who were then settled up the coast in Surat, the Company's headquarters in India. They had a 'factory' (agency) in Surat, but the town was under the control of the Moghul Emperor Aurangzeb, and if relations with the Moghuls were bad this harmed trade. The Company also resented the way Cooke traded on his own account on the side although the Company was at that time supposed to have the monopoly of all trading in Bombay. (In fact almost all the early Governors transgressed this rule.) Cooke was demoted, and a new Governor, Sir Gervase Lucas, was sent out from England. His story is typical in that he narrowly escaped capture by local Mahratta pirates before arriving in the place in November 1666: by the following year he was dead of 'a lethargy which held him 24 hours'. Neither he nor his successor were much more popular locally than Cooke had been, and one way and another Bombay seemed to be of so little use to the British that the Portuguese had hopes of being able to buy it back, and made unofficial overtures to Charles II on this subject. When this became known, the Company decided they had better acquire it for themselves: the king, uninterested in his distant island and chronically short of money, agreed to hand it over to them in exchange for a loan of £50,000, repayable at 6 per cent interest, and a yearly rent of £10. The agreement declared the Company to be 'the true and absolute Lords and Proprietors of the Fort and the Island . . . their successors and assigns for evermore to be holden to us, our heirs and successors, as of the Manor of East Greenwich in the county of Kent, in free and common soccage . . . '

Thus did the Merchant Adventurers gain their first substantial possession and responsibility, and thus inconspicuously began the process which was one day to transform the British presence in India into what Gandhi referred to as 'the most powerful secret corporation the world has ever known'. In practice, over the next 190 years, the Government of Great Britain was in piecemeal fashion to take back the powers it had so prodigally vested in the East India Company, till at last the wraith of the Company faded away in 1858, the year after the Mutiny. But in 1668 the concept that the whole sub-continent of India might one day be administered by Britain can hardly have been a remote dream in anyone's mind; the Company were no doubt sufficiently pleased with the clauses in the agreement that stated that under the terms of their charter their powers in Bombay were to apply to any other territory in India that they might acquire. The local Company men in Bombay were surprised as well as gratified when the news of the acquisition came through. The agreement had been signed in May 1668, but word of it did not reach Bombay till a passing ship brought mail in September.

By their charter, the Company were to collect all the revenues of Bombay, estimated at £2,833 per annum, make laws and see that they were enforced. Bombay was to be governed from Surat, with a resident Deputy Governor. People born on the island were to be reckoned natural subjects of Great Britain (another proviso that was to have unforeseeably far-reaching results) and were to be allowed free exercise of their religion. On their own account, the Company wanted to establish an English colony and expand trade, and for the first time it was envisaged that the port might become a centre of ship building.

At this point there comes on the scene the man who is always considered the founding father of Bombay, Gerald Aungier. Sir George Oxinden, the Governor who was in charge when Bombay became Company property, was a Surat man with little interest in the new acquisition, but he died the following year, and Aungier, who already knew Bombay, took over. Three years later, in 1672, having tried in vain to get the Company to shift their centre of government from Surat, he moved his own headquarters to Bombay, and devoted the next several years to laying out 'the city, which by God's assistance is intended to be built'.

The phrase has, in Bombay annals, become famous, but the inner significance is less readily recognised. Simply, Bombay was, like Leningrad and Washington but not like the archetypal European city upon which most general concepts of urban history are

60

founded, a conscious creation and furthermore an *urban* creation almost from the beginning. The classic concept of 'city' is of an agglomeration which has grown, by slow degrees, from a rural agricultural settlement to a prosperous village to a market town to a city, gradually acquiring the appurtenances of the final incarnation (large governmental or religious edifices etc.) along the way. But however valid this concept is for certain cities, particularly in Europe – and even there its validity as a stereotype may be questioned in many instances – it is invalid for Bombay or, for that matter, Calcutta. Bombay was never primarily an agricultural settlement, even using the term in the loosest sense: much of her eventual land surface went straight from semi-wilderness to suburban occupation. And it was a city, the final apotheosis which most settlements never reach, which was envisaged from the first. It was with this goal in mind, rather than the *ad hoc* needs of his own day, that Aungier started construction.

It was he who established the Courts of Justice under English law, as promised by the agreement with the Crown; part of the original building, Mapla Por, was still standing in the Fort in the 1930s. He also built new docks, a printing press and a mint to manufacture gold and silver coins for local use. He inaugurated a Company militia, the precursor to the East India Company Army which was eventually to become the Indian Army, plus a reserve force of local inhabitants who, on a feudal system, were liable for military service. (A subsequent visitor – Burnell – remarked, 'They are usually called up once a month to do their exercise, which they do with as much grace as a cow might make a curtsey'.) Instead of appropriating land like his predecessors, he called a meeting of local landowners to sort out their tortuous and ill-recorded land-holdings, and made a gentleman's agreement with them to start afresh on the basis of their claims. He managed to purchase for the Company the land that later became the Fort, and also Colaba and Old Woman's Island. He built forts at Sion and Mahim. Above all he encouraged settlement from elsewhere, and made plans for each religious or racial community to have its own official representatives. A French physician, Dellon, who visited Bombay during the years of Aungier's rule, wrote admiringly of it as 'a city where they grant liberty to all strangers of what religion or nation soever to settle themselves, and exempt them from all manner of taxes for the first twenty years'.

It has often been stated that under Aungier the population of Bombay, with its outlying districts such as Mazagaon and Parell, attained 60,000. I think that this is a considerable over-estimate, a figure tossed off in a day when statistics were unknown, and then repeated down the generations as if it were a received truth. But it is true that the population of the new colony grew greatly within a few years. Aungier encouraged Banians (Hindu traders) to settle: many came up from Goa, escaping the intolerance of Jesuit power there. Others came down from Gujerat, where they were already a thriving mercantile people; these were the first-founders of Bombay's present large Gujerati-speaking business community, and they brought their own ways of life and building with them. Mapla Por was in fact a typical *pol*, or Gujerati-style group of buildings round a courtyard, with one defensive external gate which could be shut against Moslems, Mahrattas and suchlike traditional enemies. In Bombay, as well as providing them with a refuge for life, Aungier gave the Banians their own burning ground for their dead on the shores of Back Bay – it remains there to this day, though time and reclamation have removed the sea from its edge and railway trains now go clanking by on their way to Churchgate Station where once the charred bones were cast into the ocean. Parsis too began to migrate from Surat, and were allowed to build what Fryer misleadingly refers to as 'a tomb' on the rocky wilderness of Malabar Hill. Their ancestors had migrated from Persia some thousand years before, so they were in a sense the first of the great waves of Middle Eastern peoples who were to help form Bombay. At the same time, Arab traders from the Gulf and the Red Sea were also coming, encouraged by Aungier with free passages. (Today the traffic is the other way, for in recent years numbers of Bombay's skilled and semi-skilled workers have flocked to places like Dubai and Abu Dhabi, drawn thither by the high earnings to be had in these oil-rich places.) Under Aungier too the Armenians began to arrive: there are few of them left in Bombay today – instead Calcutta has become the centre of their community, as Bombay is the centre for the Parsis – but they still have a small church (not, unfortunately, the original one) standing in a corner of the Fort between Hamam and Dalal streets, the street of the Turkish Baths and the street of the Stockbrokers. Today, the skyscraper block of the new Bombay Stock Exchange looms over it.

One should not exaggerate. Aungier's rule, though longer than that of many of the other all-too-mortal early governors, did not last that long: he died at Surat in 1677, and much of what he had hoped for Bombay must have been left unfulfilled. In addition, the aura of universal respect that his name still carries must reflect to some extent the extreme *dis*respect aroused by the record and the memory of some other holders of that office. Aungier openly disapproved of the drinking habits he found among the Europeans of the colony; in particular he disapproved of those who partook of the local toddy, or of the mixture of this with limejuice, plain water, rosewater and sugar that composed 'the accursèd Bombay punch, the shame, scandal and ruin of religion'.* He was a man reared in the Cromwellian era, and though he assured the religious toleration in Bombay that had been promised in the agreement, he also laid plans for a church, with the 'main design of inviting the natives to repair thereunto, and observe the gravity and purity of our own devotions . . . and at length when the merciful pleasure of God shall think good to touch them with a sense of the eternal welfare of their souls, that they may be convinced of their error . . . '

The tone is oddly suggestive of the evangelical imperialism of a much later date. Few, if any, of Aungier's contemporaries seem to have shared his lofty sentiments. At any rate, though foundations were laid for the church and the work was begun, it was abandoned after his death. For another generation the walls remained at fifteen feet – 'a mark of derision for the natives for whose conversion they were partly raised, a reproach and a scandal to the English in Bombay'. That was written by Richard Cobbe, the East India Company's chaplain *c*.1715, and it was not till he busied himself about the matter that the walls rose higher and the church was finished – St Thomas's church, today styled 'cathedral', which still stands, somewhat altered, in the middle of the Fort district, a venue for waiting taxis and bullock carts.

Just as some of Aungier's attitudes prefigured those of nineteenth-century Bombay, so his personal life-style had more in common with that of the 'nabobs' of the eighteenth-century than with the hand-to-mouth existence of Bombay's first colonisers. He lived in the Castle, the ex-Portuguese Manor House, now fortified by the 'bold rampires' mentioned by Fryer; his meals, announced by trumpets and served to music, were as grand as the resources of the Island permitted (though Fryer also wrote: 'Cows are a scarce commodity on the Island, as in truth is everything also for provision, we being beholden to our neighbours the Portuguese for almost everything we eat'). When he travelled, either in a coach drawn by oxen or in a grand palaquin with a 'sombrero' or umbrella

---

* Five ingredients. The name is from *panch* – 'five' in the vernacular.

of state held over his head, he was followed by a large retinue of servants.

It was Aungier's Bombay that Fryer was describing when he wrote in 1675 of the changes that had come over the old Manor House he had known. He continued:

At a distance enough from the Fort lies the town, in which confusedly live the English, Portuguese, Topazes [Indo-Portuguese], Gentoos [Hindus], Moors [Moslems], Coolies and Christians – mostly fishermen. It is a full mile in length; the houses are low and thatched with oleas of the coconut tree; all but a few the Portuguese left and some few the Company have built. The custom house and warehouses are tiled and plastered and instead of glass use panes of oyster-shell for their windows. There is a reasonably handsome bazaar at the end of the town looking onto a field where cows and buffaloes graze [the east end of the future Esplanade, more or less the site of the present Bombay Gymkhana] . . . The Portuguese have a pretty house and church [on the Victoria Terminus site beside the original Mumba Devi temple], with orchards of Indian fruit adjoining. The English have only a burying ground called Mendham's Point from the first man's name therein enterred, where are some few tombs that make a pretty show at entering the haven; but neither church nor hospital, both of which are mightily desired.

He also mentions that Old Woman's Island then housed 'the Company's antelopes and beasts of delight'. Were they part of Aungier's gracious life-style?

At the same period Aungier himself wrote proudly to the Court of Directors in London, where Surat silk and Indian muslins were newly fashionable:

Before the English came the trade was only in coconuts and cairo [coir]. Now the country merchants drive a great trade with Surat, Broach, Cambay and Gogo, and also to Dabull, Kelsey, Rajapore and Goa, to Mocha, Persia, Scindia, Bussora, in salt, coconuts, cairo, betel-nut, rice, elephants teeth, broadcloth, lead, sword blades and some other European goods. Last year we disposed in Bombay of 600 pieces of broad cloth, 3,000 maunds of leads, all the perpetuanes and serges, and all the sword blades.

He added: 'the trade by sea and land is interrupted by the Mughal and Seevajee's fleets and armies', but appended a further list of places with which they were attempting to open trade – 'whence we shall get myrrh, aloes, olibanum, choseed, tinkall, sena, red earth, carminia wool, pertchock, skins, corryes, pepper and cardomoms and other goods proper for Europe and the South Seas'.

The Moghul powers and 'Seevajee' (Sivaji, Shivaji) were not the only enemies that menaced the settlement in Bombay, then and for many years, but they were the most significant. The Moghul fleets were in the charge of the Sidis, Abyssinian buccaneers who had made a deal with the Emperor Aurangzeb. Aurangzeb ruled a large part of northern and central India; he was the son of Shah Jehan and the queen who lies to this day in the Taj Mahal at Agra, and he co-existed in an uneasy and often-broken peace with the British at Surat and Bombay. *His* main opponent was Shivaji, a Mahratta military adventurer who had his stronghold near Poona. It was rather hard on the British of Bombay that the power-struggle between these two, the representative respectively of the declining Moslem empire and of rising local Hindu power, should have been taking place on or near their territory. Although Aurangzeb outlived Shivaji (who died in 1680) and retained his power for another generation, it is Shivaji who is remembered in Bombay. He is said to have found a secret way across the marshy creeks that cut Bombay off from the mainland, and to have been able to get from Poona to Bombay in an unnaturally short time. He has a cult-following today among the sort of people who write 'Maharastria for the Maharastrians' on walls – surely one of the most inappropriate slogans ever for a city renowned as a free-trade city, open to all comers, from its inception?

In addition to the Moghuls, the Sidis and Shivaji, the early inhabitants of Bombay also suffered from the depredations of common pirates, both Mahratta and Malabar, fears of a Dutch attack (during the Dutch war with England) and intermittent trouble from the Portuguese, who were not above combining with one of the forces mentioned above if they thought it was to their advantage. But it was not the enemies without that brought Bombay low in the years following Aungier's death and came near to destroying it, but the enemy within, for Bombay, *a ilha da boa vida*, so promising an Eden, so lovely with its fringed palm groves set in its blue sea, had revealed itself by the 1680s to be a place of death.

Even in the first years after the British took over the west coast of India it could hardly have been said to have been famous for its health. Aungier was the fourth Governor, out of five in little more than a decade, to die in India. But death-rates are relative and so is the fact of death. At the time when Cooke was attempting to claim the Island, the Plague of London was running its course, and typhoid or malarial fever could strike a man down as quickly at Hampton Court or Greenwich as in Bombay fort. Our ancestors lived with death as a constant presence in their lives at home, and presumably were not as readily intimidated by the thought of Death lying in wait for them on the other side of the world as we should be. But by and by the odds on dying in Bombay before you had begun to make your fortune began to seem so short that even the hardiest adventurers were daunted. Illnesses that were described ranged from 'the Chinese death' (*mort de Chine*, a corruption of the vernacular *modasi*, probably cholera) through assorted fevers and 'fluxes' to beri-beri, otherwise 'barbiers', which sounds like polio in its effect – 'a man tottered in his gait like a dying sheep or span round like a teetotum'.

An account of these years comes from Ovington. He was a chaplain with the East India Company and sailed to Bombay, arriving in 1690 while the Castle and the main island were being besieged by the Sidis, who were encamped close at hand in Mazagaon. In spite of this unpropitious state of affairs, Ovington's ship anchored in Bombay harbour in May, just before the monsoon broke, and so had to stay there for three months. During that time, of the twenty-five passengers who had sailed with Ovington twenty died, and also fifteen of the ship's crew. The Bombay chaplain also died at this period, as had several of his immediate predecessors. Hardly surprisingly, Ovington refused a pressing offer to take on the job and betook himself to Surat where life was healthier and, for the time being, more peaceful. Of Bombay, he wrote that 'one of the pleasantest spots in India seemed no more than a parish graveyard, a charnel house . . . Which common fatality has created a Proverb among the English there, that *two monsoons are the age of a man*'. This last phrase has passed into the mythology of early European life in India: a condition of intensity without a future, one long hot day which will end abruptly in an eternal night.

At the time of Aungier's labours to create 'by God's assistance' the new city, there are said to have been 300 Englishmen resident, most of whom, including soldiers, would have been Company servants. By the end of 1691 there were only 80 left, many of whom were ill; only 5 of these were covenanted Company men. By the following January the 5 had dwindled to 3, and that was in the coolest and healthiest part of the year. In 1696 there were only 27 Englishmen left, plus a few dying military officers. By 1702 we find the Governor, Sir John Gayer, writing to the Court of Directors of the Company in London complaining of the small number of soldiers sent out, considering the ever-present danger of invasion, which was at that time feared not only from the Moghul armies (who had departed from Mazagaon in 1691 leaving the place burnt out behind them) but also from the French, with whom the British were then at war in Europe. Gayer pleaded: 'This number [of soldiers] sometime will not satisfy the craving of Mendham's Point [the cemetery] above halfe one month . . . it is a cormorant paunch, never satisfied with the daily supply it receives, but is still gaping for more.' Four years later the next Governor, Nicholas Waite, wrote to the Court of Directors: 'We are only eight covenent servants, including the Council and but two that write, besides two raw youths taken ashore out of ships, and most of us sick in this unhealthful, depopulated ruined island.' Later in the year he wrote again: 'We are six including your Council and some of us often sick. It is morally impossible without an overruling Providence to continue longer from going underground if we have not a large assistance.' Already, on his arrival two years earlier from Surat, he had written to the Company beseeching that his son 'be settled in the Bay [of Bengal, i.e. Calcutta] rather than in this place of mortality, without shipping or as yet trade'.

Sure enough, Bombay's abrupt decline after her fair beginnings in the seventies had allowed Calcutta to steal the advantage. Calcutta was founded c.1690 by the legendary Job Charnock, a Company servant who managed an advantageous deal with Aurangzeb. He and his successors established Calcutta, commonly then known as the Bay or Fort William, as India's premier port, a distinction which Bombay was eventually to regain, but not till the coming of the 'overland' route and the opening of the Suez Canal in the nineteenth century. De Mello's prophetic remark about India being lost to Portugal the day the British were established in Bombay turned out, in the long run, to be true, but it can hardly have appeared likely by the last two decades of the seventeenth century. Along with the crippling mortality rate, which particularly affected Europeans but did not exempt other races either, there was a drifting away of many of those traders who had come to Bombay in Aungier's day. The Moghul–Sidi siege of 1690 must have driven away many more. Again, one should be wary of population estimates made at this date, but it is said that the total had sunk by 1700 to a quarter or even a sixth of what it had previously been.

It is clear that a general demoralisation had set in; there were complaints from Surat to the Court at home of the poor calibre of the men prepared to come from England as soldiers to the Company in Bombay – 'debauched broken tradesmen and renegade seamen' – and ample evidence that the calibre of the covenanted servants of the Company was not all it might have been, either. In 1683, as the result of a wrangle between Keigwin, Captain of the Bombay garrison, and Ward, the then-Governor, a revolt had occurred. The Company, who were tired of the money the floundering colony was costing them, had ordered Ward to make cuts. Ward was a Surat man – there was considerable rivalry between the two centres – and was said to care nothing for Bombay and to be feathering his own nest. In his absence, Keigwin seized control and was proclaimed Governor. The matter was finally sorted out and an uneasy peace prevailed under Sir John Child. He, perhaps in an attempt to make the colony function better and to follow Aungier's plans, moved his centre of government from Surat to Bombay. He was encouraged in this move by the Court, who wrote from London hoping that 'an ill-grounded fancy or unmanly fear of sickness would not prevail with him'. It was easy enough for Directors, sitting in comfort under a London sky, conducting the slow-motion correspondence of the sailing ships, to make such pious remarks.

Ovington, arriving in Bombay five years later, fresh from England, was shocked by what he found there, though, as a clergyman and a slightly prissy one at that (a contemporary satirist referred to him as 'female Ovington' and 'soft Hermaphrodite'), his observations have a distinct slant:

> I cannot without Horror mention to what pitch all vicious Enormities were grown in this place, when the Infection was most outrageous; nor can I but think that the Divine Justice interposed, and forwarded these fatal Infelicities, which are not wholly imputable to an impure Contagion of the Air . . . the true Cause of the Malady lay deeper. Their Principles of Action, and the consequent evil Practices of the *English* forwarded their Miseries, and contributed to fill the Air with those pestilential Vapours that seized their Vitals, and speeded their hasty passage to the other world. Luxury, Immodesty, and a prostitute Dissolution of Manners, found still new Matter to work upon . . .

Others besides Ovington, without going so far as to intimate that sin leads to cholera, were of the opinion that the citizens' habits had something to do with their death-rate. Fryer had thought that the mortality of the Island was mainly due to the consumption of 'phul arrack (brandy made of blubber or carvill) and foul women'.

Bombay from the harbour. 18th century. The large building on the shore is the Custom house, with St Thomas's church visible behind it. The baston walls of the Castle are to the right.

The 'Fort' – fortified town – of Bombay in 1811, viewed from the Esplanade. The harbour lies on the far side.

The house at the heart of Bombay Castle, constructed by late 17th century British settlers out of the shell of da Orta's 16th century Manor House and used for about a hundred years as the Governor's house. (Photograph late nineteenth century).

The second Governor's house, built in Apollo Street in the 18th century, and for many years in the 19th century used as the Secretariat. Now put to multiple commercial uses. (Photo taken 1980).

A third Government House: the property at Parel, on the site of a Jesuit
monastery, where 19th century Governors and their wives held court.
Today the building has become a plague laboratory. Viewed from the
west, with the mountains of the mainland in the background.

Forbes's House, in the Fort, the home of a wealthy merchant.
Watercolour view from the north west made in 1815.

The same house, photographed from the same angle in 1980.

One of the 'Towers of Silence' on Malabar Hill where the Parsis lay their dead. Note the vultures in attendance round the top of it. Picture taken c.1900.

In the early 1680s the Governing body in Surat had stated: 'When men come new out, drink punch toddy and country beer, besides that are disordered and tumble on damp ground, it cannot be expected but that disease must be contracted.' The picture of the wretched English of the time, eating, drinking and making merry all the more incontinently in the extreme likelihood of death on the morrow, is a poignant one; though the effect of the damp ground seems neither here nor there compared with the doubtless half-putrid meat which, clinging to a European diet, they must often have swallowed, and the unsuitable, tight, European clothing which the early pictures by native artists invariably show them as wearing. Records of the sales of personal property when the owners had died tell in themselves a poignant tale. What further can one add to the case of Ambrose Thompson, whose property, auctioned in Bombay in 1701, included 'A Black Coat, Wastcoat and breeches . . . 3 Wiggs, 23 Neckcloths, 1 Microscope, A Carraboy of Portugall wine, A Slave boy, 48 gallons of Clarett'?

Ovington was no fool; elsewhere in his essay he speculates on the material causes of so much ill-health:

> They have abundance of coconuts, which bring some Advantage to the Owners, but very little either of corn or Cattle, but what is imported from the adjacent Country; and those not in great Plenty, nor of very good Growth. A Sheep or two from *Suratt* is an acceptable Present to the best Man upon the Island. And the Unhealthfulness of the Waters bears a just Proportion to the Scarcity and Meanness of the Diet, and both of them together with a bad Air, make a sudden end of many a poor Sailor and Souldier, who pay their Lives for hopes of a Livelihood. Indeed, whether it be that the air stagnates, for the land towards the Fort lies very low, or the stinking of the Fish which was used to be applied to the Roots of the Trees, instead of Dung . . . 'tis certainly a mortal enemy to the lives of the *Europeans*.

He does not mention, or perhaps did not realise, that many natives and Indo-Portuguese were dying also, for plague raged in western India between 1686 and 1696. But he was surely right about the water, which was to carry death for the unwary for many a year: still today only the tough or the foolhardy of all races drink the Bombay municipal water without filtering or boiling it. Although the specific nature of the waterborne cholera vibrio was not suspected till the mid-nineteenth century, the *general* principle of danger lying in impure water was appreciated by the seventeenth century, so it is hardly surprising that European settlers indulged themselves on beer, toddy and wine: these beverages were believed, perhaps rightly, to be less contaminated. Their traditional consumption in England was due, in part, to the same logic: Englishmen at home were hardly famed for their abstemiousness at that time. Another visitor to Bombay in the early 1700s, John Burnell, who was in charge of the fort at Dongri for a while and was dismissed from the Company for 'drinking and insolence', wrote of the Bombay water supply: 'Just by the gate is the well, large deep, the habitation of frogs as big as wild ducks. This is the water which serves the Fort, town and shipping; therefore I mention it and wish I could report it wholesome, but it can't be expected, seeing it is dug in a ground whose nature is salt petre, not agreeable in the least to European constitutions.'

The salt-petre seems doubtful, but the water may certainly have been brackish. It is not quite clear which 'gate' is referred to, but probably, at such an early date, it is the gate of the Castle itself, the old one with the Portuguese soldiers engraved on top of it. Later maps show a large, round tank at this place, which survived up to the mid-nineteenth century, and it seems likely that this is Burnell's 'well'. In any event, the well was obviously to the west of the Castle, and all the land to the west, stretching to the shore of Back Bay – the land that was later to become the Esplanade – is sandy gravel: water can be obtained at any point along it by digging deep enough. By the early nineteenth century there were literally dozens of wells dotted about the Esplanade (there are still one or two today). But it was observed at that period that the level of the water in them rose and fell very slightly in accordance with the tides in the Bay, which argues some degree of salt-water seepage.

The two other possible causes of sickness mentioned by Ovington, the marshy lands and the application of fish-manure to the coconut plantations, were long discussed and disputed. From the beginning of the British presence in Bombay the possibility of joining the seven islands into one and reclaiming the drowned Flats in the middle had been eagerly canvassed, but more for territorial reasons and to make the island self-supporting in crops and pasture than for those of health. The Great Breach north of Malabar and Kamballa Hill was the major problem, if the Flats were to be made usable, and as early as 1668 a scheme for damming this was suggested, for the cost 'in the judgement of sober men' of £1,000 or £1,200. However this estimate was doubtless too modest even at that remote period, and the work too difficult. At all events nothing was done about the Great Breach for over fifty years, though from the 1680s onwards it was persistently suggested that the 'pestilential vapours' arising from these Flats after the monsoon were the cause of every known disease. The swamps must indeed have been classic breeding grounds for the malarial mosquito.

Some works were done on the smaller breaches or creeks, in particular on Umarkhadi ('the Fig-tree Creek') between the main island and Mazagaon, on the opposite side from the Great Breach. There was some sort of bridge there in Portuguese days, and though its successor was presumably cut during the Moghul siege it would seem that by 1700 the creek was not only bridged but dammed. It is likely therefore that the Footwash, the tip of this creek, dried up quite early; this and the adjacent district of Mandvi* were the first of the low-lying land over which houses began, in the eighteenth century, to creep.

The other small creeks between the northern islands were closed, after a fashion, with causeways, about 1710, and presumably this all helped to reduce the swampiness of the Flats. When the causeway between Worli and Mahim was cut through two hundred years later, during works by the Bombay Improvement Trust, it was found to be solid masonry and still in good condition. In 1712 ambitious plans were again made for the Great Breach, and work started. It was to be closed in a straight line running across the little bay from Kamballa Hill to the south of Worli, taking in the small, rocky island which, today, supports Hadji Ali's mausoleum, then unbuilt. But perhaps the Moslem celebrity did not wish the site of his death (see Chapter VI) to disappear in this way, or possibly – as the current Hindu theory went – the goddess Mahalaxmi, whose temple by the Breach had been earlier destroyed, did not want the wall built either. At all events the work had to be abandoned. Not for another decade was the first semi-circular wall, following the natural line of the bay, constructed on the present site. There is a story that the contractor, one Ramji Shivji, was visited by Mahalaxmi in a dream and told that, if the temple were reinstated, the wall would hold. During the excavations, a broken statue of the goddess was indeed found embedded in the mud, and subsequently the Government granted land on the promontory for the rebuilding of the temple, where it stands today.

* It means the Custom House in Marathi: then on the eastern foreshore, it was apparently the site of the harbour customs in Portuguese days – though it should be added that in Gujerati 'Mandvi' simply indicates a market.

The fish-manure was another matter. As early as the 1670s Fryer remarked that the unhealthiness of Bombay was 'at first thought to be caused by bubsho, rotten fish; but though that is prohibited yet it continues as mortel'. But in fact the 'buckshawing' of the trees, as it was called, was itself continuing at that time, as the following letter from the Surat Council shows:

> As regards your order permitting the natives to put dry fish to the roots of the trees, buried deep underground, Mr Matthew Grey at the time of his abode on the island, remembers not any offence given by the stench of dry fish buried at the roots of trees. As this practice is beneficial to the natives, and not so offensive to the people as to prejudice their healths, we think it may continue till his Honour the President (Mr Aungier) this season, upon better information, finds to the contrary.

Dry fish? There seems to be a certain confusion there between fish-manure and the edible dried fish ('Bombay Duck') which has traditionally been a delicacy of the Island and still is today. Or were the two commodities in practice not dissimilar? At all events the manuring did continue, for in 1708 we find the Court in London writing to the Bombay Government: 'The buckshawing or dunging of the toddy trees with fish, occasions in a great measure the unwholesomeness of the Bombay air. Of this the venomous and putrid buckshaw fly which swam in such abundance as to be very nauseous to the inhabitant is a plain proof.' They add, however – this was to be another obsession of the eighteenth century: 'Another cause of the unhealthy air is the thickness of the trees at Warli and Mahim woods, which hinders the land breeze that sets in every morning from cleansing the air and cooling the ground.'

The fish-manure was prohibited, but for decades there were petitions from the inhabitants of the Island asking for it to be allowed again because the trees did not thrive without it; this presumably means that they were continuing to use it and did not want to be harassed. The petitions were in Portuguese, which had been the language in use for business transactions in the settlement till about 1700, and after that was gradually superseded by English: most of the plantations, indeed most of the land, were then still in the hands of people of Portuguese or part-Portuguese descent. The requests were repeatedly turned down, and finally in 1770 the use of fish-manure was penalised – Rs.50 for the first offence and Rs.100 for the second, half to go to the Company and half to the informer.

(The value of the rupee fluctuated somewhat, and still does today, but as a rough rule one may reckon it as having been something between one and two British shillings.) Evidently the fines did not act as a complete deterrent either, for in 1787 we find a Polish traveller, Dr Hové, noting: 'Dr Scott informed me the people of Mahim often manure their plantations with putrified fish which renders the air unwholesome to those that live in it. Not an instance is known of a European recovering of a fever if he has contracted it in these woods.' At least, it would appear, the habit of buckshawing had retreated to the groves of Mahim, a good seven miles from the Fort. Mahim remained a coconut grove into the twentieth century, though it is now a residential district.

So where did they go, all those people dead, like one of the earliest Governors of a sudden 'lethargy' that in a day and a night put an end to them – dead, according to Fryer, of 'fluxes, dropsy, scurvy, barbiers, gout, stone' and especially of 'malignant and putrid fevers, which are endemial diseases'? The Europeans at any rate went to Mendham's Point, described fearfully by Nicholas Waite as 'a cormorant paunch, never satisfied', and referred to more temperately by Fryer as having 'some few tombs that make a pretty show at entering the harbour'. There were three other tombs, remarked on by eighteenth-century travellers: a 'Jew's tomb', a 'Mussleman's tomb' (Moslem) and the mausoleum of Sir John Child, the opinionated Governor of Bombay who died there in 1690 during the Moghul War and who was to give his name to the developing East India Company, known for many years after as 'the honourable John Company'. Child's tomb had a beacon light on top of it which could be lit in time of storm; it was a mark for mariners. It is fairly obvious, from this fact and from contemporary accounts, that these three tombs did not lie near the Fort but further down, across the straits, on Colaba, but they were razed to the ground, probably in 1759 when the British were preparing for a possible attack from the French, and successive generations said of Child's tomb that 'no man may tell where it lay'. The Mendham's Point cemetery was removed a few years later and its site, too, was forgotten. When nineteenth-century writers on Bombay touched on the subject of tombs they tended to assume that Child's tomb and all the rest must have been grouped together and to try to combine various historical accounts accordingly. (In fact, there were isolated tombs scattered about in various places on the open land beyond the Fort, including another 'Mussulman's tomb' which appears on a late-eighteenth-century map to the north of Fort George.) As a result, supposed locations for the cemetery perambulate all over the place. James Douglas, for instance, a long-term Bombay resident who published a gossipy, valuable but very inaccurate work on the place in 1893, remarked with satisfaction: 'the banian-trees near the Young Man's Christian Institute are no doubt exuberant for obvious reasons', but he was at least a hundred yards too far west. Grose's Plan of Bombay, drawn with care in 1750 and accurate as far as one can judge in other respects, clearly shows the Mendham's Point cemetery lying near the eastern harbour sea-face, just south of the Apollo Gate (where the present Apollo and Marine Streets join and emerge from the Fort area, at the back of the Museum) and therefore approximately on the site of the present Legislative Council Hall.

Part of this building was constructed as a Sailors' Home in the early 1870s. It was enlarged in 1928, when its function was changed, and a correspondent wrote in the *Times of India*, for 31 January:

> Workmen came across human bones quite early in their operations and, affrighted lest evil spirits should be disturbed, they downed tools. But they were soon persuaded to resume their work, and day after day they have laid bare more bones. In many cases the bones have decayed to powder and few of them are intact; no trace of coffins have been found. As a result, almost any of these trench walls displays a kind of chess board pattern. The original soil is of a light grey colour: in the graves from which fragments of bones protrude, the soil, disturbed in the seventeenth or eighteenth century, is of a reddish colour, and so closely packed were the graves that, of the alternating patches of red and grey, in places the former predominate. The top two feet or so of soil is filling, probably of a much later date, and this fact shows that the original graves were but little below the surface. There was indeed very often scarcely time to dig deep.

Little time indeed, in that climate, and probably little inclination either, for the omnipresence of death must have made the gentlest grow blasé, punch-drunk in (no doubt) two senses. Burnell recounts that the Company's writers (the lowest grade of covenanted servant, usually young men without fortune who were sent out from England in the hope that they might make one) were buried without coffins under a slab irreverently known as 'the Shuffle Board Table', otherwise 'the jackalls tear them out of their graves, burrowing in the ground like rabbits'. He also tells us that five chaplains who died in the colony between 1640 and 1710, that company whom Ovington did prudently *not* join, were all buried under one tomb.

However interesting these tombs would be today, perhaps we should not regret too much that this place of such fearsome mortality has left behind no external trace. A lot of misery, thwarted ambition and wasted youth must have gone into that stony ground, beneath the hot dust. Graveyards present a considerable problem in India, where history, in our sense, is not much regarded, and where most of the population do not bury their dead anyway. At least one other old British graveyard (on Colaba Point) has today vanished without trace under a playing field. True, the Moslem community use burial, and indeed specialise in mausolea for their distinguished dead, but there seems to be an ambivalence in their approach. 'Happy is he,' said the Prophet Mohammed, 'whose grave disappears from the face of the earth.' If that is right, then we must count the poor chess-board dust beneath the Council Hall as happy.

IV 'That Common Receptacle'

The quarrelsomeness, brutality, and low standards of probity in early Bombay life were notorious. Not that, in the first couple of generations, these vices were confined to the island presidency: Calcutta and Madras enjoyed reputations not much better. Indeed Job Charnock himself, the founder of Calcutta, is said to have 'reigned like a rajah' and to have had natives who displeased him whipped near his dining room so that he could hear them while he ate. Forty years later Robert Clive, who had been sent out to Madras at seventeen after an unpromising career at the Merchant Taylors School, was at first so unhappy there on a salary of £5 per annum that he twice tried to shoot himself. (His third attempt in middle age, when fame and wealth were his, succeeded.) It was tacitly recognised that India was a suitable refuge and gamble for those who had few expectations at home, either because they had no means or because they had made themselves unpopular – younger sons, men unable or unwilling to pay their debts, a sprinkling of women despairing of matrimony in England.

Many of the male fortune-hunters were not servants of the Company; one of the Company's problems was the number of freebooting interlopers who attempted to establish themselves, to the detriment of the Company's trade – not to mention the Company servants who traded on the side. Company salaries were not high; the fabled fortunes of those lucky enough to survive the lethargy, drink, unclean women, putrid fevers, cholera, *bhang* and the rest, could only be acquired by those prepared in one way or another to play the system. The ruthless Thomas Pitt, who was Governor of Madras in the early eighteenth century, and was the ancestor of the Pitt who was to raise the whole standard of administration by his India Bill toward the end of the century, started his career being prosecuted for trading in Bombay in 1685: yet he was subsequently made a Company servant. Brian Gardner, in his book *The East India Company* (1945), quotes a homesick Company man of the same period as writing:

> At home men are famous for doing nothing; here they are infamous for their honest endeavours. At home is respect and reward; abroad disrespect and heartbreaking. At home is augmentation of wages: abroad is not more than a third of wages. At home is content; abroad nothing so much as grief, cares and displeasure. At home is safety; abroad no security. At home is liberty; abroad the best is bondage.

A similar view was expressed by the Governor of Bombay, Sir Nicholas Waite, when he begged the Directors to send his son to Bengal rather than to 'this place of mortality'. This same Governor was arrested some years later by his own Council for drunkenness, quarrelling and conspiracy; he exclaimed: 'Don't you know it is the custom of this place to be false and to cut one another's throats?' He was subsequently imprisoned, and dismissed the service. It would be unrealistic to pretend, of course, that everything in England was 'respect and reward . . . content . . . safety'. At home in Queen Anne's day supposedly respectable men intrigued, drank, gambled and duelled. But out in India, with the restraints of a temperate climate and a relatively organised society removed from them, and numerous irritations and risks imposed, they seemed to lose all sense of caution.

Keigwin's Revolt in 1683, mentioned in the last chapter, was merely the most extreme example of the dissension that could arise between Company servants. Sir John Child, Keigwin's superior at Surat who subsequently established himself in Bombay, was disliked by many, probably with reason, and was variously said to have appropriated £5,000 that had originally been collected for the building of the church under Aungier and to have sent a Banian to Surat to poison another member of the Council there. In 1698 relations with Surat had deteriorated so far that for a few years a breakaway Company was established in Bombay: in any case from 1701 to 1704 the Company's servants in Surat were held as virtual prisoners by the Moghuls. However, Aurangzeb died in 1707, and Surat and Bombay were reunited under the Company in 1709.

Relations between the rival ports improved after that, though it was not till the mid-century that Bombay became the centre of rule.

It was the silting up of the Swally river at Surat during that period which tipped the scales in favour of Bombay, though there are people to this day who maintain that Bombay was not necessarily the best natural site for India's west coast port, that Surat – or Chaul or Supara (Ophir) or Bassein or another of the ancient harbours down that coast – would have been preferable, and that Bombay was built up pig-headedly, because the Company had spent so much on it over the decades that they refused to admit defeat. Right up to the end of the eighteenth century the Company still debated periodically whether Bombay was worth its keep.

John Burnell, describing the Bombay of the early 1700s, wrote: 'The town of Bombay is divided into two distinct limits, the English and the Black. The English town lieth to the southward of the Fort on a large, spacious green.' This needs explanation. By 'fort' Burnell meant Bombay Castle and its immediate fortifications, not the whole district we know today as 'the Fort', since the walls round that did not go up till about 1720 and not till later in the century was 'Fort' applied to the whole settlement. Nor should his 'Black' or native district be confused with the 'Black Town' that grew up half a mile away, north of the Esplanade, towards the end of the century. Burnell's Black district is the northern part of our Fort, the part where two of the main thoroughfares were later to be known as Parsi Bazaar Street and Borah Bazaar Street. The latter name survives to this day. The bones of the nineteenth- and twentieth-century business district, the equivalent of the City of London, were already, in Burnell's time, being laid down. His 'large, spacious green', round which a church, a Government House, a theatre, the houses of prominent citizens and finally a Town Hall were later to be grouped, remained large for the next 150 years, though truly green presumably only in monsoon like the present-day *maidans*. Like the *maidans*, it fulfilled many functions: an informal meeting place, a drilling ground for troops, a place for transactions of all kinds. For many years in the eighteenth and early nineteenth centuries it became the Cotton Green, the place where bales of pressed cotton stood about in untidy heaps waiting to be sold and shipped. Anyone wanting to get an idea of what this merchandise, the raw seed of so much of Bombay's wealth, looked like on the Green should pay a visit to the present-day, rather more organised 'Green' up at Sewri, in the dockland beyond Mazagaon. Even today, I have been told, bargaining transactions are made there as they once were on Bombay Green – by means of a cabbalistic linking of fingers beneath a cloth.

Today the central portion of the Green still survives in Elphinstone Circle* the elegant hub of the Fort with its public garden and its classical circlet of buildings reminiscent of Tunbridge Wells or Leamington Spa, though heavier in touch. The whole thing was laid out in the 1860s, and is one of the rare pieces of non-utilitarian town-planning in Bombay. The ornate railings of the public garden, which were imported from a foundry in England and were once painted in respectable British green, are today picked out in the same tints of scarlet, peacock blue, pea green and yellow that are used to decorate temples; there are ancient trees there, and a children's playground and a *chokidar* (watchman) to keep out untidy settlers. It is still much used as a meeting place, and it is still possible there to get a whiff of long-ago Bombay, a place (Burnell again) 'mostly straggling. It consists not of many buildings and these but of one story; the chief are the Deputy Governor's [the Castle] before which there is a large tank. The barracks or soldiers appartment is a very good foundation, in imitation of Chelsea College; it is of a great length, answerable in breadth, on each side whereof is a fine piazza with stone pillars.' This was approximately on the site of the present Mint, which looks eighteenth-century but was not in fact built for another hundred-odd years. It can hardly have been anything approaching the size of the Chelsea Pensioners' Hospital (which is what is meant) but it is interesting to see a building in Bombay evoking a comparison with one in London at so early a date. Most of the buildings, both then and for long afterwards, were roofed either with thatch or with the curved red tiles of local manufacture. Still today, if you go up to a high building in the Fort and look out over the roofscape, quite a lot of the traditional tiled roofs are in evidence, some of them still sketchily covered with the original tiles rather than with the differently shaped Mangalore tiles which have been used for the last hundred years.

Adjoining what was later, when further fortified, to be known as Bombay Castle, Burnell noted a garden, with a summer-house made of coco-palms, but added: 'when I left the place there was neither tree nor flower nor anything else except hogs and poultry and a small kitchen ground at one corner which had hardly greens enough to compose one salad'. Alas for da Orta's 'delicate garden, voiced to be the pleasantest in India' of fifty years earlier. We do not

* Now re-named Horniman Circle after an anti-Raj newspaper editor who had his office here.

87

know exactly when Burnell was there – he went on to Bengal, and cropped up later as the cartographer of a map of the world – but a letter from the Court of Directors to Bombay dated April 1708 ordered that 'the Company's garden be planted with roots and green trade'.

The church walls were in place, but had progressed no further in twenty-five years or more – 'it begins now to decay, trees growing out of the stonework'. However, Bombay's most desolate days were now ending. In 1714 a young, energetic chaplain called Richard Cobbe came out from England, and was shocked to find that the only place of worship in use was a room made over into a chapel within the castle. On Trinity Sunday the following year he preached a rousing sermon to what must have been a normally rather apathetic congregation of sinners, and started a fund to raise money to complete the building on the Green. One among many who contributed to it was an old Company man of Surat, who had subscribed to Aungier's original fund forty years before, a rare survivor. The church, complete with oyster-shell windows, a neatly cow-dunged floor (the usual country covering) and a 'cannon-ball proof' roof, was opened for divine worship on Christmas Day 1718, as a tablet let into the side of the church to this day will tell you. The tower has been much altered since then, and the church extended; the high box pews allotted in blocks according to the social standing of the worshippers have long gone, and so of course have the oyster-shell windows. They were the type normal in India then, where windows were covered at all: you could not see out, and the light that entered was diffused and pearly; described by a contemporary as 'delectable', it also kept out the sun's heat. Glazing did not come into much use in Bombay for another century. Punkahs, the ceiling fans that wave to and fro when pulled by a rope and that feature in all nineteenth-century Indian memoirs, had not been invented then either; nor did the church have any form of artificial light, which meant that Evensong was held at four in the afternoon.

An organ had been ordered and sent out from England in Aungier's day, but Cobbe found it lying in some storeroom 'quite out of order, broken and useless'. This is in the Bombay tradition: there are a number of cases on record in the city's first 150 years of objects or statues ordered, received and then left to languish forgotten or lost till rescued by a subsequent burst of municipal or private energy. In the tradition also was the dispute about work on a Sunday that Cobbe apparently had with some of the Council during the building of the church; for a while he was suspended for 'sedition'. However, the church duly opened on time, with

Governor Boone, the Council, honoured guests and as many of their ladies as they could respectably muster drinking success to it afterwards in 'a glass of sack', followed by a grand dinner in the Castle that night. (Today, if you attend Sunday morning service, you get a cup of tea afterwards in the churchyard, which may be more refreshing.) Among the honoured guests was Rama Kamathi, the Hindu resident who had subscribed to restore the temple of Walkeshwar on Malabar Point and also donated a temple in the Parsi Bazaar Street. Not all the early traditions of Bombay were bad, and that of good and equal relations between people of different races and religions was there from the start. But this did not prevent Kamathi from being arrested for conspiracy, tried and even tortured with thumb-screws by Boone a year or two later.

Boone, who was in charge between 1716 and 1720, may have been ready to indulge in brutalities which the law had long ceased to sanction at home, but he was a man of some qualities. He was the first man in Bombay since Garcia da Orta interested enough in Indian antiquities to send home drawings of the carvings at Elephanta Island. He contributed handsomely to the church building fund – though, as the chatty nineteenth-century commentator James Douglas remarks, both his contribution and the Rev. Cobbe's were 'more in proportion to the profits they made by private transactions than to the limited amount of their salaries'. Boone also donated the church bell, which survives, cracked, to this day. He was the Governor responsible for carrying out, if not designing, the plan for the first city wall, that which was to convert Bombay from a 'mostly straggling' place of low buildings into a densely packed, high-built city of an ancient and indeed obsolete type. It was also Boone who planned the first successful sea-wall at the Great Breach; it was after this that some of the Flats were able to be reclaimed for crops, plantations and, subsequently, buildings, and the first roads were laid across them going north to Parell, Sion and Mahim. The main roads run on the same lines today. Boone was also responsible for strengthening works on the smaller breaches; one of his many criticisms of Bombay when he took office was that 'the breaches are in a very bad condition, I will do my utmost to get them finished, but he [presumably the contractor] that undertook them deserves hanging more justly than a common thief; if Mr Strutt [who had been temporary Governor the preceding year] had been the good servant he pretends to he should have opposed the presenting him with Rs.2,000 to which he now acknowledges no pretension.'

What is striking about Boone's complaints of corruption and mismanagement, made in a series of confidential letters to the Secretary of the Court of Directors, is that he regarded Bombay as distinctly worse in this respect than other places in India:

> It has been the custom of the settlement, contrary to what I have known in others, that the Purser, Master Mariner, Steward and Master of Attendance buy up the necessary stores their employ requires and conscientiously spare them to the Company at 50 per cent advance, if I am not very much deceived . . . Here is great want of regulation in the settlement, in Madras and Bengal such enormities would have been taken notice of, but were I to do this at once they would load me with curses and backbitings . . . The Chief at Mahim [there was a fort there, on the site of an older Portuguese bastion] had ¼ per cent on all duties, this I have ventured to take off. The Paymaster has had certain perquisites which I shall reduce. Everyone in Council allowed a House, Pallaqueen fellows, and the keeping of a Horse, this swells our expense prodigiously besides several other things which my time would not permit me to enquire thoroughly into.

In other words, just like the present-day business community of Bombay where taxes are – in theory – extremely high, the Company's agents were claiming everything they could on expenses. Boone successfully uncovered a number of more evil frauds, but this did not prevent him from adding in a postscript to one of his letters that he would like a 20 per cent reward for his efforts – 'you know the country custom is one-fourth part'. (Quoted by T. G. P. Spear in *The Nabobs*.)

He also – and in this too he followed the habit of some of his predecessors – confiscated a number of Portuguese estates on the Island, on the grounds that the Portuguese had been intriguing against the British with the Angrias: these were pirates who were in control of the Mahratta fleet much in the same way that the Sidis had earlier run the Moghul shipping. Among the properties acquired in this way was the Jesuit monastery at Parell, six miles north of the town. There was a garden there, laid out by the monks, with walks and flower-beds watered by stone channels, a terrace, a mango-grove and a lake. The building looked across the sweep of the Flats to the distant groves of Mahim, and had the wooded heights of Sewri and the eastern sea-face to its rear. The house, with its chapel in the centre, became a private mansion, and for a while was apparently rented by a well-to-do Parsi – the forerunner of many.

Later in the century it became the country house, and finally, extended, the chief residence, of the Governors of Bombay. The old chapel with its vaulted roof was turned into an eighty-foot-long banqueting hall, and above it, to the same dimensions, was built a ballroom. Stone channels, mango-grove and lake are gone now, and the house's fortunes are much changed, but you can measure the ballroom and see the ancient flooring and an arch or two of the chapel below to this day. We shall visit the place again.

Charles Boone's Governorship marked a turning point for Bombay. A contemporary historian, Downing, who knew him, wrote: 'he left the island in a good posture of defence both by sea and land. He found the same unguarded and very poor, but left it flourishing in trade and many merchants were come from Madras and Bengal to settle there.' This may have been overstated, but Bombay's destiny as originally envisaged by Aungier, that of being, like medieval London, a trading mecca, 'a mart of many peoples', was beginning to reassert itself. For that matter, the British destiny in India generally, though still not apparent, was beginning to take shape in those years. Edwardes,* who was Municipal Commissioner in Bombay in the late nineteenth century and whose *Rise of Bombay* is still one of the best books on the presidency, wrote of the second and third decades of the eighteenth century:

> Ostensibly we [the British in India generally] were still no more than merchants, actuated solely by the desire for peaceful commerce; and our Presidents yet affected to set more store by 'dutties', 'topsails', 'guinea-stuffs', 'chintzes with large nosegays and bunches of flowers', than by Sidi alliances and the course of political affairs in the Deccan. But slowly and surely we were exchanging the rôle of a purely mercantile community for that of a great political power, and the years which elapsed between 1718 and 1744 were pregnant with events testifying to the alteration of our character.

It must be said at once, however, that the gradual development of the rôle of the British in India from free-booting adventurers into the great pantheon of the Indian Civil Service ('the heaven-born') took place, in the eighteenth century at any rate, outside Bombay. The main theatres of political action for the whole of the century

---

* A famous name in India, where several generations of the family served. Edwardesbad, in the North-West Frontier Province, was named after one of them.

were located on the eastern side of India. It was there, between Madras and Pondicherry, that the battle for trade and hence ultimately for India herself was fought out between the British and the French. It was Calcutta, on the Bay of Bengal, with China to trade with round the Malay Straits and the whole of the fertile and heavily populated Punjab to draw on, that managed to gain for itself the rôle of premier city. It was in Calcutta that most of the legendary 'Nabob' fortunes were made – the word, with its connotations of a gouty figure reclining in luxury among a crowd of turbanned retainers, attended by parrots, pet leopards, *bibis* and pale brown progeny, comes from 'Nawab', the Moslem word for a potentate. In Calcutta, round Chowringee, some of the Nabobs' huge, white, pillared mansions still stand, crumbling witness to the fortunes made there by the 'jute and indigo wallahs'. In Bombay, however, such town houses were few, and all those that ever existed – such as the 'Fort House' in Dadabhoi Naoroji Road or the bulbous Tata mansion near the Bombay Gymkhana – date from the nineteenth century. Bombay, throughout the eighteenth century, remained provincial, other, isolated; in fact it was an island in every sense, surrounded by intermittently hostile powers – the Mahrattas – and literally cut off from communication with the mainland till after the third Mahratta War in 1782. This isolation, which at the time was to its disadvantage, was what laid the foundations for its strength and viability.

For Bombay, unlike Calcutta, was never essentially a colonial city. In time, in its late nineteenth-century heyday, it was to develop its clubs, its military hierarchy and its British *puckah-sahib* infrastructure: much of this, however, was for the benefit of families passing through on their way to and from up-country stations. The real life of Bombay was always lived elsewhere, in a more cosmopolitan and egalitarian setting: in warehouses (always known in Anglo-Indian parlance as 'go-downs'), in counting houses, in places where samples of raw cotton or opium or silk or ivory or inlay-work were passed from hand to hand, on wharves – and, most of all, in the yards of the shipbuilders, from which vessels of Malabar teak went out all over the world. It was Bombay frigates which, because of their unbeatable quality, were ordered by the British Government and fought at the battle of Trafalgar. One of them is still in existence today, at Gosport near Southampton. Another sailed the world for years with the following secret message carved on her kelson by the chief shipwright: 'The ship was built by a d -- d Black Fellow AD 1800'. The shipwright in question was

Jamshetji Bomanji Wadia, member of a Parsi family which, by that time, had risen to a position of unprecedented power and influence for native Indians who were not rulers. It has been said that it was not even the British merchant, but the Parsi shipbuilder, who was the real creator of Bombay. Certainly, for many decades, it was the success of the shipyards alone that persuaded the East India Company to keep the otherwise expensive settlement going.

But the period of creation was a long one. Bombay, though increasing throughout the eighteenth century both in size and in prosperity, remained something of a backwater till 1813, when the Company lost its monopoly of trade between England and India, and even in 1825 was described in the Directory as being 'of little importance to the Company'. Perhaps it would be truest to say that, though it was the Company's first real possession in India (for Surat did not actually belong to it), Bombay's character was from the first more heterogeneous and multi-racial, and that it tended to prosper in proportion to the Honourable Company's decline in influence. Bombay really began to come into its own once the 'overland route', from Europe through the Mediterranean and the Red Sea, became popular c.1840 with the coming of steamers: once the Company was finally extinct (in 1858) and the Suez Canal was opened in 1869, Bombay, in its west coast situation, at last achieved its destiny as India's chief port.

But throughout the eighteenth century news from the rest of India – news of Clive and Dupleix, of the Black Hole of Calcutta, of Warren Hastings and the Regulating Act – reached Bombay only as muffled thunder in the distance. In Bombay the inhabitants were for the most part preoccupied with their own local struggles, with the Sidis and the Angrias, with the Portuguese (so treacherous and at the same time so tempting to betray!) and with the Mahrattas. Only occasionally, as in the mid-century, did the news that the French might be coming to get them bestir them to greater excitement, stronger walls round the Fort, a spate of ditch-digging . . . In between these crises they lived together in a state of informal intimacy (or stifling provincialism, according to one's point of view). Some visitors to Bombay in those generations found its society unfashionable, clannish, bereft of culture and Christian virtue alike. Others found it a delightful place, full of friendly, unpretentious souls. Evidently everything depended there, far more than in Bengal, on whom you knew and what your business there was.

The Parsis have been a people curiously marked, and perhaps favoured, by Fate. Typically light-skinned and curly-haired, they are originally Persians (Iranians); by religion they are followers of the first monotheist, Zoroaster (Zarathustra). Their reputation as a special people, a race of Wise Men and teachers, goes back into antiquity; the Magi, the 'Three Kings' of Christian legend, were Parsis. About the year 650 AD they left Persia to escape religious persecution and settled in Gujerat, on the western coast of India. There they intermarried with local wives and adopted the Gujerati language as their own, but retained their religious practices, their sense of identity, and some distinctive articles of dress. They established themselves there as weavers and carpenters, and were still there when the British came to Surat a thousand years later. It is usually said that the first ones found their way from Surat to Bombay in the wake of the British in the 1660s. But a hundred years earlier Garcia da Orta described Bassein, the Portuguese walled city north of Bombay, as having some 'Coaris or Esparcis, who we Portuguese call Jews'. (Da Orta himself, it may be remembered, was of Jewish extraction.) In addition there is a persistent tradition among the Parsis themselves that one of their number, Dorabji Nanabhoy, came to Bombay from Surat as early as 1640 and acted as a go-between for the Portuguese and the local traders. At all events some Parsis were in Bombay within a very few years of its cession to Charles II, for Governor Aungier wrote to England in the 1670s that 'they are an industrious people and ingenious in trade, therein they totally employe themselves, there are at present but few of them, but we expect a greater number having gratified them in their desire to build a bureing place for their dead on the Island'. This 'bureing place' was referred to by Fryer at the same period in his description of Malabar Hill – 'a Rocky Woody mountain, yet sends forth long Grass. A-top of all is a Parsy Tomb lately reared.'

In point of fact this 'tomb', which still exists today alongside four others, standing in a private enclave above a municipal park in what has become the smartest residential district of Bombay, is not a burial place exactly. It is a *dokhma*, or Tower of Silence, a round stone construction like a Martello tower. Within the Towers are iron grids, and on these grids the Parsis place their dead, where they will not pollute the earth, nor the water, nor the air outside, nor yet fire, the fourth element and the holy one in the Parsi religion. Instead, the bodies are rapidly consumed by vultures, who are pictured in old and new engravings clustering eagerly round the rims of the Towers like pensioners in some benevolent institution jostling for places round a dinner table. This is the singular and single well-known fact about the Parsis as far as the rest of the world is concerned. Can Aungier and Fryer have been unaware of it, I wonder? Today the briefest and most superficial guides to Bombay cannot resist a mention of it, for of the half of the world population of Parsis that still live in India, the majority are to be found in Bombay. For some reason people whose imaginations seem undisturbed by the mental image of their own bodies rotting slowly in the ground, are morbidly fascinated by the brutal economy of the Parsis' method of disposal. Perhaps the contrast is too stark between the urbane, westernised Bombay Parsi you meet today in his or her well-appointed apartment on Malabar Hill or one of the newer sea-shore suburbs, and the mental image of the same body stretched naked on the lofty grid attacked by the beasts of the air. Indeed the contrast seems to be too much for some present-day Parsis, who debate whether making use of the new electric municipal crematorium would count as polluting fire; they are further put off by the fact that the vultures of Malabar Hill are no longer as numerous as they were in the days when it was 'a Rocky Woody mountain' without habitations. It seems that the high-rent, high-rise blocks that, in the last twenty years, have been remorselessly replacing the nineteenth-century bungalows that used to be there, have been driving the vultures away. 'It is one thing,' a Parsi has said to me, 'to imagine oneself being gobbled up – picked clean in half an hour. That's what used to happen. But I do *not* fancy lying there being half-heartedly nibbled at for days on end.'

> High on this hill the Parsee dead keep watch
> Snore, giggle or whatever
> Dead men do. Even now the names sound well;
> Vaccha and Dadyseth, Wadia and Talevarkhan: traders,
> Philanthropists, patrons of art; as placid now
> As when they were alive . . .
> (From *Malabar Hill* by K. D. Katrak)

To return to the seventeenth century –

It may be seen from Aungier's words that the Parsis were not slow to develop with the British the 'special relationship' they so long enjoyed. In 1690-1 when the Sidis had seized Mazagaon and were besieging the main island of Bombay, a Parsi called Rustomji Dorabji organised a militia of local fishermen and helped to drive the invaders out. For this he was afterwards granted the hereditary surname of Patel – 'lord'. Patel is much commoner as a Hindu name, but there are still Parsi Patels in Bombay. Although the illustriousness of the family was later to some extent eclipsed by that of the merchant-prince Parsis of the later periods – the Wadias, the Camas, the Jeejeebhoys and the Tatas – a descendant of the Patels has remarked to me, 'In *our* family we always considered Jeejeebhoy [the first Indian baronet] rather a jumped-up fellow!'

(The Parsis do not, traditionally, have surnames of their own, and therefore all the ones now in common use among them are of relatively recent adoption, and often reflect the rôle a member of the family played from the point of view of the British in the eighteenth or nineteenth century. For instance, there are Parsi families called Readymoney, Boatwallah, Paymaster, Confectioner, Engineer and even Sodawaterwallah – names which, their holders point out, are no odder in essence than the time-honoured Anglo-Saxon ones of Butcher, Baker and Marchant. A true Parsi name consists of a first name and a patronymic: Rustom the son of Sorab is Rustom Sorabji; his son will quite likely be Sorab Rustomji. This, as may be imagined, does not make for clarity in sorting out the different generations in a family history.)

One of the many chroniclers of Parsi history (Dosabhoy Framji Karaka, writing in 1884) has summed up neatly both the envy and the admiration that the Parsis have aroused in other Indian communities by remarking: 'Either the Parsis had the knack of ingratiating themselves in the favour of the Europeans or they were selected by them for their intelligence, business habits and integrity.' It has often been noted that the Parsis possess a marked capacity for adapting themselves to circumstances, and some commentators have voiced this less kindly by saying that the Parsis' most pronounced gift is for imitation, cultural, social and even technological. But it is also true that, though they have played something of the traditional rôle of the Jew* in Indian society, living between the two worlds of the East and West, they have seldom if ever aroused the antipathy that has traditionally dogged the Jew in Europe, and that their image is one of honesty. One commentator has gone so far as to describe their relationship with both the native Indian and the British worlds as 'a romance of tolerance'. At all events it would be true, if slightly cynical, to say that the Parsis managed, long before any other sect of India, to arrogate to themselves the key rôle of 'acceptable natives'. Many of them ceased

---

* Actual Jews did not reach Bombay in any numbers till the Parsis were already ensconced.

early to be 'Black Fellows' in English eyes, or even heathen – they did not bow down to wood and stone, they did not beat drums or wail or indulge in *suttee* or keep their women in purdah, they did not refuse to eat certain foods or refuse to perform certain jobs; they happily drank wine. From the early trading days the Portuguese, Dutch, French and English 'factories' (agency houses) all employed Parsis as their chief brokers, and were dependent on these multi-lingual and locally knowledgeable employees to organise their banking and trading operations. With their speedy arrival in Bombay, it was almost as if the Parsis sensed, in the arrival of the English, a unique historical opportunity, that was to be as momentous for them in the long run as the chance that had carried them to Gujerat a thousand years before.

'Wadia' is a version of the Gujerati *vadia* – shipbuilder. The first Wadia in Bombay, Lowji Nusserwanji, was previously a foreman in the Surat dockyard; the British were impressed by his work, and invited him and ten other carpenters to help found the shipyards in Bombay, when it had become Company policy to build up Bombay at the expense of Surat. Lowji Nusserwanji arrived in Bombay in 1736 as a fairly young man and put in fifty years' service there, handing on his skill to his sons and grandsons. He earned Rs.40 a month, but in time acquired extra gratuities, presents of fine shawls and silver rules, and a loan to help him build a house in Bombay. The three-storied house now on the site, in Cowasji Patel Street in the Fort, is not, as at least two historians have imagined, the original eighteenth-century one, but a replacement built by his descendants c.1850 after a fire. However, it is still a fine house, an example of traditional Fort architecture, and older than all the monster Gothic buildings that are most widely hailed today as representing 'Old Bombay'. Long may it remain, though its position, with land prices rising steadily, seems perilous.

The oldest Parsi Agiary (fire-temple) now in existence is the one in Nanabhoy Lane on the southern edge of the Fort. Burnell, who knew Bombay as a 'straggling' place, 'not of many buildings', may actually have seen this Agiary built, for it is said to date from 1709; if this is true, it must be a genuine contender for the title of Oldest Building in Bombay, but it is difficult to establish to what extent it has been rebuilt. It is a low, country-style building with a pitched, red-tiled roof, and is hidden today from curious eyes within a high-walled compound.

Parsi names crop up all over Bombay today, attached to streets, blocks of housing, public gardens and water fountains.

Some of these names are very old, reflecting not necessarily the ownership but simply the presence of a well-known Parsi house in the locality at a given moment. Others are relatively modern, and indicate the wave of Parsi commemorative munificence which, by the late nineteenth century, was endowing Bombay with amenities, leafy, watery or monumental. But a large number of the names form an accurate reflection of the extent to which the Parsis early perceived the value of land-holdings. It was being said already by the 1800s that they owned 'half the Island', and a proper land-census taken in 1855 proved that by then this was literally the case. The fate of the old da Souza estate in Mazagaon is a case in point. With the decline in Portuguese fortunes on the Island, the estate had been mortgaged, and, after some complications and a law case, the Company managed to acquire it around the middle of the eighteenth century and sell it off by public auction in smaller lots. Almost all of these were acquired by buyers whose names show them to be Parsis. Dongri Hill nearby, whose fort on top was then used as the British gaol, had already been bought by Narowji Manekji Sett, a prominent citizen who had erected another Agiary in the Fort: it became known as Narowji Hill, and was still owned by the same family in the early years of the twentieth century, though by that time it had, like many of Bombay's small hills, been largely eroded by quarrying. (Today only a faint upward incline in the streets at that point shows where this high, rocky landmark once stood, but there are still two or three stone-masons established in business there.)

In addition to properties purchased, a number of Parsi families also received grants of land for services rendered, initially from the Company and later from the British Government. The first of these was presumably the acreage where the Towers of Silence stand on Malabar Hill, given under Aungier c.1673. A second Tower was erected here about 1750 with money bequeathed for the purpose by Narowji Sett, and three more followed over the next century. (Today, in the 1980s, the land on which they stand is potentially some of the most valuable real-estate in the world.) Many more grants were made, for the purpose of house-building rather than tomb-building, in the course of the eighteenth century: it was the Directors' policy to encourage in this way the immigration into Bombay of desirable people. Lowji Nusserwanji Wadia's two sons, Manekji and Bomanji, born in the 1720s, received such a grant in 1783 for their work in the shipyards, from which ships were now going out all over the world. True to Parsi form, they were in no sense 'native' ships, but versions of European designs.

Under the third generation of Wadias (born in the 1750s), the British Admiralty for the first time ordered ships-of-the-line built outside England. 'Tell my old friend Nowrogee,' wrote the Superintendent of the Marine to his brother in Bombay in 1827, 'what a glorious part the *Asia* sustained in the battle of Navarino, and how proud I am of his success as a Builder.' It was Narowji's brother, Jamshetji, who had carved his secret message about a 'd-- d Black Fellow' on the *Marquess of Cornwallis* about 1800. Twenty years later, when he lay dying, he wrote to the then-Governor of Bombay, Mountstuart Elphinstone, reminding him that he too had been promised a grant of land. This was agreed, on which he wrote again, thanking Elphinstone who had 'calmed my dying moments and smoothed my descent into the tomb'. (Curious words, it may seem, for a man who, in death, was destined to be laid not in earth but high up in a tower, but Jamshetji had no doubt acquired the phrase, along with much else, as part of his Europeanised *persona*.) He continued, 'My breath is going, and you and the Service have my dying blessing. My life has been devoted to the Service and all I now pray for is that I will be remembered by the Hon'ble Board to the Hon'ble Court of Directors. Adieu to you all. God prosper you adieu.' Already, it seems we are hearing the voice of the Indian civil servant of the British Raj. In fact the grant of land did not particularly please the family who inherited it, for it was at Salsette, the old Portuguese territory lying due north from Bombay across Mahim Creek. They had hoped for some already-cultivated land on the Island itself. Today Salsette, which includes the prosperous suburb of Bandra, the area covered by Santa Cruz and Sahar airports and a long tract of seashore where newer suburbs are burgeoning at Juhu, has long been the foundation of vast Parsi fortunes.

At the same period Jamshetji's other brother, Pestonji, who was not a shipbuilder but was associated as a broker with the two biggest British mercantile houses, owned a large part of the Fort, extensive lands at Mazagaon and the Breach, and over a thousand square yards at Parell where he built himself a country house called the Lal Baug – the Red Garden. Today, both site and name belong to an estate of low-rent flats for Parsis. He had built himself another house at Mazagaon called Tarala ('Palm Green'), but this was for most of the time let to prominent English citizens, such as Sir James Mackintosh, the first Recorder of Bombay. The subsequent history of this house typifies the growth and change of the city. It was a rather grand house, neo-classical like so much London architecture of the early nineteenth century, yet vaguely un-English. Perhaps in fact it was more Grecian than any house built for the British climate could readily be: it would have looked perfectly in place on a Mediterranean or Adriatic hillside. It stood virtually in the country when it was built and then, from about the mid-nineteenth century, in a bosky residential suburb of similar mansions which, though mills and railway lines accumulated not far off, managed to retain its character into the present century. About 1850, when the family fortunes were much diminished after a disastrous fire (it destroyed the old house in Cowasji Patel Street – see above) Tarala was sold off to one of the rising stars of Parsi prosperity, Behramji Jeejeebhoy: he was a generation younger than the illustrious first baronet of that clan, who lived nearby in a monster house called Mazagaon Castle. In 1925, when the main Jeejeebhoy residence was a palatial bungalow called 'The Cliff' on Malabar Hill, which was by then far more fashionable than stuffy, decaying Mazagaon, Tarala was sold to the City of Bombay. It became the Sudder Adalat (Appellate Court) and then, during the Second World War, an Army clothing depot. Eventually, after suffering a fire in 1943 which may have been the result of arson, it was acquired by the Jamshetji Jeejeebhoy Hospital. This hospital, heavily endowed by the family, had been built nearby in the 1840s on what was then open land, and stands on the same spot today surrounded by a crowded inner-city area with a largely Moslem population. The JJ Hospital (as it is always known) used the old house for a few years as a staff hostel, before pulling it down to build a more modern one. I wonder how many, or how few, of the young doctors who occupied partitioned corners of its lofty rooms dreamed that they were lodging where one of the most successful and wealthy Indian families of modern times ate, slept, walked on the terrace overlooking their private gardens and gave parties – or where, even longer ago, a house guest of Sir James Mackintosh, Maria Graham, had written in 1809 after meeting the Wadias: 'the whole family . . . speak and write English so well, that if I did not see their dark faces and foreign dress, or read their unusual names at the end of a letter, I should never guess they were not Englishmen'.

It was meant innocently as praise, of course, and taken as such. Was it, in the long run, such a recommendation? For the final act of the Parsi 'romance' is only being played out now in the present century. In the early nineteenth century certain Parsis had long enjoyed friendly relations at work with the English, but they still, like the Moslems and Hindus, had little social life in the European sense of the term. They might dine with European associates after work in the Fort, or invite them and their wives to a wedding feast, but the latter occasions were regarded by the English in the light of picturesque curiosities rather than as normal dinner parties. Admiration and affability are not quite the same thing as acceptance on either side, and a 'visit to a prominent native' was still something to be recorded in a travelogue. In 1839 Mrs Postans visited Hormanji Bomanji Wadia in his grand house, Lowji Castle, which was named after the first shipbuilder and situated at Parell not far from the other Wadia house there – the Lal Baug:

> After entering the spacious hall of Lowjee Castle, we found ourselves ushered up a flight of broad and handsome stairs, which led to a magnificent drawing room, decorated with the utmost richness. Luxurious couches, and ottomans, covered with damask silk, were arranged with gilded fauteils of the most commodious form; good paintings, including full-length portraits of Lord Nelson and Sir Charles Forbes, ornamented the walls; and superb windows of painted glass, cast the brilliantly tinged rays of the departing sun, on chandeliers of dazzling lustre. Princely in general effect, the whole combined well with the dignified and graceful deportment of its possessor.

(Today, the site of Lowji Castle is occupied by the Raj Kamal film studios, but the shell of the old house may well still exist within the superimposed buildings, just as the shell of da Orta's house still exists, unrecognisably, in the much reconstructed core of Bombay Castle. A few of Lowji Castle's 'superb windows of painted glass' have been salvaged by a descendant of the family and now adorn a large old bungalow on Colaba. In commemoration of the family's original occupation, they depict sailing ships against a background of translucent red.)

In 1834 Narowji Wadia, son of Jamshetji the shipbuilder, allowed *his* son Jehangir and a cousin of the same generation to visit England and study the shipyards and the new wonders of steam. Their moral welfare was entrusted, successfully it would seem, to that same Sir Charles Forbes, the retired East India merchant whose portrait hung in Lowji Castle. We shall hear of him again. A daguerrotype of them survives, attired in the Persian dress the Parsis then still wore (smock, trousers, small slippers, shawls and the distinctive, stiff Parsi turban) sitting like exotic but domesticated cats in a room full of London lodging-house furniture. London lodging-house food might, however, have been a little too much:

they took the precaution of bringing their own Parsi cook with them. Such a trip still seemed a daring and questionable enterprise, in the days when high-born Hindus *never* crossed the sea, for caste reasons. The Parsis who began to undertake such journeys were still regarded as 'natives' rather than as honorary Europeans and spoke of themselves as such, but it is significant that at the time of the Bengal Uprising in 1857 their sympathies were wholly with the British – a circumstance which the British themselves, it may be said, took for granted. By the 1850s one wholly Parsi firm, Cama and Co., had established a branch office in London. There had been brief coolings in the Anglo-Parsi special relationship in 1839, when the Scottish Missionary Wilson (see Chapter VII) tactlessly converted two Wadia boys, Dhunjibhoy and Hormusji Pestonji, to the faith of Christ, and again when some more conversions took place in the early 1850s. The more conservative and less able among the community (i.e. the priestly caste) were inclined to say that no good came of all this European-style education that families such as the Camas were now advocating; but the pressures towards such an education, and to an eventual advantageous cultural assimilation on the Jewish model, were irresistible. 'We want English language, English manners and English behaviour for our wives and daughters', one Framji Bomanji wrote in 1863. The community lacked an indigenous culture of its own. The use of the Persian language was by now confined to prayers which most Parsis repeated without understanding; they were happy to adopt Shakespeare, Wordsworth and Macaulay as their own. Among the rising generation of the 1860s western-style dress became the rule, except always for the Parsi headgear, with its happy accidental resemblance to the British top-hat of the period.

The supremacy of the Wadia family declined after the disastrous fire at Dadabhoy Pestonji's house in the Fort in 1849 and his subsequent business failure, but later generations of the family were to supply India's earliest native lawyers including the first Indian High Court Judge. The most glamorous Parsi figure of the mid-nineteenth century was Jamshetji Jeejeebhoy (1783-1859),* whose 'real' name was murmured to be Bottlewallah from the circumstances that he in youth, or perhaps his father, had dealt in

---

* He sits today in the main hall of the hospital that bears his name, looking enormously wise, the subject of worshipful attentions from the cleaning staff who pamper him with garlands and small saucers of coconut as if he were a Hindu god.

empty bottles. But such was the respect accorded to money-making at the period both in England and India that 'JJ' readily established himself and his family at the pinnacle of Bombay society. In consideration of his enormous donations to charities of all kinds, both in India and in England, he became a knight and finally the first Indian baronet; references to him in the British press of the period are nearly always respectful. His coat of arms featured an island with two palm-trees, mountains, sun, two bees, a hand, wheat and a peacock. His son, following in his footsteps, was the first Parsi to encourage his womenfolk to accept invitations to soirées and dinner parties, and by the last quarter of the century a western-style social life had become the norm in well-to-do Parsi circles; Parsi daughters began receiving the same kind of education as their brothers, and Parsi sons were among the earliest Indian undergraduates at Oxford and Cambridge. Cricket, golf, tennis and bridge became Parsi occupations. By about 1905 a Parsi newspaper could write, as if it were a foregone conclusion: 'The closer union of Europeans and Parsis is the finest thing that could happen to our race . . . The complete Europeanisation of the Parsis is now a mere matter of time.'

Yet already by then the community were in difficulties. Through Parsi charities, educational and other, almost every Parsi in Bombay had been raised, if not genuinely to middle-class level, at any rate to a situation in which he expected a modestly middle-class standard of living – this, in a country where the great mass of people formed, and form today, a working class locked in a constant struggle to obtain the necessities of life. Since in any case it has been estimated that it takes about twice as much money, in India, to maintain a western-style life as it does to maintain a Hindu life-style at a comparable social level, it is hardly surprising that, by the twentieth century, the Parsis were in danger of becoming 'a race of educated paupers': a half-world of drearily respectable displaced persons, as far from the *beau monde* of the Jeejeebhoys and the Tatas as they were from that of their Hindu and Moslem neighbours. By the 1930s, when the value of savings had declined following the world recession, 40 per cent of all the Parsis in Bombay were in receipt of some form of charity from their community. Among the wealthy, too, matters were not quite what they had been. In Bombay today, while there are still many influential Parsis, Parsi money tends to be 'old money', the proceeds of Parsi business acumen of the previous century which is not necessarily being maintained. Indeed many of today's Parsi community have only continued affluent through the sale of those grand bungalows and mansions that were built in the nineteenth century at the height of the community's success, and which are now ruthlessly knocked down to provide yet another cliff-like slab of glass and concrete where once the vultures discreetly bred among the palms and the mangoes.

But the real problem, underlying the economic one, is that the very readiness to accept western ways which originally led the race into its position of power and privilege, has in the end led them into a void. The newspaper writer who declared that 'the complete Europeanisation of the Parsis is now a mere matter of time' did not foresee that what mere time would bring in another forty years was the ending of the British Raj and the withdrawal from India of the very people on whom the Parsis had modelled themselves. Where did the future of the community now lie? They could of course leave India, as many able Parsis before them had already done: the British MP for Central Finsbury 1892-5 had been a Parsi, Dadabhoy Naorowji, and another, S. D. Saklatvala, a nephew of J. N. Tata, was, of all things, Communist MP for North Battersea in the 1920s: so far had successful assimilation taken place. But assimilation into another country and culture means the loss of your own. Today, every Parsi family in Bombay seems to have relatives – usually younger relatives – in London, New York or Toronto; but these migrants in a secular age are inevitably losing their racial identity and sinking untraceably into the society of their new homes. The alternative is to remain in India; but India is now a country for Indians, not for surrogate westerners. (The much-depleted Anglo-Indian community in cities like Bombay have the same problem.) It seems to many Parsis that the only route lies back: back into the India life-style, the Indian habits of eating and sleeping and language that were forsaken two or three generations ago. As if demoralised by the prospect, the Parsis have a low fertility rate today, and many never marry – a circumstance unique in Indian society.

Meanwhile the ageing survivors of a lost era, sitting in spacious flats they could never afford to buy again today, surrounded by Victorian blackwood armchairs, French clocks, Venetian glass and family photographs full of dogs and horses, dispensing tea from Limoges tea-services, speak with regret of the 'good old days' when the British ruled India, and enquire anxiously if England itself has changed much, hoping it has not. 'An alien people, clutching their gods'. This is where the long-ago journey of the Wise Men from Iran has ended.

V Gentleman's Houses and Others

By the later decades of the eighteenth century the town on the Island had taken on the shape that is still there in submerged form today. The 'dense mass of buildings . . . like a fortified town' with the Cathedral tower rising out of them, and behind them 'a wide plain stretching from the ramparts to the sea' which Emma Roberts was to record *c.*1840, was substantially there. The dense coconut grove which had once, in Portuguese times, covered the Esplanade right up to the Manor House, had long since been partially cleared: probably a lot of the trees were cut down during the Moghul siege *c.*1690. Further clearance may have taken place in 1739 when, threatened by the Angria pirates who continued to be a menace up to the late 1750s, the merchants of Bombay supplemented the town walls with a moat or ditch dug round them, into which the sea was let. The harbour defences were strengthened in the 1740s, and new dockyards were constructed in the following decade including a dry-dock that much impressed visitors from Europe. About 1760, with fears this time of a raid by the French with whom the British had been spasmodically at war both in Europe and in India for the past four years, a new round of fortifying took place. The Castle defences were upgraded, making it for the first time into a veritable castle, and the walls round the town acquired further bastions and ravelins. In 1769 the old and useless fort at Dongri was blown up and a new one, patriotically called Fort St George like the one at Madras from which the French had now been forced, was built at Bori Bunder at the northern end of the town, the walls of both forming a continuous fortification.

Two fragments of the massive black granite walls of this date are visible today. One has been built into the boundary wall round St George's Hospital to the east of Victoria Terminus and is visible to anyone going along Frere Road (D'Mello Road). It looks rather like the stanchion of an obsolete railway bridge. At the time of writing, some of its lower stones form the back wall to a pavement shanty lived in by an untidy family of immigrants from the country. A public urinal is situated conveniently to hand. The other fragment, one of the bastions of the Castle itself – Flower Tree bastion, I rather think – may be seen from the compound of the Mint: in fact the entire Castle wall still exists, but it forms part of the closely guarded naval headquarters and is not generally on view to the public. It is curious to think that these ancient-seeming remnants, which are spoken of in Bombay today as if they did indeed date from some past as remote as the Norman Conquest, were actually being built when, in Europe, town walls were being allowed to decay as useless if picturesque structures and fortresses like the Bastille were on their way out. But the fortifications of Bombay were serious military structures, for the British were a serious military power in India. A German traveller, Carsten Niebuhr, who came to Bombay in 1764 and has left us an account of it in French, got into trouble with the local authorities for sketching the new walls. But then Niebuhr was a nuisance in a number of ways. He angered the Parsi community by attempting to penetrate into one of their Towers, and spread a silly story in his writings about the Tower having been built to protect the dead after a dead girl had been visited there by her lover.

Opinions and accounts vary as to whether the Roman Catholic church and the Mumba Devi temple by Bori Bunder disappeared as early as 1739, or whether they were swept away in the more extensive clearances of the 1760s. What is known is that in 1772 (when the American War of Independence was in the offing and the English in Bombay again feared a French attack on that account) the Esplanade was levelled, and presently cleared of all buildings and trees to create a free field of fire for 800 yards. This was later extended to 1,000 yards; the distance can still be measured across the *maidans* today from the road junction south of Bombay Gymkhana or from Victoria Terminus.

Other things also disappeared in the 1760s clearances. The gunpowder manufactory which had been conveniently but dangerously situated outside the southern, or Apollo, gate of the town, in the direct line of fire from ships entering the harbour, was shifted to a site in Mazagaon. (Gunpowder Lane, lined with old frame houses, still winds through Mazagaon today, not far from the hill where the Belvedere used to stand.) The old cemetery at Mendham's Point was removed and so, presumably, were the single graves on the Colaba foreshore, including Sir John Child's. A few years later the beacon light which had been on Sir John's grave was revived in the form of Colaba lighthouse. The cemetery was closed in 1763; for a few years burials took place in the churchyard, and apparently there was, for a period of twenty years, a burial ground outside the Church Gate a little way beyond the town walls in the direction of Back Bay, approximately where the bottom of Marine Lines is now. (See *The Story of St Thomas's Cathedral*, 1946.) All trace of this has disappeared, but it would have been a logical site for burial, bearing in mind that this area was then something of a no-man's-land. A map that today hangs in the Victoria Museum in Bombay and which I have seen nowhere else shows 'Madagascar Town' at that place, that is, the dwellings of Negroes who were either slaves or freed slaves. The British had followed the Portuguese in the practice of slave-owning: Negroes were imported from East Africa and Madagascar by Arab traders, and 431 were still listed in Bombay in 1789. This otherwise undocumented settlement, a tiny but significant detail in the huge, interlocking jigsaw that is the history of Bombay's people, may be the explanation for a baffling contemporary remark (quoted by Edwardes in his *Rise of Bombay*) to the effect that about 1760 a road was constructed 'from Churchgate to the Black Town'. The Church Gate, on the site of the present-day Flora Fountain, was the west gate, and the native districts that were later to be known as the Black Town were then only gradually beginning to grow on the far side of the Esplanade, due north of the Fort. Clearly 'Black Town' is a deceptive term in more ways than one, and historians should beware of it. (As for 'native', the word is used throughout this book in the sense in which it was used throughout the period covered – i.e. to mean a non-European inhabitant of Bombay. It is an essential word in the context, and no pejorative implication should be read into it.)

A little further up Back Bay were the Hindu burning ground given to the community by Aungier in the early days of the colony, and also a Moslem cemetery; both are still in use today, though their situation, surrounded by tall buildings and next to one of the mainline railways into Bombay, has become as inappropriate as it was once appropriate – they were originally right on the shore. Down below the foundations of the three blocks that now separate the burning ground from the sea there must be, in addition to sea-sand, gravel and shells, a great many fragments of bone and ash. I am told by Moslems that the sea, though driven further off today, still makes its presence felt in their graveyard, in that a tomb once dug rapidly becomes water-logged. The Moslem rule that corpses must be carried on foot to their last resting place has tended to keep Moslem burial grounds in the city, the community resisting hygienic late-nineteenth-century suggestions that it was high time the old grounds were closed.

It was here too, 'in a coconut garden near the water', after a lapse of a few years from the closure of Mendham's Point, that the new British cemetery was opened, together with grounds for the Portuguese and Armenian Christians. For exactly a hundred years it remained the principal burying ground in Bombay, for Colabá Cemetery on the far tip of the Island was mainly military. The district of the graveyards was known as Sonapur, which means 'the city of gold'. Samuel T. Sheppard, who edited the *Bombay Times* for many years, thought this evocative name derived from the Hindu saying on the death of an aged person, *tyachen sone jhalen* – 'he is turned into gold'.

More coloquially, the British graveyard there was long known as 'Padre Burrows' go-down', from the name of the Company's chaplain in the late eighteenth century. Bombay was by then no longer quite such a 'charnel house', but such was the death-rate among Europeans still at this period that you might have expected the Padre's warehouse one day to receive his own corpse in store till the Day of Judgement; but in fact the Rev. Arnold Burrows survived his forty-five years' service with the Company and retired at last to England in 1813. Five years later, when a lane was made through the coconut grove to connect the cemetery with Girgaum Road, one of the main north-south roads, it was called Burrows Lane. It exists today, as an alley between high buildings, but it no longer gives access to the old cemetery, which has itself been shut for burial since 1866. In about 1960, when its tombs were broken and overgrown, the 'city of gold' was at last cleared and made into a public garden and children's playground. There on that ground that received so many European children and infants, succumbing like pallid flowers to the sticky, heavy climate, the young of the well-to-do families from Queen's Road and Marine Drive swing and jump and slide down the trunk of a giant model elephant; they are protected by a watchman, and by a paling of Disneyish animal cut-outs, from the street families that would otherwise infiltrate. Across the forgotten British dead, westernised India and Indian

St Thomas's church and part of Bombay Green in the early 19th century.
Note the box-like palaquins being carried, and the collection of men in
the forground in Parsi headgear.

Another view of Bombay Green in 1811, showing signs (to the left) of its use as a cotton mart. One of the Parsis toward the right of the picture has adopted European dress.

Above The Town Hall and Green before Elphinstone Circle was laid out – pre 1864.

Below The same view today. The skyscraper in the background is the new Reserve Bank of India building.

Mazagoan as it once was – early 19th century.

What might almost be the same house, photographed in Mazagoan in 1980.

Mazagoan Bay in the late 18th century. Mazagoan Hill and the Belvidere house on the left, Narowji Hill on the right, in the centre distance Bombay Fort.

Above Elaborate vernacular architecture in an old and dateless house in Gunpowder Lane, Mazagoan.

Below the simpler traditional abode of Mazagaon Christians.

Mazagaon grand-style: 'Tarala', the late 18th century house built by the Wadia family and subsequently the home of Sir James Mackintosh. Photographed just before its demolition (?) circa 1960.

India confront and ignore one another.

Several accounts of Bombay around the mid-eighteenth century have survived, including Grose's *Voyage to the East Indies* and his invaluable map of the Fort, which enables one to locate precisely many of the buildings. The one straggling main street that Ovington and Burnell had seen had developed into many more, with a network of cross-lanes, especially in the northern, more native part of the Fort. Grose, who came out as a writer for the Company in 1750, recorded that 'the houses of the black merchants as they are called, tho' some are far from deserving the appellation of black, are for the most part extremely ill-built and incommodious, with small window lights and ill-arranged rooms. Even the best have a certain air of meanness and clumsiness.' He admitted, though, that their verandahs (a Portuguese word and, to him, a novel invention) were a good idea. Others might have said that the large windows obstinately favoured by the Europeans, even before glass was available so that they had to be covered by wooden or bamboo blinds in the wet season, were not particularly well-suited to the climate. The days when 'confusedly live the English, Portuguese, Topazes, Gentoos,* Moors, Coolies and Christians' in the same section were numbered. In 1742 there had been an attempt to reserve certain sites in the Fort for 'Europeans, topasses, sepoys and the better sort of Christians', and in 1754 the Government of Bombay tried to curb the casual native construction habits by passing a regulation for the summary demolition of shanties and outhouses put up without permission, and to prevent building materials from being left lying around the streets. Anyone who has seen the way shanty-constructions spring up almost overnight in modern Bombay, and creep like a tropical fungus over any unpoliced open space, may doubt whether these early attempts at town planning were entirely successful.

However, further attempts were made in the 1770s: the part of the town lying south of Church Street (today's Vir Narriman Road where it runs between the Flora Fountain and Elphinstone Circle) was to be reserved for European building; whether because of this or by established custom, that was the area in which most of the European firms that settled in Bombay toward the end of the century had their premises. Evidently the town was trying to urbanise itself and develop an ordered air, in the way that towns were at the same period on the other side of the world – this was the

* From 'gentiles' in the biblical sense of 'heathen', i.e. Hindus.

117

time when the great London estates of squares and terraces were beginning to be laid out. Plans were made for the demolition within the Fort of 'small houses at present occupied by *hamals* [servants] and other indigent peoples', the sort of rural slum-cottage that lurked by the gates of great houses in Europe up to the eighteenth century, and still, in spite of two centuries of municipal legislation, tends to lurk beside more substantial dwellings in India today. There were also orders to owners of coconut *oarts* within the walls to let their land go for further building, in spite of their protests: the concept of Bombay not just as a fortified trading post but as a properly organised and prestigious city, the metropolis of a larger outer domain, was at long last reasserting itself.

One result of the increasing urbanisation of land within the walls was that 'garden houses' first began to appear, suburban European bungalows set among the shore plantations north of the Esplanade, on the old Mazagaon estate and along the shore of Back Bay. They were to become, in time, a great feature of Bombay, whose centre, corseted within walls and moat, was unable to expand. Indeed by the late eighteenth century the inconvenience of this in itself was already becoming apparent: complaints about shanties thatched with palm leaves disappear, and by 1787 we find a commentator writing: 'the confined extent of their ground has led many of the black inhabitants to raise their houses to so great a height as may be injurious to the healthiness of the town . . . little attention has been given to the breadth of the streets'. However, I doubt myself if 'confined extent' was the only reason: there was a pre-existing tradition of tall houses in western Indian cities to give a precedent. Unlike Calcutta, where buildings were traditionally low, the conditions of medieval European cities were being reproduced in Bombay, even to the overhanging wooden balconies and projecting eaves. One early-nineteenth-century visitor – Bishop Heber, the first bishop of Calcutta – was put in mind of the rows at Chester, but then he was peculiarly apt to seek homely comparisons by which to render India more compassable. And, as so often in Europe in earlier centuries, the result of this dense wooden building was a disastrous fire (1803) which swept through a large part of the city and accelerated the most prosperous citizens' move to out-of-town houses.

A similarly medieval lack of drains cannot have helped the healthiness of the town. The need for sewers was debated in the 1770s, at which time it would appear that the town-ditch – the moat – was the chief receptacle for sewage, for it was said to be in urgent need of cleansing. But it was to be another hundred years before Bombay acquired a proper drainage system. In any case views on the state of the town seem to have varied widely. One visitor at the period under review stated that 'the town is all lying low and swampy and is generally esteemed unhealthy for the European constitution', while another remarked: 'The soil is a sand, mixed with small gravel, which makes it always so clean, even in the rainy season, that a man may walk all over the town within half an hour after a heavy shower, without dirtying his shoes.' The same witness (Abraham Parsons) provides a concise description of the town's layout:

> The town of Bombay is nearly a mile in length from the Apollo Gate to that of the bazaar, and about a quarter of a mile broad in the broadest part of the Bunda, across the green, to the Churchgate, which is nearly at the centre, as you walk round the walls between the Apollo and the Bazaar Gate [i.e. the south and north gates respectively]. There are likewise 2 marine gates, with a commodious wharf and cranes built out from each gate, besides a landing place for passengers only. Between the two marine gates is the castle, properly called the Bombay castle, a very large and very strong fortification, which commands the bay . . . Here is a spacious green, capable of containing several regiments exercising at the same time; the streets are well laid out, and the buildings (viz. the gentleman's houses) so numerous and handsome as to make it an elegant town . . . The esplanade is very extensive, and as smooth and even as a bowling green, which makes walking or riding round the town very pleasant.

He added that on Colaba island, where there were then no houses, only military barracks, people would sometimes camp after an illness 'for a change of air'. A causeway made the place reachable on foot at low tide.

A few of the 'gentleman's houses' of this era or only a little later may be seen to this day. An elegantly bow-fronted house, its original pillars lurking behind shops, fills the fork of Apollo and Marine Streets and is known to this day as 'the Writers Building'. Then there is a large old house with two side wings and some rather elaborate iron-work balconies in the central block, standing on the west side of Apollo Street south of Elphinstone Circle, with its pillared verandah likewise filled in. It is occupied by a variety of different businesses including a printing shop and looks rather run down, but this building, which originally stood in a garden compound shaded with mulberry trees, was for many years in the late eighteenth and early nineteenth centuries the home of the Governor of Bombay and later his Secretariat. An inconspicuous plaque high up on the side wall records that Governors lived there from 1757 to 1829, but the dates should probably be treated with caution. The actual date when the house was built does not seem to be known, as the governor, when he moved from the Castle, may possibly have occupied an earlier house on that site: the usually authoritative *Bombay Gazetteer* (1909) gives a very confused account of the building's history and is apparently unaware that two plots of ground it mentions in this connection are one and the same. Personally I think that the move from the Castle was probably made as a result of the further militarisation of the Castle around 1760; in October 1764 a house whose site approximates to that of the building we now know as the Old Secretariat was purchased from a Mr Whitehall. There does not appear to be any direct evidence of rebuilding, so it is quite possible that the house we see today was already there c.1750, if not before: it was apparently built by Mr Whitehall on the site of a tank, and possessed a deep well of its own in the compound and 'a staircase like that of a Genoese Palace' – which may still be there somewhere in its entrails. Pictures of similar fine houses, indeed in the italianate style which suits well with the local climate, appear in Grose's book, and also in a picture of the Green by James Forbes (see below). But by the 1770s the tendency for wealthy Europeans to have additional 'garden houses' out of the confines of the city was becoming apparent, and successive Governors adapted and enlarged their property out at Parell, the erstwhile Jesuit house and garden five or six miles from the Fort. Duncan, who was Governor for sixteen years, eventually died in the old house in Apollo Street in 1811, a fact which is also recorded on the wall plaque, and after that no Governor seems to have made it his chief residence – a pattern of town-growth and mortality which was later (see Chapter VII) to be repeated at Parell itself.

Another ancient stone house of the mid to late eighteenth century is still standing at the lower end of Marine Street, next but one to St Andrew's Church and opposite the elegant dockyard gate and clocktower of the same period. It belonged to Hornby, who was Governor from 1771 to 1784, but it was known for part of that period as Admiralty House, as it was occupied by the Secretary of the Marine Board. After Hornby's return to England, it became the Mayor's Court – the local Magistrates' Court. This institution was, with the passing of time, upgraded to Recorder's Court and finally High Court, but it remained in Hornby House all that time till it was removed in 1879 to the new and magisterial Court buildings on the Esplanade that were part of the late-nineteenth-century building boom. After that the house in Marine Street became the Great Western Hotel (conveniently situated near the port for disembarking guests) and was recommended in *Murray's Guide* of 1887 for its 'large airy rooms'. It is remembered as the hotel by elderly people today. Most of them believe it to have disappeared, but it still stands, occupied by offices and looking rather shabby minus its pillared verandah, which has been removed for summary road-widening. Its progression, from private, rather grand house, to Government department, to Law Court, its social decline into an hotel and then its physical decline into little-regarded obscurity, follows a classic pattern for inner-city buildings. (Compare the *hotels privés* of Paris, or the once private residences of London's Covent Garden.) Any time now it might be swept away.

One more house of this period does indeed, as I write, appear to be trembling on the brink of extinction, but let us hope that, like many another ramshackle-looking structure in Indian cities, it will survive nevertheless. This is Forbes's house, situated in the lane of that name on the south-west edge of the Fort. Forbes is a trap of a name in Bombay, for two separate illustrious citizens, overlapping in time, bore it. The best-known to the rest of the world was James Forbes, a Scot born around the middle of the eighteenth century who, in the fashion of his time, was sent out to Bombay at only sixteen as a Company servant. He remained there for the best part of twenty years, when he retired to England with the material, in the form of letters, notes, paintings and drawings which was to furnish his *Oriental Memoirs*, a sumptuous book published in 1813. But we are concerned for the moment with the family of John Forbes, also a Scot, who was born a few years earlier; he too came out to Bombay very young, and founded the agency house of Forbes & Co. which was to be one of the city's leading commercial enterprises for several generations. He amassed a considerable fortune, with which he was generous to his Scottish birthplace, but never married. In 1788, among the family papers, we find his brother George, who was Minister of Lochell, writing to John to commend to him his son, John's nephew Charles, who was to be sent out to Bombay in his turn at barely sixteen. His elder brother had already been sent two years before, but the ship he was in went down and all on board were drowned. Such were the hazards then of sending your sons out to seek their fortune. The Minister wrote: 'I am sure he [Charles] will please you, for he has not a fault just now I would wish mended, though perhaps I may be partial. I only wish he may continue equally well and avoid all bad company.' Later, when Charles was established in Bombay, he wrote to him: 'Your frequent letters are a great cordial to us and make us infinitely happy, happier than anything would except a sight of you, which we never expect to live to be blessed with, but while we have agreeable accounts of your health and happiness we ought to bless God and be satisfied.'

This was not idle pessimism. The father lived on another ten years, but it is highly likely that he never saw his son again, for in the days before steamships a voyage to India had to be considered a definitive step, at any rate for many years. Numerous are the examples of people who spent twenty, thirty or even forty years in the colony, and who went Home once during that time, if at all; the voyage cost the equivalent of several thousand pounds in our money. Numerous others went early to a more final resting place, hence that oft-quoted pathetic tombstone, 'Here lies X . . . who was to have gone home next year'. Of the nineteen young men who had sailed with *James* Forbes in 1765, he was, twenty years later, the sole survivor. Letters normally then still took seven months or more between England and India, though an overland route via the Mediterranean, Persia and the Gulf was beginning to come in by Charles Forbes's day, which cut the time to between three and four months. The letters therefore tend to be faintly desperate communications of essential information on health, with lists of other people's fortunes and misfortunes, news that would be months out of date by the time it was received. George Forbes would commend the sons of friends and acquaintances coming to Bombay to Charles's notice and kindness, and the latter would entrust others with similar commissions to his family. We find him writing to a local acquaintance who was going home: 'The small parcel for Mrs Lumsden may be delivered to my father. It contains a pair of buckles, a China seal and a comb which belonged to her son, who died in this country last year. These things are trifling, but you know they will be valuable in her eyes.'

Charles himself did not die but, taking after his uncle in amiability and diligence, prospered very greatly. On two occasions he or his firm lent large sums of money to the Government of Bombay. He was a close friend and business associate of the Wadia brothers. His portrait, it may be remembered, adorned the drawing room in Lowji Castle. He was a proponent of the principle of equal rights for Indians – he thought, for instance, that there should be Indians among the JPs who sat in the Mayor's Court, an advanced idea for the period. He left Bombay definitively in 1811, became a Member of Parliament (he was popularly described as the 'Member for India') and finally a baronet. A statue of him by Chantrey was ordered and paid by public subscription, and today stands in the Town Hall, but for some reason he is in a side room on his own, and not in the anteroom where other larger-than-life marble Governors and the like keep each other company, including some that were his friends in life. He himself ended his days at an advanced age at a house in Fitzroy Square in London where his uncle had lived before him, and it may be that his house in Bombay, which is the one that concerns us now, was also built by his uncle some time in the 1770s before Charles' arrival. Two water-colours of it, drawn from different angles, have come down to us and are in the Victoria Museum, Bombay. These permit a careful comparison with the house still standing today in Forbes Lane near the nineteenth-century synagogue, and visible also from the site of the old town walls by the Jehangir Art Gallery: though much changed it is undoubtedly the same house, surviving through time and chance.

For a description of the life once led in the now darkened and rabbit-warren-like old houses, we must however turn again to the other Forbes, James. Looking back in 1813 to a period some thirty or forty years earlier, he wrote:

> The English houses at Bombay, though neither so large, nor elegant as those at Calcutta and Madras, were comfortable and well-furnished; they were built in the European style of architecture, as much as the climate would admit of; but lost something of that appearance by the addition of verandahs, or covered piazzas, to shade those apartments most exposed to the sun; when illuminated, and filled with social parties in the evening, these verandahs gave the town a very cheerful appearance.

He adds, however, that no artistic, scientific, literary or charitable institution existed then in the town, and that 'early hours prevailed'. Dinner was normally at one, as in England, unsuitably so in the hottest months, and was commonly followed by an un-English siesta. (Later generations shifted the main meal to the evening and began to look upon the siesta as a debilitating and old-fashioned habit – by which they really meant that it was immoral, and had been known to lead to another habit that had come to be looked on askance, i.e. the fathering of mixed-race progeny.)

In an often-cited passage in his *Oriental Memoirs* James Forbes describes himself as a young man newly apprenticed to the Company – we would say a mere boy in his teens – sitting on the roof of the Custom House at night reading Shakespeare by moonlight for lack of candles. It must be noted that the tropical moon is very bright and that wax candles were relatively expensive commodities at the period, particularly in Bombay, but Forbes also complained that he used to go supperless to bed: his annual salary (accommodation found) was only thirty rupees a year. This was a frequent complaint among the Company servants of his day, and the Company's answer was always that complainants had the opportunity to make fortunes by trading on the side, which was officially tolerated in Bombay till 1806. Some, including Forbes himself, eventually did, but many fell by the way. Coming to India and enduring a term of years there was still, and for long afterwards, seen in the nature of a lottery for high stakes in which, however, many 'drew a blank'; these ended up either in the bankruptcy court, seeing their furniture and palaquins auctioned off, or in the shallow soil of Mendham's Point or Sonapur. Between those extremes the writers, factors and merchants must have led, in the main, a life only redeemed from its provincial boredom by the constant imminent threat of death – a life, it has been said, without apples, ice or quinine, where claret and Madeira and the ill-famed Bombay punch and toddy were the only solace (apart from siestas) and where you met the same faces all the time round dinner tables. As late as the 1790s, by which time the population of the whole island was something in the region of 120,000 or more, the entire European population probably did not exceed 1,000.

These figures tell their own tale. So indeed does the fact that the larger figure is only a very rough estimate – some authorities place it considerably higher. The Island population by the early 1700s is thought to have sunk, from its peak under Aungier, to the level of 10,000 where it had been when the British had first arrived forty years before. For the first half of the eighteenth century it crept up only gradually. In 1760 it was probably only 60,000, though again some retrospective estimates put it much higher. It seems that after that date the rate of increase did itself increase; in 1780 the population was officially estimated at 113,000 and by the first Census in 1816 it was 161,550 – which probably, like most formal Censuses, under-represented the real figure. (General estimates, on the other hand, tend to overstate numbers.) But the point is that no one really knows or ever did know. Figures for Europeans were never hard to obtain: most of them were still Company servants (civil, military or marine) and their families; their occupations otherwise – tavern keeper, barber, surgeon, hospital super-intendent etc. – were known and listed. But the great bulk of the people, those who, through the eighteenth century, were gradually creating the new 'native town' north of the Esplanade, spreading from Mazagaon across Mandvi, where there was no longer a custom house, across the Fig-tree Creek and the Footwash which were now dry, beginning to settle in what was eventually to be the great bazaar area of Kalba Devi – they were a different matter. It is obvious that it was with them, their crafts and their trade, that the true growth of Bombay lay. Yet this great, stealthy swelling has been little documented either at the time or after.

It is clear in general terms that the traditions laid down by Aungier in the 1670s were being maintained. Already in the 1750s Grose had written: 'Nothing . . . has more contributed to the population of this island, than the mildness of the government and the toleration of all religions, there not being suffered the least violence or injury to be offered, either to the natives or Europeans on that account.' He contrasted unfavourably the behaviour of the Portuguese and Moslem authorities elsewhere in western India: this in itself produced a steady trickle of refugees into Bombay.

It is known that Moslem weavers from Ahmedabad were encouraged, like the Parsis, with grants of land, to come and settle around the middle of the century. Other 'Moors', traders – Borahs – the descendants of eleventh-century Hindu converts, came later in the century and were allowed to settle in the Fort. Many of these too distributed themselves in the eastern part of the growing native town, near where the Jumna Musjid (the Great Mosque) was built c.1800 on a garden belonging to a Konkani Moslem, a descendant of Arabs. Indeed the presence of Moslem shrines and mausolea in many parts of the town indicates the widespread nature of Moslem settlement, though the shrine that is the most famous today, Hadji Ali on an island in the little bay that was once the mouth of the Great Breach, does not appear in any account or map of this date or much later. We know from Niebuhr that Greeks had settled in the city by the mid-century, and it is probable that the first of the Beni Israel (see Chapter VIII) had arrived by this date. A colony of Jains (a Hindu-Buddhist sect) from Gujerat began to arrive at the end of the century, driven from their homeland by the Mahrattas: they reinforced the Gujerati-speaking trading community already established by the Parsis, the Borah and

Khoja Moslems and some of the Banian Hindus. In time there were many others, Mahratta Brahmin clerks from Poona, other Mahratta castes such as goldsmiths, coppersmiths and jewellers, Bhatias – toddy growers who sought to escape their caste of origin by adopting vegetarianism – Moslem converts from Sind, a few Pathans from the north, Goans, even some Chinese in the silk trade. The story of Bombay's development could have been written from the viewpoint of any one of these separate communities, and it would in each case have been different. But it has not been written.

In the bazaar areas today there must be many houses quite as old as the ones I have picked out in the Fort, but, built of wood in a timeless, high-galleried style, and embedded like fossils in commercial accretions of a later date, they are nearly impossible to pick out with any accuracy. Some seem to show distinctively Gujerati features, in their carving and in their inner courtyards, but their builders remain anonymous, unstudied. One of the very few scholars (Dr V. S. Pramar, MS University, Baroda) who *has* attempted to document this kind of building (though not in Bombay) remarked to me that Indians who have done well in business and moved up the social scale have none of the twentieth-century European's pride or interest in the humbler past, and that those whose families have not been so upwardly mobile and have therefore stayed within the bazaars are still less equipped to survey the past and its products. At best, the present-day inhabitants or neighbours of an old house can sometimes date its construction back to an illustrious local figure or personal ancestor – date, that is, not by years, but by an unreliable counting of generations. For example, the house of the prominent Konkani Moslem ship's captain, Mahommed Ali Rogay, who enlarged the Jumma Musjid in the 1830s, is still there in the crowded Bhendi Bazaar, in Nakhoda Mohulla – 'Captains' ghetto' – and is still occupied by Rogays. I have been inside it, and in its spacious, private first-floor rooms are the carved and rose-wood inlaid furniture of a past era and a revered portrait of Mahommed Ali's son in black jacket and waistcoat, tie, collar and *dhoti*. But it is significant that the present occupants seem to have got the generations confused and telescoped in their account: they do not realise themselves how venerable their house is. It is hardly surprising, then, that where less distinctive houses are concerned, no one seems to know or care what their history may be; they are just 'very old', and it is considered part of the natural course of things that they will eventually fall down and disappear. Every year several *do* fall down, precipitately, with a crash of timber or masonry, clouds of dust and loss of life. Large as many of these much-lived-in houses are, they were not really built to last.

In so far as preservationism has touched Bombay, it has, as a European import, only attached itself to buildings deemed by Europeans to be 'important' (the Town Hall, the big station, etc.). Indeed it sometimes seems to me that the Hindu attitude to the body at death (that it should be dissolved in fire and its ashes irretrievably scattered) and to the soul (that it migrates into another form) is applied equally to buildings. The concept that an individual building may, just because it is old, have accrued to itself layers of historical interest and be, in a sense, an embodiment of that lost past, seems foreign to Indian ways of thought. Perhaps this is, once again, because Hindus know time to be cyclic, while we know it to be linear. Or it may, in the case of Bombay, relate also to the fact that most of those who have settled there over the last three centuries have, by definition, been essentially nomadic, opportunist peoples – traders and itinerant craftsmen – not people whose deepest identification is with the land, the quintessential place.

Just as Indians seem, by British standards, to have no proper mental maps of the past, so mapping actual streets and buildings appears to present them with problems also. The parts of Bombay that were built up by Europeans, or by those honorary Europeans the Parsis, were always the readily mappable and mapped from the earliest days. The parts, however, where the rest of the population were left to construct their own dwellings in a piecemeal and individual way developed without a plan – without, indeed, proper streets at all: just spaces between the houses which presently solidified into meandering lanes and gullies. When these districts *did* come to be mapped by police and ordnance surveyors in the mid-nineteenth century, they presented great problems which have never, to this day, been entirely solved. Is a road a road if it runs through someone's courtyard? Is a lane a Public Highway if it is simply the spare space left between one private house and the next?

In any case, at a fundamental level, the mental image that is so familiar to Europeans of all social levels – that of a town as a network of thoroughfares bisecting denser masses of townscape – seems to be foreign to the Indian way of thought. Nor, typically, do such thoroughfares as exist in a native town actually go anywhere. They are there, it appears, simply to service the surrounding area. Thus names of main roads in Bombay are used indiscriminately to signify areas rather than the roads themselves, and still, today, the name of one road in a district is frequently confused with another running parallel or at right-angles to it, as if the two were indeed interchangeable and, once again, the linear concept did not apply. The visitor to Bombay today soon discovers that its taxi-drivers have no mental map of the city that corresponds to a western-style street map: they orientate themselves by a series of landmarks. As they are frequently illiterate this is hardly surprising – but what is more surprising is that many educated Indians too have difficulty in reading a street plan when it is presented to them. How, I have often wondered, does a Bombayite see his city? As a series of concentric circles, perhaps? Or, knowing the compartmentalisation of Indian life, as a swarming, inchoate mass in which there are just a few clearly seen, fixed points which are to him real – the buildings or streets connected with his own family, job, caste and religion?

The British urban historian, accustomed to the estates-system, under which a chunk of land would be divided up in the eighteenth or nineteenth centuries into separate roads and individual houses but would still retain an individual identity, feels particularly adrift in a city like Bombay, which superficially looks so British but actually is not. He seeks vainly for the key to the city's land-use and development, which he feels must be there and which he only gradually realises does not exist as a master-key at all. At the beginning of the twentieth century a body styled the Bombay Improvement Trust imposed some superficial order on the labyrinthine, unventilated mass of building on the Flats that had become central Bombay, by cutting a few new roads through it and widening a few of the existing ones. Some of the development in the most northern part of the island, beyond Parel (as it is now spelt) owes a good deal to their interest. But the fact remains that the greater part of the city north of the *maidans*, where the true commercial and popular heart of Bombay lies, grew up as an anarchic jumble of individual properties and this it has remained. Ownership there clearly was, and is – the landlord is a perennial figure in Indian life – but it is ownership divided for the most part into literally hundreds of thousands of separate parcels of land, hundreds and thousands of separate bits of paper, as originally spacious *oarts* and paddy grounds were gradually split up. Moreover, the transformation from planted land to housing land did not, as it often did in European cities, occur at a defined moment on the decision of a big landowner, but typically seems to have taken place by degrees, so that early accounts of the native town speak of 'houses thickly clustered within a coconut wood'* which later and

128

imperceptibly become 'houses standing in gardens'. Indian land records are just that – they do not describe the buildings on the land. Later, these individual gardens themselves were divided and sub-divided, as land in each district in turn became increasingly valuable. At this stage, plots that had originally been used by master-craftsmen and traders to lodge their labourers must have been laid out in lucrative tenements, the beginning of the *chawl* system. Today, with rents on old properties frozen at unrealistically low levels, the block or blocks of dwellings built on the spare land of the original proprietor as a profitable investment have become a dilapidated and often unwanted liability for the original landlord's descendants, and the landlord's house itself is now almost unrecognisable; its once-elegant tiers of carved wood balconies sag ominously above a row of minimal shacks that have attached themselves to the façade and both support and destroy it, like ivy on an ancient tree.

To see what these older houses in the bazaars looked like when they were built, we have to turn to a commentator of the early years of the nineteenth century (Maria Graham) who wrote:

> . . . the dwellings of rich natives are surrounded by verandahs, equally necessary to guard against the intemperate heat of the sun and the monsoon rains. They are generally painted in flowers and leaves of a green or red colour; those of the Hindus have usually some of the fables of their mythology represented on their walls. The houses are necessarily of great extent because, if a man has twenty sons, they all continue to live under the same roof even when married. The lower classes content themselves with small huts, mostly of clay and roofed with cadjan, a mat made of the leaves of the palmyra or coconut trees plaited together. Some of the huts are so small that they only admit of a man's sitting upright in them, and barely shelter his feet when he lies down. There is usually a small garden round each house, containing a few herbs and vegetables, a plantain tree and a coconut or two.

Herbs and vegetables, plantains and coconuts have virtually disappeared from the populous quarters of central Bombay, except from the baskets of the pavement sellers, who sit all day with their polished aubergines and onions in front of them near the vegetable markets at Byculla railway station, or hawk coconuts to thirsty strollers or bananas to office clerks. But the huts are still there. Not

---

* See, for example, Benham Hall Lane in present-day Girgaum, which is an anglicised version of *ban mahal* – the house in the wood.

the same huts, of course, that were there in the 1800s: their individual mud walls were swept away countless monsoons ago and their leafy sites have long been overtaken by more substantial buildings. But collectively and in general the huts are still there: the same archetypal constructions of mud, the same exiguous size, even sometimes roofed still with the coconut matting. Today they cling to scraps of waste land, to corners of unguarded private compounds; they squat on the verges of railway lines and invade any slope too steep for conventional houses; they huddle on the very pavements. But clearly they are not the hideous urban excrescences they are today so often imagined to be, obscure products of something called 'urban poverty'. On the contrary, these are displaced *rural* dwellings. Their poverty is essentially nothing to do with the city; they are, rather, imports from India's even poorer countryside. They are, like the ones Maria Graham saw in 1809, village huts, and the people who tenaciously occupy them, spreading their washing on nearby railings to dry, cooking their evening meal on tiny charcoal braziers, are ex-country people, attempting to continue life in the big city in the only way they know.

A number of factors encouraged the development of Bombay, after its long, slow beginnings, as the eighteenth century drew to its close. From a purely practical point of view, the construction of a proper wall at the Great Breach, to deal once and for all with the inroads of the sea, was important in permitting the gradual spread of settlement westwards across what is now central Bombay. The wall constructed with difficulty in the 1720s had only partially achieved the effect of land-drainage. Grose wrote in the 1750s: 'There is still subsisting a great body of salt water on the inside of the breach, the communication of which with the sea, being less free than before the breach [wall] was built, must be in proportion more apt to stagnate and breed noxious vapours.' A proper closure was eventually achieved by the causeway-road known to this day as 'Hornby's Vellard' (from the Portuguese word *vallado*, a barrier); one must suppose that it was planned by Governor Hornby (1771-84), although it does not appear to have been constructed till after his day. In Maria Graham's time there was a small house at the end of the Vellard nearest to the town, bearing the inscription 'Vellard begun 1797, finished 1805'.

Hornby was perhaps the most forward-looking and distinguished of the eighteenth-century Governors. It may or may not have been a coincidence that he presided over Bombay at the period when far-reaching changes, that were to affect Bombay's whole future, were taking place within the East India Company itself. The image of the rapacious merchant, enduring his term of years in India for what he could get out of the place, was giving way to that of the highly educated civil servant and 'selfless' Empire builder. By the 1770s many of the Company's merchants, trading on the side, had amassed the legendary Nabob fortunes, particularly in Calcutta, yet the Company itself was on the verge of bankruptcy and had acquired a reputation for indolence and corruption both in India and in Leadenhall Street – a reputation of which the unfortunate Warren Hastings was eventually made the symbol in a showcase trial. In 1773 the British Government bailed the Company out of its immediate difficulties with a substantial loan, and took the opportunity to pass the Regulating Act. This put the British possessions in India under the joint control of Company men and others, including a Governor General, appointed independently by Parliament and the Crown. The interference of these outsiders from 'some dirty corner of Westminster Hall' was much resented by the old guard of the Company. It meant that for the first time there was some formal recognition that the Company had administrative responsibilities above those of 'a ramshackle company trading in tea and opium', but in fact this was only the delayed enactment of an aspiration that had been expressed by the Company itself long before, in 1689. In that year the Company had issued a formal declaration of intent, stating that its purpose should be 'to make us [the British] a nation in India. Without that we are but a great number of interlopers, united by His Majesty's Royal Charter, fit only to trade where nobody of power thinks it in their interest to stop us.' Now, the best part of a century later, this transformation began to take place, and at considerable speed. This was just as well since, at the same period, the British were acquiring virtual control over larger and larger tracts of India, wrested from the French, the Dutch, from the last of the Moghuls in Delhi, and from Tipu Sultan the flamboyant ruler of Mysore, who fought the British for the last three decades of the century finally to die at the fall of Seringapatam in 1799. (His life-size clockwork model of a tiger devouring a red-coated Company soldier was taken to the Company's museum in Leadenhall Street and can be seen today in the Victoria and Albert Museum in South Kensington.)

A further Act of Parliament, Pitt's India Bill, was passed in 1784, the year after that in which America was definitively lost as a colony: it has indeed been suggested that in the busy creation of her

Indian Empire Britain was compensating for the loss of her previous New World. Pitt's Bill continued the principle of joint control between Company and Crown, but also set up a board of control at Westminster made up of the Chancellor of the Exchequer, the Secretary of State and four Privy Councillors – in effect a Ministry for India at the highest level. The Company remained in existence for another seventy-four years, till the Bengal Uprising ('Indian Mutiny') of 1857 provided the British Crown with the pretext for taking virtual control of the whole sub-continent, but from the end of the eighteenth century the Company's powers and trade monopolies were in any case steadily eroded.

The British gain which most affected Bombay was the piecemeal acquisition of territory from the Mahratta Confederacy, which then held most of central India. Much of the impetus for this came, naturally, from Bombay itself. In the first part of the eighteenth century the Government in Bombay, feeling that they had enough European enemies and also pirates to contend with, maintained a devious friendship with the Mahrattas: for instance they let them overrun the Portuguese town at Bassein and the surrounding territory of Salsette in 1739. However, by the 1770s Hornby felt strong enough to undertake a series of skirmishes with the Mahrattas, presently acquiring Salsette and the other neighbouring piece of semi-mainland, Thana, and the outer islands of Bombay harbour such as Elephanta. By a treaty of 1782, the town of Bassein itself, by then already half-derelict, was handed over to the Mahratta Peshwa of Poona, which was the key town to the Deccan – the western mountainous region which is the hinterland between Bombay and the rest of India. The British had decided to support the Peshwa for the time being, as an ally against other enemies including Tipu Sultan, but obviously their eventual hope was to acquire the Deccan also. An attempt had already been made on Poona, in 1780, when the American War of Independence was being fought out in India as a trade-war between the British and the French, but the expedition from Bombay was beaten back, and a greater disaster was only averted when there appeared on the scene a company of infantry all the way from Calcutta on the far side of the continent. It was the first time such concerted action had been achieved, and Warren Hastings, the then-Governor General of India, reported back to the Company in London that 'the way was long, through regions unknown in England, and untraced on our maps'.

The local Mahrattas were an essentially warlike, predatory

people, and the supposed ruling powers in Poona never in practice had much control over them. One of the freebooters turned against Poona itself in 1802, and the Peshwa escaped ignominiously to Bassein. Under Lord Wellesley, the Governor General of India, he was reinstated at Poona with the military assistance of Wellesley's younger brother Arthur, the future Duke of Wellington, then on the first of his much-celebrated visits to Bombay: naturally concessions to the British were part of the price exacted. Thirteen years and numerous intrigues later, the further opportunity for the British to gain control occurred. The Peshwa had unwisely agreed to join forces with assorted other Indian leaders to overthrow the British, and British troops, again including Arthur Wellesley, re-converged on Poona. The battle of Kirkee, which was fought near where the famous Poona military cantonment was later built, spelt the end of native power over a large section of western India, and opened up the trade routes through the Deccan which were to bring Bombay so much prosperity. The Peshwa was allowed to retire to a town on the Ganges with a handsome pension. There, the Bombay *Gazetteer* of 1909 remarks, 'he doubtless instilled into the mind of his adopted son, Nana Sahib, that hatred of the British which bore such terrible fruit in 1857'. It adds that, having annexed all the territories, 'the Bombay Government settled down to the task of peaceful administration'.

The White Man's Burden had been assumed, with a certain ruthless alacrity, one might say, but also with a becoming top dressing of *noblesse oblige* which is apparent in commentaries of the period. For instance:

> What infinite advantage, what incalculable benefits must accrue from a wise and liberal administration over those extensive realms which now form part of the British Empire, is not for me to judge. What immense good was done by the wise policy of the Bombay Government alone during the late famine [which devastated western India in 1803] we learn from the address of Sir James Mackintosh to the Grand Jury of that island in 1804 . . . Fifty thousand human beings have been saved from death in its most miserable form by the existence of a British Government in this island . . . I am entitled to presume that if they had continued subject to Native Governments, they would have shared the fate of the neighbouring province which are still so subject . . .
>
> (Forbes, *Oriental Memoirs*)

The rooted British Raj idea that Indians were extremely

fortunate to have responsible adult Europeans looking after their interests was quick to develop.

Yet James Forbes himself was a merchant, and a very successful one; in spite of the imperialist (and indeed missionary) sentiments he developed in middle age, back in England, he cannot have failed to know at some level that trading wealth was the growing Empire's rationale, and that it was not primarily to do the natives of the Deccan a favour that the British acquired their territory. Elsewhere in his *Oriental Memoirs* he wrote, describing his own days in Bombay in the 1770s and 80s:

> Bussorah, Muscat, Ormuz, and other ports in the Persian Gulph, furnished [Bombay's] merchants with pearls, raw silk, Carmenia wool, dates, dried fruits, rose water, attar of roses, and several other productions. Arabia supplied them with coffee, gold, drugs and honey. A number of ships annually freighted with cotton and bullion to China, returned laden with tea, sugar, porcelain, wrought silks, nankeens, and a variety of useful and ornamental articles. From Java, Malacca, Sumatra, and the eastern islands, they brought spices, ambergris, perfumes, arrack, and sugar: the cargoes from Madagascar, the Comorro isles, Mosambique, and other ports on the eastern coast of Africa, consisted chiefly of ivory, slaves and drugs: while the different parts of India produced cotton, silk, muslin, pearls, diamonds, and every precious gem; together with ivory, sandal-wood, pepper, cassia, cinnamon, and other luxuries. This valuable commerce was carried on by vessels belonging to the European or native merchants settled in Bombay; totally independent and unconnected with the trade of the East India Company.

Cotton, it will be noticed, is only mentioned in passing, as something that was exported to China. Forbes saw the beginning of this: a famine in China in the 1770s caused the Chinese to plant grains on much of their land that had hitherto been under cotton, and thus a demand grew there for cotton from India. This was regularly supplied by merchants in both Calcutta and Bombay. After 1784, when the duty on tea imported into Britain was lowered and the demand soared, tea became part of this trading cycle: much of the tea came from China, so it suited both British and native merchants to carry raw cotton from Indian ports to China and use it there to pay for the tea which they would take on board instead.

It was cotton which, with the nineteenth century, was to become *the* great export of Bombay; cotton raw, later spun, and finally in the forms of finished products, which provided the foundation on which most Bombay fortunes rested. Still today cotton is King in Bombay, as it once was and is no longer in Manchester and its satellite towns: indeed India today has to *import* some of the cotton she needs to feed Bombay's flourishing textile industry. An irony becomes apparent here: there is a case for saying (as Gandhi did, among others) that the village tradition of textile manufacture in India was all but destroyed by the imposition of British manufacturing and trading methods; but it is also true that the textile trade of Britain in the present day has, in turn, been much affected by the mills and workshops of Bombay.

But the cotton trade, for much of the nineteenth century, was not the only booming one. The opium trade too was a growth industry, for opium, extracted from the poppy, was the other Indian commodity that the merchants of Bombay traded with China in return for tea. It was one which, we would now say, they and the British Government itself thrust upon China with brutal and immoral opportunism. A discussion of this inglorious and prolonged phase in imperial politics would be outside the scope of this book: it is enough to say that Chinese surnames, which are still quite common among the Parsi community in Bombay today, are at least as likely to be due to the family's one-time involvement in the opium trade with China as they are to cotton trading in that country. Because Parsis experienced difficulties, in the days of Company monopoly, in trading with Europe, it was natural that they should concentrate on the China trade: the Jeejeebhoy, Cama and Dadysett families all originally had opium interests. It was not true, however, though it was sometimes pretended subsequently, that it was only the native merchants who dealt in opium. The East India Company itself did in the eighteenth century, and later most of the big well-established European firms did also, directly or indirectly, trading under Company licence. In the 1840s the newly-formed Bombay Chamber of Commerce, containing British business men such as William Nichol and Stewart, were actually urging Lord Palmerston, the British Foreign Secretary, into the Opium Wars, demanding 'vigorous action' against 'the trickery and deceit of Chinese diplomacy'. (Palmerston, incidentally, needed no urging.) Many of the eminently respectable city fathers of commerce – men like Dinshaw Wacha,* who ended his life with a

* He lived to over ninety, and stands today on a plinth near Churchgate station, with his Parsi headgear, sticking-out ears, and gentle, eroded face.

knighthood and has left a fat treasure-trove of boyhood recollections entitled *Shells from the Sands of Bombay* – could remember a time when city magnates themselves were not above working late in the warehouses on Marine Street adjoining the old Law Court: '. . . those large go-downs smelling of "Afim" or opium . . . After office hours a large quantity of opium or poppy leaves dried were seen strewn on that part of the Green.'

It is said that Sir Charles Forbes, almost alone of the early European merchants, always refused to deal in opium. In everybody else's defence it should be added that the idea that opium and its derivatives were relatively harmless was widely held in nineteenth-century England, at a time when even respectable pillars of society could be found taking laudanum by the decanter-full in the way they might now swallow whisky, tranquillisers or aspirin. In the East too opium was traditionally considered beneficial: it had originally been marketed as a specific against leprosy! By 1859 it constituted 42 per cent of the total value of merchandise exported from the port of Bombay while cotton accounted for under 30 per cent, and, in addition, a lot of opium trade out of Calcutta was owned by Bombay firms. Not until the 1870s did a new morality – or discretion – prevail. Opium-dealing was finally outlawed in 1880, but by then the balance of trade had swung firmly in the direction of cotton. The great mills that were going up in northern Bombay, and the industrial tenements that were presently built to house the workforce, may be seen, with hindsight, to raise moral and humanitarian questions of their own. But to consider this now would be to move too far ahead in Bombay's history.

VI *First Ladies and Inferior Women*

Few women have so far appeared on the Bombay scene. Among the Europeans who ventured there in the early days there were certainly a sprinkling of female gold-diggers, but their lot can hardly have been a happy one. Ovington, recording his voyage there in 1690, summed up the situation which was to prevail, only slightly modified, for the next hundred years:

> The Company allow marriage to their Factors, and Liberty to young Women to pass thither to gain Husbands, and raise their Fortunes. But so very few of their Children live, and of those that do, so many of them are set for *England*, that fresh colonies from thence are very necessary for supporting the Government and Affairs of the Island. A Modish Garb and Mien is all that is expected from any Women that pass thither, who are many times match'd to the chief Merchants upon the place, and advance thereby their Conditions to a very happy pitch. As considerable trouble attends the Passage, especially of Women, considering the Hazard, as well as the length of the Voyage, with some other Casualties that sometimes happen on Board, a modest Woman may very well expect, without any great Stock of Honour or Wealth, a Husband of Repute and Riches there, after she has run all this Danger and Trouble for him. And indeed the fond Indulgence of the Husbands, as well as their Wealth, is another valuable Recompense to Women for the Toil and Trouble of the Voyage.

This sounds like Ovington, as Company Chaplain, doing propaganda on its behalf. He does not mention the inevitable tendency of merchants, lacking white, Church of England women to marry, to form alliances regular and irregular with whatever was on offer locally, which was 'Portuguese' Roman Catholics, many of them of mainly or entirely Indian blood. This had already, ten years before, caused Aungier such concern that he had tried the experiment of having the Company pay the passages out to Bombay for 'needy English women' who would, it was hoped, provide the settlers with more suitable wives. However, the experiment was not an unqualified success: a place which had difficulty, at that date, in attracting respectable men to it, could hardly hope that the women drawn thither on the promise of a meal-ticket for life would be much better. Some indeed behaved so badly that they were threatened with confinement on bread and water, and subsequently sent home again.

The general precariousness of life, and the prospect of rearing 'not one in twenty' of any infants she might bear, was not likely to appeal to any woman whose main quest was for security. Mrs Elizabeth Arwaker, whose goods were sold by public auction in Bombay in 1701, cannot be said, poor thing, to have made a successful bargain with fate. Her husband had presumably died: among the goods on which she was trying to raise money there were, in addition to the usual disproportionate quantity of liquor, '2 old Landskipps, a Box of Pipes, Gowns, Petticoats and Fanns . . . '

The ground-plan for St Thomas's Church that was opened in 1718 shows high box pews, each section allotted to persons of a specified rank from the Governor down to 'Visitors' and 'strangers'. The womenfolk are similarly graded – 'Senior Merchants' Wives', 'Free Merchants' Wives' and so forth, with one set of pews for 'Inferior Women'. This may have meant simply ladies' maids and the like, but I suspect that it was a catch-all appellation conveniently covering all those female companions who, if they professed Christianity and wore some sort of western dress, could not, by any minimally Christian standard of behaviour, be excluded from Sunday Morning church. The church registers for the greater part of the eighteenth century show actual marriages to have been few and far between, and when they did occur in nearly every case the names indicate a British man marrying a woman with a Portuguese name, or sometimes one with no surname at all. As late as 1739, there were said to be only eight unmarried English women in all the island of Bombay, twenty married ones, 'between four and eight' widows (mortality perhaps taking its toll even as the figures were being computed) and the merest handful of children. And this was in spite of the fact that the East India Company were still making spasmodic attempts to encourage more suitable English women out there. For instance in the 1730s it paid the passage (a very substantial sum of money in those days) of John Cleland's sister and several other women. Cleland, having been born a gentleman and having then blotted his copybook in some unknown way in his teens, joined the Company's Army as a common foot soldier, but distinguished himself sufficiently in Bombay to be accepted a few years later as a writer. He became a factor (the step on the way to becoming a junior merchant) within three years rather than the usual five, and by the age of thirty had risen to be Secretary of the Council and a senior merchant. No wonder the Company thought that his sister and her friends might be an embellishment to the society of Bombay (though she does not, in fact, appear to have married there). Would they, I wonder, have been so keen on the family had they been able to foresee that ambitious young Cleland was the future author of the notorious *Fanny Hill: the Memoirs of a Woman of Pleasure*? (Sixty years later the book, which had been published in 1748 after Cleland had left the Company service and India for good, was brought out to India in the luggage of Arthur Wellesley, the future Duke of Wellington, possibly to beguile him on the long voyage. But I doubt if he knew that its author had passed thirteen formative years in Bombay.)

The only woman associated with eighteenth-century Bombay whose name has been known to future generations was Eliza Draper. She it was who eloped, on the night of 14-15 January 1773, down a rope ladder into a boat from the Belvedere House on Mazagaon Hill; a sentimental cult grew up later about her fragile ghost, which was said to haunt the place. She was born in 1744 at Anjengo, 600 miles south of Bombay, where the Company had a small factory. She was sent to England to gain the kind of education that fitted a girl only for attracting a husband who would provide her with 'an Establishment'. She was returned to India at fourteen, and six months later docilely married Daniel Draper, an East India Company servant twenty years older than herself. He had then been newly appointed Secretary of the Council, the job that Cleland had once held, and later became Accountant General. He is said to have been 'a noble and good-humoured man', but no doubt he and Eliza had little in common: she complained to a friend that 'our minds are not pair'd'. Two children were born, in 1759 and 1761. Eliza travelled back to England with them in 1765 to leave them there, in the British-India tradition which was already becoming established, and, while there, seems to have been ill: perhaps it was the thought of a return to Bombay alone. She was taken about in society, was flattered and called 'the Brahmine' and *'la belle indienne'* by the writer Sterne, among other people, who was himself more than old enough to have known better. She took seriously his suggestions that she had the makings of a literary lady *à la* Mrs Montagu and the Blue Stockings: in fact those of her letters which have survived show little trace of intellect or wit. One must suppose that she was pretty, in an oval-faced eighteenth-century way, and she is said to have played and sung charmingly. At all events, when she returned to Bombay, which was then admittedly provincial to the point of brutality, she found there 'a Dearth of everything which could charm the Heart – please the Fancy, or speak to Judgement'. More Madame Bovary really than Mrs Montagu, she solved her *ennui* by the drastic expedient of an elopement: it should be said that Daniel Draper, with whom she had ceased to share a bed, was by then carrying on an open affair with a maid. To a woman friend the day before, she wrote: 'My heart is full. The next 24 hours will, in all probability, either destine me to the grave or to a life of reproach . . . I had deserved a better, if chance had not counteracted the good propensities assigned to me by nature.' To her husband she wrote: 'I go, I know not wither, but I will never be a tax on you, Draper . . . I am not a hardened or depraved creature – I never will be so.' She added, in apparently unconscious bathos, 'The enclosed are the only bills owing that I know of, except about 6 rupees to Doogee, the shoe-maker. I have never meant to load myself with many spoils to your prejudice, but a moderate provision of linen has obliged me to secure part of what was mine, to obviate some very mortifying difficulties.'

The almost incidental rôle of abducting lover in this carefully orchestrated drama was played by a Sir John Clark of the Navy; he was then in command of a frigate in Bombay and so was conveniently placed for carrying Eliza off by water. The liaison does not seem to have lasted much longer than the immediate need for it. Eliza sought refuge for a while at Rajahmandry with a 'kind uncle' called Tom Whitehall, relative of the Whitehall of Bombay who had sold the Company the property that became Government House in the Fort. Tom Whitehall may well have looked indulgently upon Eliza, for he himself was the father of many mixed-race children, but naturally the double standard applied in Anglo-India as in England. She later returned to England where, as Sterne had published his *Journal to Eliza*, she once again aroused a certain amount of flattering curiosity. From then on she seems to have declined, via a further self-conscious relationship with another old literary lion, the Abbé Raynal, and a less platonic affair with John Wilkes, the political pamphleteer, into relative obscurity and poverty; she died in Bristol at the age of thirty-five.

Her pathetic story is significant, not for the legend that accrued around it in nineteenth-century Bombay, but for the incidental light it throws on the East Indian life of the time. Eliza's flagrant behaviour made her an exotic oddity, but for Englishmen in India throughout the eighteenth century and into the nineteenth, unsanctified liaisons were the rule rather than the exception; the *bibi-khana*, the 'lady-house' in a corner of the compound, separate both from the main house and from the servants' quarters, was an accepted feature of many a European bungalow. It was inevitable: as late as 1809 European men outnumbered their female counterparts in Bombay by three to one, and many of those men would have spent virtually their whole adult lives in India. George Dick, for instance, who was Governor of Bombay between 1793 and 1795, and whose memorial tablet is in St Thomas's Church, came out as a writer for the Company in 1759 and remained in Bombay almost uninterruptedly until his death in 1818. What the tablet does not record is that for many years he kept a Mahratta woman openly in considerable state. Not till after 1806, when both the pay and the qualities required of a civil servant had been upgraded, and Company servants in Bombay were no longer allowed to trade on their own account, did society begin to be both more compartmentalised and more respectable; even so there must have lingered in Bombay for many years longer old India hands who regretted the passing of the good-bad old days, the hubble-bubble and the *bibi*, the afternoon siesta, and the nights spent in drinking and cards.

Naturally all this unofficial activity left its results, in the form of a growing race of Eurasians. These, in Bombay, merged to some extent with the local Portuguese, themselves of mixed race, but they were not really acceptable to either the native community or the European, and became less so with time, as the image of the British as a separate ruling caste began to take shape. Ironically, the rise in standards of probity expected from the British led initially to *less* real fairness and participation between different races. After 1791 Eurasians were no longer appointed to the Company's Civil, Military or Marine service, though those who were already there could stay. Colonel Skinner, born 1778, was the son of a British officer and a Rajput lady. In 1803 his mixed blood caused his dismissal, for a while, from the Company's Army, but he went on to found Skinner's Horse which was to become the crack cavalry regiment in India. He was a distinguished scholar and ended his career as a Companion of the Bath, though he in turn married an Indian lady and their large family were said to be 'quite black'. Charles Forjett, born in Madras about 1810, whose origins are obscure but who rose to become Chief of Police in Bombay in the 1850s and finally Municipal Commissioner, must have been a Eurasian, though by the mid-nineteenth century such a fact was no longer so freely mentioned; oblique references are made instead to his 'sun-burnt skin', his 'capacity to disguise himself as a native' (very useful for gathering information) and his 'proficiency in the native tongues'. Forjett, nevertheless, after a lifetime in India elected to retire to England, where he built himself a large house at Hughenden in damp, green Buckinghamshire, perversely named Cowasji Jehangir Hall after a prominent Parsi.

The fact that even these outstanding men suffered slights during their careers shows how unenviable was the position of the less gifted and socially prominent Eurasians, particularly as they were often illegitimate as well. Sons were sent to England to acquire the education of English gentlemen, but this, when unsupported by the appearance or the means, did them little good back in India once Company service above the level of clerk was denied to them. Half-caste daughters received, in theory, even fewer benefits, but with the prevailing wife-shortage many of them must, in practice, have managed to land English husbands and thus 'pass', at any rate in Bombay's rather mixed society. Others, at a lower social level, were the progeny of loose Indian women and common soldiers or seamen, and presumably many of these disappeared in turn into the developing red-light district of the native town. The vulnerability of such women, adrift in an Indian society which then, as now, provided security only within a closed family and caste structure, is poignantly conveyed by a tombstone which stood for many years in Sonapur burial ground. It was that of Captain Thomas Samuel Tydd of the Company's Army, who died, so the stone informed, in 1797, at the age of thirty-seven, after twenty years' service with the Company during which he had twice been wounded: 'He has left an infant daughter unprovided and her unhappy mother who had been cherished for some years by his bounty.' It seems an unusual message to put on a tomb, but perhaps the friend who paid for its erection was trying by these means to shame Captain Tydd's other acquaintances into 'doing something' for the girl and her child.

Gradually, with the decline of piracy and the improvement of ships, the number of women prepared to venture out from England increased. However, the route was still the long one round the Cape and was hardly undertaken lightly. Each passenger embarking on the six- or seven-month adventure was advised to bring for the voyage 'a sofa, with mattress, a pillow and a chinz covering for the day-time, a Hanging Lamp, a looking glass with sliding cover, a swing tray, a chest of drawers in 2 pieces, a foul-clothes Bag, an oil cloth or carpet (this merely for the sake of Appearances), a bucket and rope for drawing salt water' – salt water was used for washing the person and the clothes, since fresh water was strictly rationed. In addition, it was suggested that a lady should bring hair powder, 'papillate paper', hartshorn, aromatic vinegar, aperients and cologne water.

Some of the women who ventured out complete with aperients, cologne and sofa did not live long to enjoy their destination. Elizabeth Rivett, a well-known beauty who was painted by Sir Joshua Reynolds and came out to India to marry the elderly General John Carnac, died in Bombay in 1780 at only twenty-eight: she is buried under the floor of the Church, and her brother, who added the Carnac name and monies to his own and fathered a future Governor of Bombay, is buried near her. Four years after Elizabeth Rivett's death a pretty 23-year-old girl called Charlotte, niece of the General John Bellasis whose name is remembered in Bellasis Road in Bombay, sailed there already engaged to marry Daniel Christie of the Bombay Engineers. (Mrs Bellasis herself had sailed out in the same way to marry her John a decade previously.) Charlotte's wedding was promptly celebrated, but she died two months later; a cart drawn by white oxen carried her body to the sad city of gold at Sonapur and the doctor who had attended her wrote an elegy to her in thirty-one verses. It is not necessarily true that in times or places where death is commonplace people become hardened to it.

Not all the women who came out to Bombay were already engaged. Charlotte's brother Joseph, who came out the following year, married a girl he probably met during the voyage. A Bellasis brother, George, married a girl who was one of seven good-looking but penniless sisters: these sisters came out to Bombay in turn to try their luck. The unwise exploits of one of his sisters-in-law compromised George Bellasis into fighting a duel with a young relative of Charles Forbes. He narrowly escaped with his life on the subsequent murder charge. It seems clear that by that date the old idea of women coming out to India expressly to seek husbands had been revived in an unofficial way, and for the whole of the nineteenth century it was to flourish under a thin veil of gentility that deceived no one. Not for another 40 years, by which time the steamship route made matters so much easier, was Thomas Hood to write his satirical poem *Going to Bombay* (see Chapter VII) but there is a telling passage in an early work by Jane Austen, *Catharine, or the Bower* (c.1790) in which a penniless girl is 'obliged to accept the offer of one of her cousins to equip her for the East Indies'. Like Eliza Draper, she there marries a rich man twice her age, which one of her friends comments is 'no hardship'. Another, however, sees the matter differently:

> ' . . . to a girl of any Delicacy, the voyage itself, since the object of it is so universally known, is a punishment that needs no other to make it very severe.'
> 'I do not see that at all. She is not the first Girl who has gone to the East Indies for a Husband, and I declare I should think it very good fun if I were poor.'

Jane Austen's own aunt, Philadelphia, a generation before, had sailed to Madras and there married a man twenty years older than herself. They eventually separated, she staying in England with a daughter after a voyage Home and he returning to India for good. The pattern was not an uncommon one. Sir James Mackintosh, the first Recorder of Bombay (1804-12) and perhaps the most intellectually distinguished citizen of that period, lived for much of the time as a bachelor, his wife having gone Home. While she and their daughters were with him, he was lent Parel by Governor Duncan, himself a bachelor who had lived in India for thirty-nine years. (Duncan's views on Indian culture and its importance were progressive for his time. Mackintosh considered him an honourable man, but 'brahminised' and lethargic.) After his wife left him, Mackintosh rented Tarala (see Chapter IV) and it was there that Maria Graham stayed with him. Let us hope that this visitor, who was the future author of *Little Arthur's History of England*, sympathised with his own literary and historical interests, and distracted him temporarily from the Bombay 'languor' of which he complained. In the *Journal of a Residence in India*, which she subsequently published, she wrote:

> The parties at Bombay are the most dull and uncomfortable meetings one can imagine. Forty or fifty persons assemble at

seven o'clock, and stare at one another till dinner is announced, when the ladies are handed to table, according to the strictest rules of precedency.

The conversation consisted exclusively of local gossip, especially of 'rupees and bales of cotton'; afterwards, when the ladies withdrew, they talked of

> . . . lace, jewels, intrigues and the latest fashions; or if there be any newly arrived young women, the making and breaking of matches for them furnish employment for the ladies of the colony till the arrival of the next cargo . . . I found our fair companions like the ladies of all the country towns I know, under-bred and over-dressed, and, with the exception of one or two, very ignorant and very grossière. The men are, in general, what a Hindu would call of a higher caste than the women; and I find the merchants the most rational companions.

As for the meal itself:

> . . . it is as costly as possible, and in such profusion that no part of the table cloth remains uncovered. But the dinner is hardly touched, as every person eats a hearty meal called tiffin, at 2 o'clock, at home. Each guest brings his own servant, sometimes two or three . . .

It was hardly surprising that topics of conversation should have been parochial. Other travellers note that many English in India at that time had, for lack of contact with Europe, lost any interest they might otherwise have possessed in European affairs, including such events as the French Revolution and the rise and fall of Napoleon. And those that did retain an interest hardly enjoyed a constant flow of up-to-date information to sustain it. Not till the 1830s did books begin to be sent out to India in substantial numbers – along with those other much desired and still more transitory commodities from colder climes, ice and apples – and not till the steamships were well established toward the middle of the century did recent English periodicals and newspapers appear in Bombay. Mrs Sherwood, the future writer of *The Fairchild Family*, *Little Henry and His Bearer* and many other improving works for the young, who sailed to Madras with her husband in 1805 and there suffered considerably from loneliness, boredom and what we would now recognise as culture-shock, wrote later:

> The scarcity of books in India was in my time a great evil, and I have on reflection laughed at the various schemes and contrivances which I used to put in action to get a book into my

possession for a little while, and how vastly civil I used to be to any person who could lend me a book! . . . No one can imagine what the solitude of a large house in India is – when the heat and glare without renders it totally impossible to go abroad, and when no sound meets the ear through all the weary morning, but the click of the punkah within and the cawing of the crows without . . .

The obscure sense of horror which India generates in many Europeans, now as then, first finds clear expression in the writings of Mrs Sherwood. As an early Evangelical and a friend of the pioneer missionary Henry Martyn, she formulated this feeling to herself as a dread of heathenism, 'the horrible darkness of the most corrupt and abominable superstitions'. It was as if this were inextricably bound up in her mind with 'the clamour and the smell of burnt manure, and the creeking of the wheels of bullock-carts, and the cry of unhappy babies, with the scorching heaven above and a parched earth beneath'. Perhaps the 'under-bred and over-dressed' ladies met in Bombay by Maria Graham were not unduly troubled by such things. But an equal sense of homesickness, and a kind of formless dread, is expressed in the letters of another Bombay lady, Lady West, wife of Sir Edward West, the first Chief Justice: she was a much simpler person than Mrs Sherwood, but for this very reason her writings make poignant reading.

An engraving from a picture of her made in 1822, the year of her marriage and her journey to Bombay, shows a pretty, soft-faced girl in the muslin-trimmed Directoire dress of the period; the material for such dresses was by then being imported from both Calcutta and Bombay in ever-increasing quantities. No portrait was ever made of her husband, a circumstance which was to cause her much grief on his sudden death a few years later: a contemporary describes him as a slight but well-built man whose 'countenance betrayed a considerable degree of susceptibility; where his mind was in the least degree excited his sensations appeared like lightning on his countenance'. Although a lawyer by profession, he had also written pamphlets on economics and was known for his sincerity and integrity: perhaps he was too intelligent, and also too essentially innocent and sensitive for his own time in India and for the post in Bombay that was now offered to him. Did he know, I wonder, when he set sail with his young bride, that he was going to wrestle with corruption and enmities in a place where the power-struggle between Westminster and the East India Company was still being fought out? And did he also know that hardly any of his predecessors, except Sir James Mackintosh who renounced his post prematurely on the grounds of ill-health, had lived to return home? His wife was also his cousin and childhood playmate, and seems to have been no better fitted for her new rôle than he was:

> The society here is very formal, and the Ladies very self-sufficient and consequential, thinking of little but their fine Pearls and *local* rank. We of course dine out a good deal, and give a Dinner of about 22 once a fortnight. From my being the first lady, Edward the 2nd gentleman [Mountstuart Elphinstone, the urbane and sociable Governor was a bachelor, and his successor, Sir John Malcolm, was unamicably separated from his own wife who remained in England] we are terribly observed, and of course I doubt not pulled to pieces, but thank God we are still quite English and domestic, taking our walk together every evening, our tea and our bath afterwards . . .

Her earlier, first impressions of India reveal much:

> I enjoyed my ride extremely in the Palaqueens. I only felt for the heat and fatigue the Bearers must have experienced, but I am assured that one shall soon lose that proper feeling of humanity . . . I went to see our house, with which I was much disappointed, not as to its size, for it is immense, more like a Barn; in fact it looked unfurnished and wretched, but I hope I shall be able to make it more comfortable.

'Comfortable' was a favourite word with Lady West; poor dear, it was not one she very often felt like applying to her new and difficult life. Her reaction to her house, which appears to have been one of the big, old colonnaded houses in the Fort, is, incidentally, a typical outsider's one of the period: both those accustomed only to English houses, and those who had experienced the pretentious mansions of Calcutta, found Bombay's houses unnervingly simple; one visitor considered his country-style residence 'like a cow-shed'. Presumably Lady West learnt later, as Mrs Sherwood did, that 'were rooms in India to be curtained, carpeted and littered as they are in England, even supposing that the temperature of the air in such rooms could be endured, yet the inhabitants would speedily be ejected by the nests and swarms of every species of vermin, which would harbour themselves in every corner'. But at first Lady West was particularly unnerved by the incomplete partition walls and doors left ever-open for air to circulate – 'Nothing is ever shut in this country, so that one seems to dress to amuse others' – and never happier than when, in the rainy season, she was able to recapture

147

some semblance of Home – 'The weather reminds me of dear Tunbridge Wells, so damp and chill. I long for a fire – thermometer 75. . . . The esplanade looks like the environs of Ely, but it is very cool.'

The 'country houses' in which most of the Wests' social equals were now established were nearly all bungalows in the English sense of the term, i.e. they were all on one floor, although 'bungalow' in India simply means a 'country-style' house and can be a high, galleried building like many now found in the Bombay bazaars. At this date only the grander houses had two storeys, like Tarala and also Parel – now styled without a second 'l' – which Mountstuart Elphinstone had further extended and beautified with imported furnishings. Inevitably the Wests were frequent visitors there: 'It is a magnificent Place, with an abundance of beautiful Chandeliers . . . It reminded me of the Arabian Nights' Tales.' The painted ceiling of the ballroom (which still exists in the house today) dates from this period. The garden was planted with all kinds of exotic trees and flowers, including ancient cypresses which another visitor of the 1820s described as 'entirely covered with flame-coloured bignoria, like pillars of fire'. There was also a willow grown from a slip of the tree planted on Napoleon's grave in St Helena, brought to Bombay by an East Indiaman that had called there; and wild animals in a paddock including deer, a tiger, an ostrich, a wild ass from Cutch, and an ape from Sumatra which the servants called 'wild man' and overfed with fruit.

Lady West at first liked the cultured Elphinstone very much, but later fell out with him over a number of matters. Like her husband, she was in her own natural way something of a mid-nineteenth-century Progressive before her time, and she found herself in Bombay put down in a Georgian setting that was more redolent of the century that was past. She plucked up her courage to complain to the Governor in a letter of having met at Parel 'ladies of spotted reputation who are not visited by anyone'. A few days later she received his reply and recorded in her journal: 'Mr Elphinstone tells me he has enquired as to the 2 ladies' characters I named to him, and finds them both so very bad, that he shall never ask them again to his house. He thanked me, but in his heart, I am sure, he must hate Edward and me, as he worships popularity, and cares for no one, and wishes to make no distinctions.'

The Wests were both shocked also by the readiness of some Europeans to flog natives for trivial offences; one magistrate even used to do so without examining the case – 'A Friend sends a note to

Lady West, wife of the first Chief Justice of Bombay, who died there
in 1827.

The view into the Fort from Apollo Gate c. 1830. On the left, the Scotch church, above it the porticoed Hornby House (the law court), opposite the dock-gate with a clock tower.

A view from the same angle about eighty years later. Hornby House has become the Great Western Hotel, and between it and the Scotch church stands the circular ice-house, erected by public subscription. Visible at the end of the street is the bow-fronted Writers' Building. Note the tramway.

Above The four-storey building is Pestonji Wadia's house in Cowasji Patel Street in the Fort, rebuilt c. 1850.

Below The Jeejeebhoy mansion on the edge of the Fort, now a shipping agents and a store.

Above The Sassoon mansion at Byculla – 'Sans Souci' – now the Massina Hospital.

Below J.N. Tata's 'Esplanade House', built in the grand manner in the late 19th century.

Gowalia tank – 'Cow-herds tank' – circa 1900. One of Bombay's
many vanished reservoirs.

Near Gowalia tank stood the bungalow of Dr John Wilson, missionary and founder of schools. Today it is a local post office.

Above The 19th century wealth of Bombay: cotton bales, and brokers.

Below The Cotton Green at Colaba, well stocked.

him and says "Pray flog the Bearer", and it is done'. Optimistically she adds, 'Edward will have it all corrected'. Doubtless she did not know that on leaving the same job eleven years earlier, Mackintosh had written an emphatic memo on this very subject, but it had been ignored. The Wests were also exercised by the way people were kept in prison without trial, sometimes in chains; and the occasion when Edward West passed sentence of death on a British soldier accused of shooting a native affected them both. Lady West wrote of her husband, 'He suffered very much before the judgement and after it; he has so much feeling', and, later, 'The poor man being hung today has never been out of my thoughts'. It was soon after this that Edward's post was upgraded from Recorder; he was made a Chief Justice, a promotion from Home which did nothing to endear him locally, where the shock at the death sentence passed for the murder of a native had been of a different order from his own. It was because of Edward West's principled stand on such matters that Elphinstone's successor John Malcolm wrote to the Board of Control in London that the next Chief Justice 'must view himself as an aid to the Company'. He wrote at the same time to his wife: 'I am now engaged in a battle with the Supreme Court [to prevent] the Government over which I preside being trampled on, not by honest fellows with glittering sabres, but by quibbling, quill-driving lawyers.' This was a month after Edward West's sudden death. Malcolm himself is enshrined in marble, by Chantrey, in the Town Hall. He looks fierce.

There is a particular poignancy in reading Lady West's comments on the ever-presence of death in India when one knows all the time what her own end and her husband's were to be. Quite early in her stay she was writing: 'I know not when I have been so shocked as I was last evening to have Mrs Newnham's death announced to me. She took Tiffin here last Thursday, had an attack of fever that night, expired last evening.' Ten days later she recorded, 'To my English ideas it appeared very unfeeling and indelicate, that yesterday poor Mrs Newnham's* Pianoforte, Drawing-room Furniture, Chandeliers, and all her little things were sold by auction.' Over the first years the Wests spent in Bombay a number of such events are recorded, typically with some comment as 'These frequent sudden deaths make one tremble' . . . 'Oh Lord, preserve my husband and me'.

* She was wife to the permanent Secretary to the Bombay Government and founder of the Byculla Club – see Chapters VII and IX. They lived at the Belvedere. She is buried in St Thomas's Church.

There were respites from anxieties, quarrels and duty-dinners: a daughter, Fanny, was born. There were a few real friends such as the Stewarts, relatives of Charles Forbes; there was a visit to 'Hormaji [*sic*] Bomanji Wadia in his house at Parel' – which appears to refer, not to the Lal Baug, but to Lowji Castle. There were pleasant evenings spent during the hot season in tent-like structures on the Esplanade; there were trips to Elephanta and Bassein, the latter in company with Bishop Heber, then newly appointed to Calcutta. His cheery and uplifting presence produced a temporary amnesty in the Elphinstone–West relations: he, like the Wests, was a natural Victorian, imbued with high missionary and colonial spirit, though in fact death lay in wait for him in Trichinopoly after less than three years in India. It was he who wrote the well-known hymn:

> *From Greenland's icy mountains*
> *From India's coral strand,*
> *Where Afric's sunny fountains*
> *Roll down their golden land,*
> *From many an ancient river*
> *And many a palmy plain –*
> *They call us to deliver*
> *Their land from error's chain.*

Such were becoming the rooted beliefs of Englishmen who 'laid down their lives' for India. India, who did not care, was to claim the Wests too. During the monsoon of 1828 they were in Poona, the hill-station that had become the favourite resort of Europeans in the last ten years since it had been taken from the Peshwa. Edward fell seriously ill. On 17 August his wife wrote in her journal, 'The night has been a dreadful one, with hiccough and fever and his dear mouth so parched. God have mercy upon him, and support me in the awful trial which I fear awaits me.' He died the next morning. The next entries are about the funeral, marks of respect – there was a gun salute and 'a Ball was put off' – and tributes from all classes. But these were feeble comfort – 'The last week I have seemed so lost, and my nerves so shattered, I have scarcely had the power to do anything, and seem as if I must close my eyes to the future . . . ' By the beginning of September the child, Fanny, was ill, 'which always makes me anxious, especially as Dr Ducat was obliged to leave this yesterday to see a sick friend at Sholapore, 200 miles off, and may be absent a fortnight. I am not very well myself, so weak.' She was shortly expecting another baby. The next entry reads, 'Dear Fanny coughed a good deal in the night, but is, thank God, better today. I was so unwell, *and am*, that I thought it prudent to see Dr Bryden.' There, the journal ends.

Lady West was taken back to Bombay, to the house* of the Chambers – Sir Charles Chambers was a fellow judge – and there, having given birth to a child who did not survive, she herself died. She is buried in the aisle of the Church, near Mrs Newnham, and her infant son is buried outside. Sir Charles himself died within the same week.

Fanny survived, and was returned to her relatives in England at the end of the year, 'every provision being made for her being carefully attended to'. The phrase comes from the letter to her uncle that was written by Sir John Peter Grant, the sole surviving judge who, the following year, was to become so angry with the Bombay Government that he locked the Court, put the keys in his pocket, and sailed for England. With the coming of the 1830s and the further erosion of the Company's power and monopolies, the long-term enmity between Company and Crown administration gradually subsided, and the expansion and civilisation of Bombay began in earnest.

What was it like, the Bombay of the first quarter of the nineteenth century in which people like the Wests and Elphinstone and Mackintosh and Duncan and Charles Forbes and John and George Bellasis lived and quarrelled in the last of the 'bad old days'? Some, at any rate, of the old buildings in the Fort, particularly in the northern section, disappeared in the fire of 1803. Just as at the Fire of London, which had destroyed comparable close-packed wooden houses in 1666, there was a shortage both of water and of the means of conveying it. Duncan, the Governor, wrote afterwards to the Directors in London:

> So great and violent was the conflagration that at sunset the destruction of every house in the Fort was apprehended. The flames directed their course in a south-easterly direction from that part of the bazaar opposite to the Cumberland Ravelin quite down to the King's Barracks. During the whole of the day every effort was used to oppose its progress, but the fierceness of the fire driven rapidly on by the wind baffled all attempts; nor did it visibly abate till nearly a third part of the town within the walls had been consumed.

* This was 'The Hermitage', one of several large bungalows lying below Kamballa Hill on the way to the Breach – present day Pedder Road. The house was pulled down *c.*1970 and Kemp's Corner flyover now occupies part of the site.

Four hundred and seventy-one houses were destroyed then, and some of the buildings that replaced them in Parsi Bazaar Street and Borah Bazaar Street and in their cross-lanes must be the ones that still stand today. Others, in the southern part of the Fort, date from rebuilding after a second serious fire during the hot season of 1823, which Lady West records in her journal:

> Last evening at 9 o'clock a fire broke out in the Fort among the bales of cotton near the Church and Mr Stewart's office; and want of water made the people very apprehensive it might extend to the Castle where the Gunpowder is kept. If so the whole Island might have been blown up; it was fortunately a calm night, and the loss of about 3 lacks* of Rupees is all the damage that has been done. Mr Stewart and Edward were actively moving away all the books and papers from Mr Stewart's office; it was an awful sight . . .

Several days later she wrote: 'Everything has been in such a disordered state. But already it wears quite a different aspect. I am told that the natives say God has sent an angel to protect them.' In fact fires in the native town north of the Esplanade, also by then known as 'the Bazaars', were so frequent as to be almost commonplace.

The following year the monsoon partially failed and there was a shortage of water for all purposes, in Bombay and throughout the surrounding Deccan that now made up the much-extended presidency. Famine followed in the countryside. There had been another serious one ten years earlier. These various calamities had two results: an increase of population pouring into Bombay, much of which proved permanent, and a preoccupation on the part of successive Governors and commercial leaders with the need to create more wells and tanks in the city; fortunately, perhaps, for the essential quenching of thirst, the connection between tank-water and malaria had not then been realised. Today, virtually all the tanks that date from this period have been filled in, but so much were they a part of the nineteenth-century life of Bombay that their names are permanently attached to the districts where they once stood – Dhobi Talao, Kharatalao, Gowalia Tank, etc. But then, for a people apparently unconcerned with the past, the inhabitants of Bombay are oddly attached to the wraiths of vanished landmarks. 'Mazagaon TT' is still the favourite designation for the place where the trams once had their terminus; taxi drivers know the Jehangir

* A 'lakh' is 100,000 rupees.

Art Gallery, on the site of the one-time Apollo Gate of the Fort, as 'Kala Gora', though the Black Horseman who used to stand there (actually Edward VII) has vanished from the place as completely as the Apollo Gate itself.

I have already dealt with the steady, unregulated and unplanned expansion of the native town during the early nineteenth century. Actually there was one piece of planned road construction shortly before the turn of the century which was fortunate, since, without it, central Bombay would have begun to develop with no east–west cross-route at all, though this may not have been what the originator of the plan had in mind. This was General John Bellasis who, in 1793, as part of a famine-relief effort, employed men at his own cost to make a road lined with trees from the foot of Malabar Hill (the road to the Breach) due west in the direction of Mazagaon. In both localities European houses were accumulating, and a communication between the two districts was obviously going to be useful, even though Bellasis Road when first made is said to have been 'a straggling, uneven, jolting pathway'. It was in fact a causeway across the lower part of the Flats, which, with the planning of Hornby's Vellard to stop the Great Breach to the north-west, could now be expected to dry out.

The coming of this European-style communicating highway helped to create a new European-colonised locality, that of Byculla, where it crossed the northward road to Parel. Within a few years of the building of the road a race-track was established on the erstwhile drowned land just north of the road. (Not the present Race Course, which is a little further north.) By 1800 the races had become so popular that the Bombay Turf Club was established, and in that year presented a prize of 100 gold mohurs – the traditional Indian coin corresponding to the British guinea – to be added to the proceeds of a sweepstake of Rs. 100 apiece. The intention was to encourage the breeding of horses in Bombay and its surroundings 'by gentlemen'. Evidently it was successful, for a little later in the century Bombay became well-known as a centre for horse-trading, and its stable of imported Arab horses in the Bhendi (hibiscus tree) Bazaar were famous throughout Anglo-India. But at the beginning of the eighteenth century the available horses were rather a job-lot, and the 'hounds' used for a scratch hunting-pack even more assorted, to judge from cartoons of the period. This 'Bobbery Hunt' met for many years on Sundays in front of the Church, and used to hunt hyenas and jackals at Mahim and Sion. An advertisement in a Bombay newspaper during March 1811 runs:

Meet at gunfire this morning on the Byculla Course, where the hounds will throw off a numerous field, and great sport is expected; afterwards Bobbery Hunting Etcetera till breakfast, which has been ordered for fifty at the stand at nine; the party will then proceed to Lowji Castle, where various Hindustanee gymnastics, wrestlings, pigeon shooting, juggling and tumbling will be exhibited till four o'clock, when a dinner in the best English style, will be served up for the same number as at breakfast. The sports of the day to conclude with music, fireworks Etc.

Such were the unsophisticated pastimes of the typical Bombay officer or merchant and his wife.

Because of the lack of horses on the Island all through the preceding century, humped oxen were still the normal carriage beast. They would go at quite a pace, swishing the occupants with their tails; one had to stop every so often to wipe away the froth from their muzzles, otherwise (it was said) they would suffocate. Within the Fort and its immediate neighbourhood palaquins were still, in the early nineteenth century, the usual mode of transport, but the version in use by the Europeans had developed by then from a curtained oriental litter into something like a complete carriage-body with doors and sliding windows, merely minus the wheels. 'Palkies' were carried traditionally by Kolis, who were supposed to perform this service without any definite pay: they were said to do well out of tips, but naturally enough resented the obligation, and by the 1790s had managed to demonstrate successfully against it. Palaquins, however, continued for many a year, long after the sedan chair had become obsolete in England, and did not finally disappear till the *gharry* (victoria) became the general form of transport in the 1870s. Many of these same old victorias, complete with leather hood and buttoned upholstery, are circulating in Bombay even today: they are cheaper than taxis. Their horses are well-groomed but thin. As for the oxen and their carts, they are still to be seen, even in the centre of the city, among the hooting motor traffic.

Very gradually Bombay's physical, and hence social, isolation was diminishing. In 1798 a regular though expensive monthly mail was established via the Persian Gulf: twenty years earlier there had been only one mail-boat a year. Sion Causeway, the first proper route linking the Island with the mainland, was opened in 1803; a ferry to Thana, another section of the mainland, was opened at much the same time. (Mahim Causeway did not come till 1845, when it was built largely with Jeejeebhoy money.) Rough roads began to be established up to the hill towns of the Deccan – to Matheran and Mahableshwar and, after the decisive battle of Kirkee, to Poona. There was still no causeway to Old Woman's Island and Colaba that was usable to high tide. That had to wait till the 1830s, but Colaba's future as a cantonment area, which it still is today, was taking shape: after 1796 requests from individuals to build houses there were refused on the grounds that the area was for troops only. Hitherto troops had been stationed in the Fort – the 'town barracks' were where the Mint was later built c.1830 – and also out at Matunga, between Parel and Sion. No vestige of this ancient cantonment remains in the busy, dusty, lower-middle-class area that is present-day Matunga. In the late 1830s, only a few years after it had been abandoned, a visitor (Mrs Postans) wrote, in a passage which captures the essence of so many undated and unregarded ruins in India, whether Moghul, Hindu or British:

> Graceful boughs of shadey trees droop upon the broken roofs of crumbling dwellings; gaudy blossoms, and the paler moonflower peep from amid the fallen stones; and gardens, once gay in 'bloom and fruitage bright' are tangled and overgrown with thorns. Matunga is now abandoned: the demon of disease claimed it . . .

Gradually at first, constructions that still survive in present-day Bombay began to appear. The original Apollo Pier – narrower than today's and minus the Gateway to India – dates from this era: it was another of Bellasis's works. On the very site of the old Fig-tree Creek, now long dry, a new gaol was built: it was here that Edward West found men kept in chains and without trial, and here, outside, that public executions took place, including that of the European soldier sentenced by West for the murder of a Hindu. How many people in present-day Bombay realise that this place, with its thick, lumpy outer wall like that of some country stronghold of the remote past, still survives unchanged? Today it is designated a 'Boys' Remand Home' and the inmates who wander in the bleak compound are all under sixteen, but it is still known locally as 'the gaol' and there is no mistaking the atmosphere of ancient repression and privation that pervades the place. It is on no one's tour-itinerary, yet it should be, for it is at least as characteristic of 'old Bombay' as the Mint and the Town Hall, two buildings readily shown to visitors as the oldest examples of British architecture.

Both the Mint and the Town Hall, with their pillars and Grecian porticoes, could have been carried to Bombay intact from an English town at any time in the latter half of the eighteenth century, but both in fact date from the 1820s. The long-drawn-out history of the Town Hall is not untypical of the way things were still done then in Bombay. The idea for a worthy building on the Green, a symbol of British civic pride, was first mooted in 1811, when Mackintosh solaced his dissatisfactions in Bombay by founding the Bombay Literary Society (later metamorphosed into the Asiatic Society): it was always intended that the building should house, not only civic offices, but also a library and a museum. A lottery was launched to raise funds but did not raise enough, and the Company could not be persuaded to authorise the whole thing till another ten years had passed. It was designed, if that is the word for so conventional, though pleasant, a structure, by a Colonel Cowper of the Bombay Engineers, and was not completed till 1833: Cowper was by then dead, and the British Government had to supply the balance of the money required. It cost £500,000 in the end, far more than was estimated, even though the original plans were curtailed. The line of Ionic columns along its frontage was originally to be a double one, and the full number of columns was supplied, like much of the building material, direct from England, but by the time they arrived the plans had been modified. The surplus columns were economically used for a new – and thus inevitably classic-style – church at Byculla, to cater to the new suburban population there.

There are intermittent references to theatres in Bombay, but visiting professional companies were few and amateur productions eked out the rest of the season. There was a theatre built on the Green as far back as 1770 by public subscription; it was in a dilapidated state by 1818 and was repaired largely at the expense of Charles Forbes's company, but it was never very successful and was later abandoned. At about the same time there was also the Artillery Theatre in Matunga – this was before the cantonment there was deserted. A Parsi (Sir Dinshaw Wacha) has written:

> Dramatic high jinks were held amidst all the suburban picturesequeness of the spot, now made so hideous by industrialisation on the one hand and the operations of the precious Bombay Improvement Trust on the other, chiefly, in erecting chawls to here, there and everywhere. It is recorded that in 1820 all Bombay society, including the Governor, flocked there to witness a performance called 'Miss Teens and the Padlock'.

FIRST LADIES AND INFERIOR WOMEN

If Elphinstone really went to that I doubt if it was much to his taste. Worldly he may have been but he was one of the most intelligent and far-sighted men in India at that time, and was the moving spirit behind the Native Education Society. This, after his retirement, became the Elphinstone College, and today occupies the grand Gothic-Italianate building on Mahatma Gandhi Road.

Later in the century another theatre existed for a while on Grant Road, a new route cut through central Bombay c.1840, and later still there was a theatre near the Bombay Gymkhana, but both are now vanished or transformed. Present day Bombay has the obligatory late-nineteenth-century Opera House, and any number of well-patronised cinemas, some engagingly still known as 'Talkies', but the town lacks those rococo theatres that are so much a feature of western metropolises. In the days before air-conditioning such structures were simply too hot in Bombay, and perhaps cultured European support for them was limited also. For an evening's recreation a carriage drive, either up and down the Esplanade where the bandstand stood or to the Breach and back, was greatly preferred; literally dozens of accounts of this simple and repetitive evening pleasure have come down to us:

> It was nearly dark when we reached this 'prado', and as there is scarcely any twilight in the tropics, we sat for half an hour in the dark, with our faces turned to the western breeze. The only lights were those for the musicians, who were playing from notes, and the lamps of the numerous carriages. The ladies remained in the britzas, and the gentlemen flitted about from carriage to carriage, paying their devoirs to the fair occupants, who were just recovering from the unusual and overpowering heat of the day. The children were led by their attendants round and round the band-stand, which I thought would give the little things a decided taste, or dislike, for music in future years.
>
> (Lady Falkland)

(That particular bandstand disappeared when the open Esplanade Road began to have a phalanx of grand public buildings laid out along it in the late 1860s; its site is somewhere underneath the Institute of Science, next door to the Elphinstone College. However, a similar one was constructed not far away and still stands today near the foot of the Oval Maidan: it is charmingly wreathed with creepers, though reclamation works have robbed it now of its sea-view and shifting residential patterns have removed its clientele. A middle-aged man of my acquaintance, however, has vivid childhood memories of it – 'That bloody bandstand, we were

165

always going there. The ayah used to walk us round and round it . . . ')

Fewer nineteenth-century accounts mention that it was not only the European community that liked to 'eat the air' on the Esplanade in the evenings. Dinshaw Wacha records that, while the Hindu and Moslem communities did not take to outdoor recreation till the later part of the century, Parsis long before this had their own informally established quarters on the level, open plain where they used to congregate at sunset. By tradition, Parsis gather for prayers when the sun sets into the sea, but the air-eaters of Wacha's mid-nineteenth-century childhood used the Esplanade to stroll, play chess or draughts, or gather to hear stories recited and eat sweets from a confectioner in the Fort.

As a prime site facing the western sea, the Esplanade would long before then have been covered with bungalows had it not been still maintained by the authorities as a defensive 'field of fire' on which no permanent buildings might be erected. Instead, tents or 'temporary bungalows' used to be put up on the Esplanade for part of each year, and these were a distinctive feature of Bombay for several generations. Nearly all travellers to Bombay refer to them: they were unknown in other presidencies, and to the European mind there was something daring about the idea of ladies and gentlemen camping out like natives, however elaborately. Lady West, otherwise condemned to her grand 'barn-like' house in the airless Fort, enjoyed staying at the Stewarts' temporary bungalow, though she was troubled by 'musk rats running about our room [who] perfumed the air very disagreeably, and a troop of ants [who] lodged themselves in our bed'.

A dozen years later in 1839, Mrs Postans had no such complaints:

> During the hot season, the Esplanade is adorned with pretty, cool, temporary residences erected near the sea; their chuppered roofs and rustic porches half concealed by flowering creepers and luxuriant shrubs, which shade them from the mid-day glare . . . The material of which they are made is simply bamboo and plaster, lined with stained dungaree, dyed a pale straw colour . . . which affords no attraction to the depredating presence of loathsome insects seeking what they may devour . . . Elegance combines with comfort, in making these pretty abodes truly pleasant; and a fine-toned piano, and a good billiard table, are the usual additive to varied articles of luxury and convenience . . .

166

By that date the steamships were coming, and 'varied articles of luxury and convenience' were, for the first time in Bombay, becoming readily procurable. However the new conveniences tended, in the long run, to drive out the old, simpler pleasures, and by 1859 *Murray's Guide* recorded, 'By a recent order, it is not allowed to erect temporary banglás on the Esplanade or to pitch tents there'. However, this order was apparently not complied with. Temporary bungalows are recorded in a guide of about 1870, and a picture-postcard view of the Esplanade looking towards Colaba *c.*1900, showing the bandstand in its present position, shows rows of what would appear to be tents facing the airs of Back Bay in the time-honoured way.

As for the progress of the *puckah*-built, or proper suburban bungalows, out among the coconut groves, we have for the first time in the early nineteenth century a properly surveyed map of these and indeed of the whole Island, made by Captain Thomas Dickinson of the Royal Engineers. Malabar Hill, which was later in the century to become covered in rather grand bungalows (excepting always the land where the Towers of Silence stood), was then still more or less an attractive jungle. There were only three bungalows on the hill itself – 'The Beehive', 'The Retreat' and the one on Malabar Point which was later to succeed Parel as the Governor's 'country' residence, and is today Government House – but there were a number along the shore of the promontory, including 'Surrey Cottage' where Wellington stayed. I think that Randall Lodge, the home of one branch of the copious Bellasis family, was near here also: a later water-colour shows that it had two storeys, with a verandah all round the lower one, a flat-roofed side-wing, and a garden laid out with a rectangular lawn, cypresses, and vegetables at the side. Other family connections lived along the road to the Breach, and there the Stewarts, who were the Wests' friends and Charles Forbes's relatives, had their *puckah* residence. Nearby in Hermitage Pass between Malabar and Kamballa Hills, was the house where Lady West was to die. Further north again, at Love Grove on the far side of the Breach, a place to which there was attached a romantic Moslem legend concerning two drowned lovers today commemorated in Hadji Ali's mosque, there had been at least one European house since the end of the eighteenth century. It had, like many of the houses in Bombay, a banian (pipal) tree in the garden, one of those sacred trees whose aerial roots descend from the branches to form a natural shelter; this one had Milton's lines on the banian tree from *Paradise Lost* engraved on its trunk. This tree has long gone: its approximate site is currently occupied by a skyscraper designed by Charles Correa, India's best-known architect. But banian trees, some of them even occupied as homes by street families, are still to be seen today in central Bombay, the isolated remains of all the lost gardens.

The greatest concentration of European (and Parsi) occupation by the early nineteenth century was at Mazagaon, subsequently spreading from there into the adjacent suburb of Byculla. The Belvedere was there, and the Grove and the Mount and Mazagaon Castle and Tarala (renamed Claremont) and Belmont, and further up the road were Chinchpoglie House, Belair, Lowji Castle, Storm Hall, Parel House and the jokily-named Non Pareil. Each of these substantial houses stood in its own grounds: the whole place was becoming a pleasant, populous residential district, a kind of grand, European-style counterpart to the thickly populated Girgaum Woods on the Back Bay side of the Island. Today, you have to seek carefully in Mazagaon–Byculla to find any trace of most of these large old houses: it is as if St John's Wood had been swallowed by Whitechapel. A few, however, survive, against all the odds. One is now the Mazagaon Magistrates Court: the building is decrepit but the garden is still tended. Another is occupied by a dealer in ornamental shrubs; another, originally the family house of the Parsi Patels, is hidden away in a quiet spot just off Gunpowder Lane, complete with pink paint and an ornamental pool filled with green water. It now belongs to a Moslem printing firm, and its elegant Regency staircase leads to an upper room full of swing beds and presided over by old, old gentlemen in skull caps. Flying squirrels, similarly capped, charming in black and white, still disport themselves on the overgrown trees that surround this oasis.

Bombay was growing. In 1780 it had 113,726 people; by 1806 this was considered to have risen to 200,000 and by 1814 to 240,000. These last two figures include the floating population of people who travelled in temporarily from the surrounding country to trade or find work or escape famine, and therefore (like a great many other population estimates up to and including those of today) probably over-represent the true figure of settlers, but there is no doubt that numbers were then generally on the increase. The population probably did not grow much in the 1820s, but in the early 30s it took off again, rising between 1832 and 1842 to 270,000 or possibly considerably more. Some commentators even put it as high as 500,000 by the mid-century.

Various dates during this period are commonly adduced as the 'turning point' for Bombay, when her real transformation from struggling provincial port into successful metropolis, *urbs prima in indis*, began. The defeat of the Peshwa in 1818 and the annexation of the Deccan was obviously important; so was the legislation of 1806 which meant that merchants and administrators would henceforth develop as separate species without a conflict between official interests and private ones. More important, probably, was the Charter Act of 1813, which abolished the rule that private merchants could only trade from Bombay with a Company licence; henceforth any British firm could trade with Europe and the Middle East – though the Company still had a British monopoly of the China trade. Many new British, and especially Scottish, firms were added to the two old-established leaders, the house of Forbes and the house of Fawcett. A road for wheeled vehicles going up into the Deccan was open by 1830, which greatly increased Bombay's potential as an export point. But I think myself that the most crucial development of all occurred in 1833, when the Company's remaining trade monopolies were swept away and it effectively ceased trading in its own right. International traders were thus able to establish businesses in Bombay – the Greek Ralli brothers, whose firm flourishes to this day; the Baghdadi-Jewish Sassoons, who were to make Bombay their stepping-stone to international wealth and prestige. At last, then, Bombay was on the way to becoming what Aungier had long ago wished it to be: a latter-day Venice, a world free-trade city.

VII 'Going to Bombay'

'No ship from England', Lady West wrote in her Journal on 13 September 1823. 'We have been expecting one the last month, and begin to get quite impatient. Oh for steam vessels!' Presumably she had been talking to Mountstuart Elphinstone, for that same year he made an official proposition to the Court of Directors for the establishment of steam-communication between England and Bombay via the 'overland' (Red Sea) route which, since the turn of the century, had been supplanting the old route round the Cape. But the request was not granted. The first steamboat actually arrived in Bombay harbour, having raced another one there, in October 1827, to considerable local excitement, but the regular service was not to be established for another ten years.

Among those who were not slow to take advantage of the new, swifter and supposedly safer mode of transport were a number of literary-minded women. Already, in 1830, a Mrs Elwood made the trip and subsequently published her *Narrative of an Overland Journey to India*. (She found suburban Bombay growing so fast that it reminded her of London, which had also expanded greatly since the ending of the Napoleonic Wars, while the Fort itself, with its wooden houses, reminded her of Switzerland. The persistent tendency of travellers of this period to evoke Switzerland surely tells one more about the other journeys they had made than about India itself? Switzerland, plus 'the Holy Land' – usually known only in imagination – are the main points of comparison for nineteenth-century travellers.) Emily Eden, sister to the then Governor General, Lord Auckland, arrived in Calcutta in 1873 and stayed in India several years. While her subsequently published Memoirs and

Letters relate to the Bengal presidency rather than to Bombay, she is a rich source for general material on British society in India during those years. Emma Roberts, a middle-aged English woman of already-guaranteed literary ability, arrived in Bombay in 1839 with a commission to edit the newly established *British United Services Gazette* and also to write a book on western India. She stayed at Parel with the Governor, Sir James Rivett-Carnac, and has left an interesting account (*Overland Journey to Bombay*), but she died at Poona, poor lady, the following year. From the point of view of posterity her place has fortunately been taken by Mrs Postans, who arrived in 1837 as the wife of a military man. He died a few years later, but she survived to return Home, remarry and enjoy a permanent reputation as something of an expert on India. In her *Western India in 1838* she wrote:

> Few places have undergone greater change and improvement than the Presidency of Western India, during the last six years; and if we venture to become prophetic on the present appearance of political affairs connected with the east, its career of progress promises to be even yet more singularly rapid. If the affairs of Sindh, Kandahar, and Caubal, terminate as all such affairs have terminated when British force has been employed . . . Bombay will spring at once into the important position for which later events have so well prepared her. The work of Improvement has been gradually, but surely, progressing, and the tone of society is changed. The native gentry now form a recognised, and important part of the community; their sons are educated to fit them for any mercantile or political appointment, to which they may be called; the English merchants are daily considered as forming a more valuable class. Men of science are organising branch Societies, which offer every encouragement to enquiry and research . . . the fine Government steamers, with their six weeks news from England, now ride in the harbour, which wanderers of the olden times were glad to make after the dangers and delays of a twelvemonth's voyage.

The tone of energy, optimism and a degree of self-satisfaction, plus an anxiety to reassure the reader of the extent and rapidity of Bombay's change of heart, is one that is replicated in the nineteenth century in writer after writer. Hindsight was to prove them triumphantly right: * Bombay did become a major and thriving

---

* Bombay was regarded as important enough to be the subject of a panorama, painted by Burford and displayed in Leicester Square in 1831.

metropolis, so much so that by the closing decades of the century many people regarded it as only a matter of time before she would usurp Calcutta's position as the imperial capital (a dream which was finally scotched by the building of New Delhi in 1911). But it is also probably true that, in the 1840s and 50s, Bombay-partisans rather tended to exaggerate Bombay's amenities at the expense of Calcutta's; although a historian might well date the beginning of Calcutta's long, inexorable decline from the establishment of the overland steamer-route via Suez to the more convenient Bombay, this decline did not really become apparent till the twentieth century. Also, though it is true that the Bombay of the mid-century was cosmopolitan in the genuine sense, for those who worked there, there are indications that those who passed their days at home in bungalows at Byculla or at the Breach enjoyed, as ever, a somewhat provincial and narrow existence, despite the improvements to life of which Mrs Postans and others make much: 'The present rapid communication with Europe * has introduced a very superior class of ideas and interests; and among other advantages, are many of a literary kind – reviews, papers, periodicals, and books, arrive before their novelty is dimmed in Europe; thus all intelligence of interest is discussed, and every means of getting information easily acquired.'

Other commodities equally important to comfort and even to the preservation of life began to make their appearance. Accounts vary as to when the first cargo of ice arrived in Bombay: it is said that a rogue consignment found its way there by accident in 1833, and that this demonstrated the practicality of transporting it regularly in blocks from North America now that the journey-time was much shorter. The coolies who hauled this first consignment from the docks into a go-down complained in bewilderment that this unknown commodity 'burnt' their bare backs: still today one sees large ice-blocks being dragged around the city on handcarts, but they are normally wrapped in sacking and sawdust. The firm of Jehangir Wadia and Co. began importing it on a regular basis from Boston in 1836, but not until an ice-house was built by public subscription in the following decade, on a space next to St Andrew's

* The traffic was not all one-way. Ivory, Benares brass-ware (later copied and produced in Birmingham), elephants' feet, tiger skins and Kashmir shawls poured into Britain, plus some less desirable imports. Cholera, which originated in Bengal, first reached London and Paris in 1832, to devastating effect.

church, was it possible to keep the stuff for long in Bombay's everlasting warm climate. It was sold to the public at a few annas a pound (sixteen annas then made up one rupee) and was always much in demand; the 'ice-famines' that occurred when the weather was at its hottest were a source of much complaint. During such times head servants had to resort to the old method of dressing bottles in 'wet petticoats, fancifully arranged round the necks. Port, claret and burgundy were usually dressed in wetted cloths of crimson with flounces, while sherry and Madeira appeared in bridal white'. (Samuel T. Sheppard) Not till an ice-making plant was built in Mazagaon, on the garden of an erstwhile Wadia residence in the 1880s, was the supply assured. Its greatest use was of course in preserving food-stuffs: the luxury of ice-cream was only gradually introduced – Sir Jamshetji Jeejeebhoy began to serve it at dinner parties, though the first time he did so it was alleged that everyone caught cold. It seems to have been believed that iced water was automatically pure, regardless of the provenance of that water, and by the 1850s glasses of the stuff used to be offered to guests at bedtime in Bombay households, in replacement for the eternal sack and punch of the Old Days. But probably a more important factor in the greatly improved health of the Bombay inhabitants by the mid-century, a decline in mortality on which everyone commented, was the introduction of bottled soda water. The main source of soda water was Messrs Treachers, a chemist and lynchpin of European life, which stood for the middle decades of the century in Rampart Row, just inside the Fort walls, near Forbes's old house and the Apollo Gate. All memoirs and guide books of the period mention this palm-thatched shop appreciatively. In 1865 the business moved elsewhere, and the modest house was replaced by the ponderously italianate Oriental Bank Building which stands there to this day: such is the natural development of cities. Opposite Treachers in the mid-century were the premises of the Palkiwallah family, the Parsi firm who were by then constructing not only palaquins, but, increasingly, carriages on the English model.

The old Bombay tradition, good or bad according to your point of view and your personal experience of it, had been for visitors to stay either with friends (which frequently meant friends of friends) or in tents on the Esplanade. The new influx of visitors of the 1830s, both from Europe and from other parts of India, was obviously straining the well-intentioned but inadequate system of old-fashioned hospitality. Mrs Postans wrote:

Every family visiting Bombay, must feel the great inconvenience of there being neither a hotel, or other place of public accommodation, at which they can put up, in the event of their not possessing an acquaintance, whose hospitality they may venture to claim . . . The Victorian Hotel solicits the patronage of travellers; but as it is situated in the very dirtiest and narrowest street of the fort, the additional annoyance of flights of mosquitoes, a billiard table, a coffee and a tap room, place it without the pale of respectable support. The Sanitarium [a long bungalow on Colaba, still in existence today] affords shelter to invalids, and is delightfully situated, where the smooth sands and fine sea breezes render it a tempting locality for the convalescent; but the rooms are far too small for family accommodation.

A few years later the first of the residential clubs (that archetypal British Indian institution) was established in premises adjoining the stand at the Byculla Race Course, with the expressed intention of providing respectable and reasonably priced lodgings. The Committee's deliberations about the site are instructive. Land within the Fort was by then expensive, which is why the suburbs were decided upon; initially it was proposed to acquire and renovate 'The Grove' at Mazagaon; the fact that adjacent Byculla was regarded in the end as more suitable shows that the social shift away from the old Portuguese township, which became so marked a generation later, was already under way. The same year (1833) that the Byculla Club opened, the new church there was also completed, and almost at once overtook St Thomas's in the Fort as the fashionable place for Morning Service. With its frilled punkahs, venetian blinds, cane-work armchairs, and chits put in the plate instead of cash, it seemed to one newcomer 'very unlike a church in England', but externally today it still looks exactly like dozens of the churches constructed in English towns before the Gothic revival swept the country – a piece of changeless Home, spired, pillared, white-stuccoed and tree-shaded, standing back from the seething main roads that now surround it, half-hidden in the oasis-like compound of Christchurch Schools.

I am inclined to think that the 'Victorian Hotel' mentioned by Mrs Postans was the place usually known simply as the British Hotel: it has long disappeared, but one street in the Fort, still one of the 'dirtiest and narrowest', bears its name. Around 1840 it was owned by one T. Blackwell, who also ran a registry office for servants from the premises. By the early 1860s it was owned by one Pestonji Sorabji but he seems to have been in difficulties, for the place was to let and he was inserting notices in the *Bombay Gazette* asking creditors to pay their bills. Within three or four years Watson's Hotel was to rise from the Esplanade, 'something like a giant birdcage', in imitation of the palatial new hotels then going up in London and Paris, and a new era in Bombay was opening. In the 1850s, twenty years after Mrs Postans wrote her complaint, Murray's *Handbook to India* had been able to list five hotels in Bombay, of which only the British Hotel and one other were in the Fort. The best seems to have been the newly-opened Adelphi at Byculla, where a Parsi cook was soon to master the art of ice-cream making and begin to supply all Bombay. The favoured family hotel was Hope Hall at Mazagaon, which, like the Great Western Hotel later in the century, occupied one of those great houses of former times by then subtly come down in the world.

The overland route gained its name because passengers embarking at Southampton and sailing round through Gibraltar and into the Mediterranean disembarked from that ship at Alexandria and proceeded by Nile steamer to Cairo. (A more genuinely 'overland' and rather *chic* variant in the 1850s, once the European railway network was established, was to cross France by train and embark for Alexandria from Marseilles.) From Cairo, the passengers were taken by carriage to Suez. From Suez, they embarked on another boat down the Red Sea, and frequently changed into a third one at Aden, according to whether their ultimate destination was Bombay, Calcutta or Madras. (The British, in an expansionist mood, had annexed Aden for this purpose in 1839, in a manoeuvre now generally regarded as reflecting no credit on anyone.) The P. & O. vessels, which began plying this route in 1840, were said to be passable, while the East India Company steamers which, for a number of years, continued to carry many of the passengers between Suez and Bombay, were the subject of travellers' horror stories: they were reckoned to be manned by officers who resented the whole coming of steam. A merchant (Sidney Terry) who arrived in Bombay in 1844, wrote to his wife, whom he had left for the time being in England:

> All the Bombay passengers were sent off from Alexandria without the least attention being paid to their comfort and were huddled on board the Steamer like cattle or slaves without even a sitting room. We were therefore obliged to sit up 2 nights. Bad provisions and wine also of the commonest description.

But then Sidney Terry was always inclined to be pessimistic about his lot: almost alone among the newcomers of the period, he failed to find Bombay beautiful. Ten years later, when J. S. Stocqueler compiled his invaluable *Handbook of British India,* conditions had somewhat improved:

> Our baggage having been sent forward to Suez on camels, we prepare to cross the desert. The uninitiated reader will doubtless picture to himself the complete Oriental cortège, such as we find in the illustrations of the works of Buckingham and Burckhardt, turbaned travellers, long strings of camels, rude tents, guards bristling with arms, a flaring sun, drought, privation, a single palm-tree and the apex of a pyramid in the distance. *Ah, nous avons changé tout cela!* Thanks to the exertions of the British agents and associations, who make it their business to promote the intercourse with India, there is little difference now between travelling seventy miles over a post road in England, and going over the same space of ground on the isthmus of Suez. Forty vans, each drawn by four good horses, and driven by an Egyptian jehu, carrying from four to six inside and none out, transport the living contents of two crowded steamers across the arid and desolate plain which divides Cairo from the Sea . . . The seats are carpeted and the whole thing is roomy and commodious. At the end of every ten or twelve miles, horses are changed at a sort of road-side inn, erected for the purpose; at two or three of which the traveller will get a capital dinner, or breakfast, or luncheon, of eggs, mutton-chops, roast pigeons, stewed fowls, potatoes, bread and good bottled ale, with tea or coffee if he prefer them . . . Let the travellers, therefore, shun the tempting advertisements of outfitters and guide books. All the urgent recommendations, that people should provide themselves with camel-saddles, canteens, bottles of water, parasols, braces of pistols, green veils, carpets etc, are superfluous.

On board the P. & O. ships too, there was no longer any occasion for the sofas, mattresses, lamps, buckets, ropes and oilcloths listed as indispensable for previous generations in their odyssey round the Cape. Stocqueler's reader was recommended to take with him 'only' – only? – '6 dozen shirts, 3 dozen pairs of socks, a couple of brown Holland blouses, 2 dozen pairs white pantaloons, a couple of pairs of merino or gambroon trousers, six dozen pocket handkerchiefs, 2 dozen pairs of long drawers, a forage cap, a straw hat, shoes, slippers and your razors and tooth brushes'. Lady readers are not instructed in such detail, but the *Handbook* carries numerous advertisements on its end-papers including several for 'Readymade linen warehouses . . . specialising in Ladies Outfits for India', not to mention shops dealing in maps and histories of India and in Hindustanee primers. The British Raj, with all its traditional paraphernalia, its merits and its defects, was not yet quite established in fact – the Bengal Uprising was to accomplish that a few years later – but, fuelled by steam, the Raj was beginning to be very much there in spirit and detail. At Aden, Stocqueler assured his reader, 'Barren rocks, and a few yards of sandy shore, once tenanted only by the sea-gull and the crab, are now covered by cheerful domiciles, and animated by a small but busy and contented population who live by unloading the fuel-ships, storing and protecting the coal, and embarking it upon the steamers . . . The people are evidently more than reconciled to British authority.' There was also a new hotel there, started (superfluous to say) by 'some enterprising Parsis from Bombay'. And this whole marathon journey, including 'meals . . . so numerous and blended into each other so felicitously that life on board a Peninsular and Orient Company's steamer is one vast *monstre* refection', could be had for as little as £105, rather than the £1,000 that the Cape route had once cost, or the £350 it had cost overland by Government sailing ships only twenty years earlier. (Significantly, the Cape route, which continued in existence, had by then lowered its fare to a comparable figure.)

It is not hard to guess which was the principal social group to take advantage of the quicker, cheaper passage. It has become a truism of Anglo-Indian history to say that the appearance of the white memsahibs from the 1830s onwards in far greater numbers than before radically changed the nature of life in India: it was a 'civilising' force which, paradoxically, also served to make society more rigid than it had been before, gentler in some ways and yet more radically intolerant. A returning visitor wrote in 1858: 'The good old hookah days are past; cheeroots and pipes have now usurped the place of the aristocratic silver bowl, the cut-glass goblets, and the twisted glistening snake with silver or amber mouthpiece . . . The race of Eurasians is not now so freely supplied with recruits . . . There is now no bee-bee's house . . . ' Instead, the appearance in India of the more suitable British wife, or would-be wife, turned in a few years from a minority movement into a mass one. Thomas Hood's poem on the subject, 'Going to Bombay', is well known, but it is worth quoting several verses from it, so perfectly does it capture the note of genteel vulgarity and determined opportunism inherent in such a venture. A generation earlier 'Bengal' or 'The Bay' would have been the most likely goal of such a fortune-hunter. Now, it was flourishing, growing Bombay:

> *By Pa and Ma I'm daily told*
> *To marry now's my time,*
> *For though I'm very far from old,*
> *I'm rather in my prime.*
> *They say while we have any sun,*
> *We ought to make our hay –*
> *And India has so hot a one,*
> *I'm going to Bombay!*
>
> *My cousin writes from Hyderapot*
> *My only chance to snatch,*
> *And says the climate is so hot,*
> *It's sure to light a match.*
> *She's married to a son of Mars,*
> *With very handsome pay,*
> *And swears I ought to thank my stars*
> *I'm going to Bombay!*
>
> *Farewell, farewell, my parents dear,*
> *My friends, farewell to them!*
> *And oh, what casts a sadder tear*
> *Goodbye, to Mr M! –*
> *If I should find an Indian vault,*
> *Or fall a tiger's prey,*
> *Or steep in salt, it's all his fault,*
> *I'm going to Bombay!*

Other verses name tropical outfitters of the period, and describe 'Pa' as having booked the girl's passage with the agents 'Nichol, Scott and Gray'. A firm called William Nichol & Co. was long established in Bombay, and was one of the founder members of the Chamber of Commerce. The girl's expectations of an exciting death by drowning or attack from a tiger are less up-to-date, though it is true that in 1840 the East Indiaman *The Lord William Bentinck* was shipwrecked on Colaba rocks with great loss of life, and that tigers were still seen in the Bombay suburbs during the first half of the nineteenth century. One was even seen in the densely populated area of Kalba Devi as late as 1859, and another near the Towers of Silence on Malabar Hill two years later.

The cousin 'married to a son of Mars with very handsome pay' had not done badly for herself, but traditionally civil servants were regarded as the best prizes to be had in the marital lottery: they were

irreverently known as 'Three-hundred-a-year-dead-or-alive-men' from the circumstance that this sum was both the salary of a newly appointed man, and the pension that a widow might eventually expect to collect. One young wife, when she discovered that her husband would, however, have to survive for a few years if he were to make the necessary contributions for her to receive this pension, exclaimed at a dinner party, 'John, John, it's a *do* after all!' This was quoted by Lady Falkland (see below) who was First Lady in Bombay in the early 1850s. She also wrote in her memoir of the place: 'The arrival of a cargo (if I dare term it so) of young damsels from England, is one of the exciting events that mark the advent of the cold season.' She added that most married within the year. However, the marriage market obeys the laws of supply and demand like any other. By the late 1860s and 70s 'the Fishing Fleet', as the annual influx of hopeful girls cruelly became known, had overfished the waters, and many had to return home as virginal, or at any rate as unmarried, as they had come ('The Returned Empties'). Up-country stations were a different matter, but cities like Bombay no longer had a surplus of eligible bachelors drinking themselves silly every evening and only waiting to relinquish their native mistresses for Some Nice Girl – or, if they were, they preferred to do their own fishing when on furlough in England, for by that time 'running home' every three or four years had become the usual procedure. Exile still existed, of course, but it was no longer a life-sentence; nor, as several writers remarked, was there the same sense of desperation at parting from parents or lovers once news could be dispatched in both directions with reasonable speed. In 1813 letters from London had taken the best part of four months to India by the fastest route. By 1843 they were reaching Bombay within one month or less, carried by special mail that was galloped through Egypt on relays of horses. (By 1880 it was down to seventeen days.) In 1864-5 the first telegraph cable was laid, via the Persian Gulf; it was extremely expensive to use, which led to early messages being brief to the point of obscurity, but it put an end once and for all to the sense of living in a time-scale separate from that of Europe which had haunted earlier generations of Anglo-Indians. *
It also, incidentally, was to play its part in the pattern of hysterical

---

* The word is here used in its usual nineteenth-century sense of 'British temporarily living in India'. Eurasians were not known as Anglo-Indians till the twentieth century, by which time the fact that they frequently *claimed* to be this led to the debasement of 'Anglo-Indian' – and 'domiciled European' – into euphemisms for 'of mixed race'.

boom and slump which was to characterise the Cotton Mania of that time: there is a tradition (but it sounds almost too neat to be true) that the first news sent via the cable was that of the abrupt ending of the American Civil War. (See Chapter VIII.)

It has been customary to write of social change and evolution in Bombay, and indeed in all India, as if these local phenomena were mainly or even entirely the result of local developments. Obviously local developments matter – but they are not, it seems to me, the major or indeed only causative factors that some historians have suggested. Moreover, they count less in the later period of Anglo-Indian history than in the earlier ones, since the very coming of improved communications between Europe and Asia made Indian society less self-contained and more liable to influences from Home. Thus, while it is correct to say that the general, heterogeneous growth of Bombay after 1833, and the increasing numbers of resident European wives and young children, had the effect of making society more segmented, and the British segment (excepting soldiers' wives) both more middle-class and more respectable, the same can also be said of society at Home. The early-to-mid Victorian era was characterised by an unprecedented growth in the middle classes, and a corresponding distancing from them of the really wealthy and/or aristocratic on the one hand and the working classes on the other. Notoriously, at that period in England, the wives of minor landowners who would earlier have called themselves farmers, and the wives of wholesale drapers who in a previous generation would have been merely shopkeepers, set up as ladies with fashionable gowns, drawing rooms and servants. In a similar way, in the microcosmic British society of each Indian presidency, the quite ordinary wives of run-of-the-mill Company or Government servants arrogated to themselves a pseudo-aristocratic degree of social standing, while retaining the touchiness of their middle-class origins. Lady Falkland, who was a genuine though bar-sinister aristocrat of the Regency variety (she was the daughter of William IV and Mrs Jordan) and had far too much personality to be intimidated by anyone, even had she not been the Governor's wife, commented:

> The ladies of Bombay are more tenacious of their rank than we are in England. A 'burrah bibi' (a great lady) or wife of a gentleman high in the East India Company's Service, is a very great person indeed . . . I once saw a lady, far from well, after a dinner party at Government House, and wishing very much to

go home; who, on my urging her to do so, hesitated because another person in the company – the wife of a man of higher official rank than her own husband – did not seem disposed to move. I took the opportunity of impressing on the poor sufferer, that the sooner the custom was broken through the better. However she did not like to infringe it, and so she sat on.

The anonymous but probably civilian author of *Life in Bombay*, writing at the same period (*c.* 1850), stated that he found there 'an absence of broad vulgarity . . . We have neither "parvenus" not "nouveau riches" among us . . . with a very few exceptions, no one comes to this country without either having laid the foundation or completed the accomplishment, of a gentleman's education.' Objectively, this is nonsense. As Mrs Postans and others, writing only a few years earlier, make clear, fortune-hunting or general social advancement on a shaky foundation was still a major motive in many a young man's decision to join the East India Service, or the Indian Army, or to settle in Bombay as a merchant, even if life frequently proved more expensive there – because of the very insistence on a 'gentlemanly life-style' – than he had bargained for. Moreover the writer of *Life in Bombay* goes on directly to describe the career of the typical Indian Army officer who then still arrived in India at a bare sixteen or seventeen. But the hidden message of his remarks is clear: an *air* of refinement was clearly by then the order of the day, in India as at Home, along with the latest Paris fashions now readily available, the latest three-volume novels, and even the latest craze in Berlin woolwork – though it, like the Paris fashions, was liable to be devoured by white ants during the rainy season unless packed away in camphorous trunks.

The writer was clearly impressed by life among the British community of Bombay, as he was no doubt meant to be. He does describe one gruelling dinner party in the hot season where guest after guest round the table fell asleep while one delivered an interminable speech lauding the details of someone's commonplace career, but he admired 'the general aspect of English residencies, which are usually lofty and stately-looking mansions, with façades adorned with spacious porticoes'. He also speaks of the relatively sheltered nature of life in India for Europeans, of the absence of 'those heart-wringing cases of sudden destitution . . . As regards our compatriots, we are spared all close proximity to poverty under its abject and most repulsive form; while the simple habits of the native poor . . . render it easily practical for everyone to administer efficient relief . . . Though the aggregate amount of happiness may

181

not be so great in India as in England, unquestionably the awarded proportion of pain and suffering is less.'

Less pain and suffering? The twentieth-century reader reflects on the intensity of the poverty and deprivation visible today in some parts of Bombay, as in all Indian cities, and wonders what alarming social change has occurred in India since the mid-nineteenth century and how much worse matters can become. But the answer, of course, is that India has *not* changed in this respect whereas the western world has, and that that is why we are now struck by a poverty which our ancestors took for granted. It is clear from contemporary accounts that many of the nineteenth-century native inhabitants of Bombay lived in the same minute huts of temporary encampments that we would now characterise as 'shanty-towns' and imagine to be a modern phenomenon. But to the nineteenth-century British settlers, accustomed to scenes of absolute destitution in colder climates – to the beggars and homeless street hawkers of London, to colonies of boys sleeping rough in Covent Garden – the Indian poor seemed relatively less deprived, less diseased and certainly less depraved. Moreover, the very fact that they were Indian poor lessened identification with them: a naked brown heathen beggar was less distressing than a white, presumably Christian one wearing a ragged parody of respectable clothes. ('As regards our compatriots, we are spared all close proximity to poverty under its abject and most repulsive form.') Among the white communities in India there were, after all, no very old people, no abandoned children, and indeed virtually no members of the working classes except the soldiers, who may have been brutal and licentious on occasions, and whose wives may sometimes have been regrettably dissolute and drunken (according to Mrs Postans) but who were hardly starving. The working classes, including the servant classes, were all natives.

Thus, in India, race-consciousness effectively took the place of the class-consciousness that characterised nineteenth-century England, and, like class-consciousness, grew as the century went by. It is unpleasantly exemplified by Stocqueler in his *Handbook of British India:* ' . . . Considered in the gross, there is not perhaps a people in the world who are so little distinguished by the virtues which adorn the human race as the inhabitants of Hindustan.' He makes the by-then-traditional exception for the Parsis, as typified for him by the first Sir Jamshetji Jeejeebhoy ('His private bounties are illimitable, and he seems to seek every opportunity of doing public good') but condemns also the Indo-Portuguese (' . . . may be known by his sallow countenance, slovenly gait, and mimicry of the European fashions'). Eurasians he allows to be 'an orderly and intelligent and, in one line, an industrious race of people; but they are generally devoid of both mental and personal energy'. The 'true Briton', however, is 'energetic and active, courageous and speculative . . . Even his pastimes [hunting the tiger, for instance] partake of the loftiness of his character'. After this, it comes as quite a surprise to learn that Stockqueler nevertheless considers that the British have occasionally been 'overweening' in India, and even have not always treated India quite as they should.

But Stockqueler was not a Bombay man, and it is fair to say that, whatever generalisation may be made about growing race-prejudice and the place of racial hubris in the British Raj, Bombay frequently provides an exception to this rule. It had a relatively small military establishment for its size (the main military cantonment was up at Poona) which meant that society in Bombay was not dominated by military officers, who had the deserved reputation of showing more ignorance and prejudice toward the natives than the civilians did. It lacked local princes and maharajahs; its native 'aristocracy' was, like that of nineteenth-century London, an aristocracy of wealth; this was democratic in that a really successful businessman of any community was likely to find himself co-opted to the egalitarian club of the great. It has those key between-two-worlds figures, the Parsis, to oil the wheels of social intercourse, and these, by the mid-nineteenth century, were joined by Sephardi Jews from Baghdad. The long-standing Bombay tradition of commercial co-operation between different races and creeds (a classic example of 'enlightened self-interest') had protected Bombay from the worst rapacity of Nabobery in the eighteenth century and now, in the Victorian era, was to protect it against the extremes of imperial snobbery. Mountstuart Elphinstone, who was Governor in the 1820s, remarked even at that early date, 'on this side of India there is really more zeal and liberality displayed in the improvement of the country, the construction of roads and public buildings, the conciliation of the natives and their education than I have yet seen in Bengal'.

It may be remembered that this Elphinstone was the founder of the Native Education Society which, after his retirement, was metamorphosed into the College that was named after him: one of the key figures in the setting up of the College was the most prominent Hindu citizen of the mid-century, Jagannath Shankershet (Sunkersett, etc.) who became a member of the

Bombay Board of Education. His was an old-established Bombay family – Gunbow St in the Fort was called, not after some piece of nautical equipment, but after his grandfather Gamba-Shett, who had been a banker and moneylender. Today Girgaum Road, where Jagannath built for himself a large house standing in grounds stocked with deer, bears his name. He crops up frequently in nineteenth-century records – endowing a school, donating land in Grant Road for a theatre: he was of the *sonar* or goldsmith caste, and perhaps this made his association with the European community the easier. Anglo-Indian relations were perpetually complicated by the fact that, in India, education and wealth are not traditionally combined in the same caste; the best-educated class – the Brahmin *babhus* – traditionally held aloof from the money-making classes. Shankershet came under suspicion during the Bengal Uprising, but fortunately the time was past when the Governor of Bombay would clap a prominent Hindu into jail on mere suspicion: otherwise he might have suffered the fate of that earlier friend-to-the-British Rama Kamathi. His name was subsequently cleared, he became the first Hindu member of the Bombay Legislative Council, and today he sits majestic in marble and native dress in his own corner of the old Town Hall. * Colonial administrators and military men may stand – Bartle Frere, the energetic town-planner of the 1860s even holds out his hand, in a harassed and faintly propitiatory manner – but a wealthy Hindu businessman knows his own dignity.

Jagannath Shankershet was the first Indian member of the Asiatic Society; later in the century other clubs began to appear in Bombay, but the assorted dietary and social reservations of the various native communities kept them aloof. It is false to imagine that the Shankershets or the Muhammed Ali Rogays of the nineteenth century actually wished to eat or drink with their European counterparts: prejudice can work both ways. Parsis, however, were, as always, a slightly different matter: at the Byculla Club in 1857 a member brought a Dr Rustomji Byramji to dine, and there was a subsequent fuss. On being told by the Committee that there was no ruling on the matter, another member suggested that guests should be excluded who were not 'European in manner, habits and ideas', to which the Committee retorted that 'when a guest was objected to [they] could not be expected to go into

* When the idea of his statue was first mooted, the *Bombay Gazette* asked rudely 'if successful money-lending is to form the *beau ideal* of perfect humanity?'

184

considerations of whether the objections to him arose from the cut of his hat, the absence of gloves, or the want of polish on his boots'. The reference to boots has more in it than meets the eye. When you reflect that in western society it is unthinkable to remove your footwear when entering a formal reception, whereas in India this has long been a mark of respect, some of the difficulties of mixed socialising at a formal level become apparent.

The social history of Bombay contains various examples of Governors and their wives making overtures to native Indians, and more especially to their womenfolk, which were only gradually reciprocated. The first Governor to entertain many natives at Parel was Rivett-Carnac (1839-41) but they came without their wives. The Moslem ladies were all respectably in purdah, and many of the higher-caste Hindu families had adopted this habit as a piece of social emulation during Moghul days: at any rate their husbands explained that they were 'too shy' to come. In 1840 Jamshetji Jeejeebhoy gave a European-style ball (as distinct from the traditional Indian *nautch*) at which his own wife and his three daughters-in-law were present, but it was not till the early 1860s that Lady Frere managed to get Parsi ladies to come to balls at Parel: she achieved this by refusing to go to the second Sir Jamshetji Jeejeebhoy's numerous parties unless all the ladies were there. By the 1880s it was possible to invite Parsis and Moslems to dinner parties (though not Hindus, because of their stricter dietary and caste rules) and again successive Governors gave a lead in this. On one occasion Lord Reay (1880-5) entertained at dinner a mixed party which included the future High Court Judge Badruddin Tyebjee (a Moslem of the Borah community). A Mrs Andrew Hay, the wife of a broker on the Bombay Stock Exchange whose husband must certainly have spent his working life dealing and competing with Indians, refused to have Mr Tyebjee take her into dinner, and she and her husband left. The next day the Governor sent a note telling them not to come to Parel again.

I have said that the progressive 'civilisation' of Bombay in the middle decades of the nineteenth century had an equivocal effect as far as race relations were concerned. Nowhere, perhaps, does this equivocality show up as clearly as in the area of missionary activity. You might suppose that the Christian gospel, with its message of democracy and brotherly love, might serve to make the native more visible to the British settler as a human being, and to some extent this was so. But it was also a fact that the rising tide of Evangelical

Christianity, as personified by Henry Martyn, Mrs Henry Sherwod and, in Bombay itself, by the Rev. Dr Wilson, bred a new horror of heathenism, a conviction that an absence of belief in Christ must express itself by a general 'moral turpitude'.

The overall subject of the effect – or lack of effect – of missionary work in India is far too large a one for this book. It is sufficient to say that, in Bombay as elsewhere in India, the East India Company discouraged missionaries on the grounds that they were trouble-makers. In 1813 Charles Forbes, who had by that time returned Home from India and become a Member of Parliament, wrote to Hormanji Bomanji Wadia:

> I opposed the Padres being sent out to India, not that they would alarm you or my other friends in Bombay who have never thought that our Government would interfere with their religion – that is not intended – but the ignorant part of the population would perhaps think otherwise and if the idea of converting the natives should once get into circulation there is no saying what uneasiness it might create throughout India generally . . . The measure is merely to please the religiously mad part of the people in this country.

However, religious 'madness' was increasing, and ideas wafting from Home could not be resisted indefinitely. In the 1820s Mountstuart Elphinstone, the Wests and the Chambers were all members of a newly formed Bombay Committee for the Propagation of the Gospel. The powers of the Company to forbid entry to those whom they considered undesirable, including zealous preachers, had been curtailed by the Charter Act of 1813, and they were unable to prevent John Wilson, the Scottish missionary, from settling there in 1829. (He had been going to settle in Poona, but the Bombay Government under Sir John Malcolm refused permission for that on the grounds that it would irritate the entrenched Brahmin community there.) In Bombay he and his wife quietly settled down to founding schools for both boys and girls, while nagged for more spectacular results from the Mission's headquarters in Scotland ('No baptisms yet?'). He became proficient in Sanskrit, Gujerati and Mahrathi, and his wife Margaret was the first white woman to learn fluent Mahrathi, a fact that was recorded on her tombstone in the small Scotch cemetery in Marine Lines near the Cross Maidan. Almost 150 years later, long after the cemetery had become disused, the stone still stood there, battered and ignored. Street dwellers used nearby flat-topped tombs as convenient surfaces for beating their washing, and at night the place was – and is – a thriving centre for more dubious activities, such as the manufacture of illicit liquor. At last, in 1980, Margaret Wilson's memorial inscription was saved from extinction by being removed to the compound of the girls' schools she helped to found, a habitat she must surely find more congenial. She died after only six years in Bombay; her husband remarrried and lived and worked there for another forty-seven. He survived the Disruption in the Scottish Church in 1843 and the consequent loss of St Andrew's, and founded a Free Kirk of his own and two schools in central Bombay which are still flourishing; he went Home only twice, briefly, in all those years. The Wilson College, facing the shore of Back Bay at Chowpatti Beach, is named after him, and it and the schools still employ predominately Christian staff – though today they tend to preserve a decent reticence on the subject of conversion, and particularly on the row with the Parsi community which the conversion of Dhunjibhoy and Hormusji Wadia provoked in 1839.

Many contemporary accounts tell of Wilson's combination of sagacity and good humour, of the spartan nature of his own life and the tolerance and lack of prejudice he extended towards others. I wonder how many present-day Wilson College students realise that the 'cottage at Ambroli', which was his home for many years and where he is immortalised as sitting in an ill-cut coat reading Milton and enjoying a bottle of cold tea, is still standing? It is today the Post Office of the Ambroli sub-district of Khetwadi, a crowded central area of Bombay which retains, among its high, old-fashioned houses, a whiff of charm, a hint of the tree-shaded suburb it once was. Wilson's bungalow has lost its garden and the interior is full of notice-boards and clerks, but its one-time verandah and arched windows betray its origins.

John Wilson's son Andrew by his first wife, who grew up to become one of that army of late-nineteenth-century travellers and writers on the East, wrote in 1881:

> *. . . Ten years hence I see*
> *A city grand and pleasant to the eye,*
> *Bombay, as it will doubtless one day be*
> *Freed from caste prejudice and rivalry;*
> *Broad roads to view, and noble buildings fair,*
> *Green shaded walks beneath umbrageous trees,*
> *With fountains playing 'neath the sunny blue,*
> *Tempered and softened by a cool sea-breeze.*
>   *(Songs after Sunset)*

The verse epitomises the loftiest hopes that the nineteenth-century British had for India. Places like Bombay were to be a kind of New Jerusalem, where the separate and often-conflicting Victorian goals of material Progress and spiritual Progress were to be harmoniously woven into one.

A curious dimension is added to the nineteenth-century desire to convert 'the poor Hindoo' by the circumstance that, to the European newcomer's eyes, the native life of Bombay very much resembled the life of Palestine in the time of Christ as recounted in the Bible. Commentator after commentator makes this comparison. The packed bazaars and temple courtyards were, for them, Jerusalem and the story of the Money-Changers brought to life, the women in flowing garments drawing water at the wells on the Esplanade were the living images of 'the daughters of the Patriarchal tribes [who] went forth to fill their brazen water vessels, beside the shaded wells of Palastine' (Mrs Postans).

All writers agree that it was the variety of different people living and trading in Bombay, that city of perpetual immigration, that gave her street scenes their particular richness: the same is still to some extent true today, even though the time is past when each race, each sect, caste or profession, had its distinctive dress. If Mrs Postans could return today she would still find 'half naked porters' weighted under enormous head-loads, but she might find other groups harder to pick out from the mass:

> Arabs with ponderous turbans of finely checked cloth, and Abas loosely flowing, lounge lazily along; Persians in silken vests, with black lamb-skin caps, the softest produce of Bokhara, tower above the crowd; Banians, dirty and bustling, wearing red turbans bristling with pens and memoranda, jostle roughly to the right and left; Bangies with suspended bales, or well-filled water vessels; Fakirs from every part of India; Jains in their snowy vests, with staff and brush, like palmers of the olden times; Padres with round black hats and sable cloaks; Jews of the tribe of Beni Israel, all mingle in the throng; while every now and again, a bullock hackerie struggles against the mass, or a Parsee, dashing onwards in his gaily painted buggy, forces an avenue for an instant, when the eager crowd, rapidly closing in its rear, sweeps on a restless torrent as before.

Bombay was (and is) a centre for furniture making; its speciality was blackwood furniture, indifferently jointed but beautifully carved, with ivory inlays. The men who did this 'Bombay work' were in fact Sindhis from Lahore. Each trade tended to be associated with a particular group of incomers: As the *Bombay*

Above Girgaum Road, about 1860.

Below Girgaum Road in 1980, re-named Jaggannath Shankersett Maarg.

Above Burrows Lane 1980: this was once the main access from Girgaum road to the 'Coconut garden near the water' which became Sonapur cemetery in 1766.

Below Bhang Wadi ('Dope Alley'): an equally ancient and still narrower lane off Kalba Devi is today surmounted by this elegant expression of vernacular taste.

These possibly 18th century houses in Bazargate Street in the Fort (earlier known as Parsi Bazaar Street) show the construction methods and wood carvings typical of Gujerat, from which many Parsi and Moslim immigrants to Bombay came.

Architectural elaboration on a grand, British scale: Victoria Terminus and the head-quarters of the GIP railway, designed by F.W. Stevens (1878).

Above Also designed in the 1870s, this 'Swiss chalet' style station at Churchgate was apparently the BB&CI's riposte to the rival company's grandiose Terminus. (Photo c. 1900, station since rebuilt).

Below However in the 1890s the BB&CI company also commissioned a grand building for its headquarters from Stevens, seen here c. 1900 shortly after its opening, commanding a view of Back Bay to the west, the Oval maidan in front and Cross maidan and the Esplanade maidan to the rear. The latter appear to have more trees on them than they have today.

Above The BB&CI building in 1980, its facade much disfuged by hoardings and traffic barriers. To the left, the block on top of the rebuilt Churchgate station, and the statue of Sir Dinshaw Wacha, author of *Shells from the Sands of Bombay.*

Top right Cuffe Parade: villas for the rich with a sea view, built on reclaimed land off Colaba Causeway c.1900.

Bottom right Another Bombay: a mill and Moslem textile workers in Lower Parel, 1980.

Queen Victoria: retired to a hidden corner of the Gardens originally named after her, 1980.

Times (founded ten years previously) put it in 1848: 'Our best shoemakers are Chinamen; our stone-cutters are all from the interior. Our armourers and perfume dealers are mostly Persian; our horse dealers are Afghans and Baluchis.' The itinerant peddlers, who had been a traditional feature of Bombay life, were all Moslems – Borahs. Their day was now passing. As Stocqueler put it,

> In olden times, before steamers brought out crowds of ladies attired in Paris fashions, and before it was considered necessary to send to England for regular supplies of tasteful attire, the Borahs, who purchased vast quantities of goods strangely thrown together in the lots of a hurried auction, were looked to for all that was required, from a paper of pins to a balldress. But things have changed, and the Borahs are daily becoming of less repute; their taste is questioned, their fashions laughed at, and their self-importance shaken . . .

However, Lady Falkland, at the same period, does not seem to have been above enjoying the Borah's visit to her verandah, and she even called her book on Bombay *Chow-chow*, after the Borah's 'chow-chow' or mixed-oddment bag:

> 'Lady Sahib want fine cheese? Here "Uncle Tom's Cabin" (which the Borah had just purchased at a sale). I got good pickle. There box of French gloves. Take soap Lady Sahib?' then he tempts the lady's maid with a gay ribbon . . . side by side stand a bottle of anchovy sauce and one of tincture of rhubarb. There lies a Wiltshire cheese surrounded by Goa lace, English tapes and French ribbons. There are bottles of ink, blacking and hair dyes in the neighbourhood of fringes, pins and needles. There are gun and gauzes lower down, tooth brushes, flannel jackets and cigars . . .

More western-style trading was carried on in the Parsi shops in the Fort, where accounts could be run up for bills sent out later – with added interest. But, by Mrs Postans' account, their stock was almost as mixed as that of Borah's pack:

> The best is kept by Jangerjee Nusserawanjee, who vends goods of all descriptions, from purple velvet to raspberry jam . . . The shop is large and dark; the walls surrounded with glass cases, filled with fine French china, bijouterie, gold lace, sauces, brandied fruits, riding whips, and other European superfluities. A central avenue is flanked with cases containing jewelry, French clocks, and all descriptions of nicknackery. On the floor have subsided Cheshire and Gruyere cheeses,

197

hams, cases of sardines, salmon and other edibles; and from the ceiling depend bird cages, lamps, and coloured French lithographs, in handsome frames. Large *go-downs*, or store rooms, are attached to the premises, containing beer, wine, brandy, and liqueurs of all qualities, with mess supplies of every description.

Elsewhere Mrs Postans remarks that 'The dinner tables are now admirably supplied; hecatombs of slaughtered animals have given place to lighter delicacies; and there are few European luxuries which may not now be placed on the convivial board', but she does not add that these were only obtainable at a luxurious price: Bombay, to which provisions had always had to be carried from a distance whether over sea or land, had long had a reputation as the most expensive by far of the three presidencies. It is worth comparing her experience with that of Mrs Sidney Terry, the wife of the depressed merchant quoted earlier in this chapter, who lived in Bombay between 1844 and 1847. Her letters Home, which have never been published, are instructive in that they show her and her family to have belonged, like many others, to the sector of 'persons of limited means' which Mrs Postans referred to but did not frequent:

> Substantial dwellings . . . are to found either within the fort, or at Girgaum, Byculla, Chintz Poogly [Chinchpoglie] and other places beyond the bazaars, where European residents have erected groups of pucka built and handsome houses, with excellent gardens and offices attached. The rents of well-situated residencies of this description are usually very high, and persons of limited means are constrained to retire to smaller dwellings, many of which are scattered about among coconut woods, at a distance of about four miles from the port; these are considered feverish locations, and moreover swarm with insects of every description.

Such a locality was the small bungalow in 'rather a pretty situation in a garden' that Sidney Terry eventually found for his family before they travelled out to join him. He added in his letter, 'I hope you will like it. The frogs are croaking, the crickets singing while I am writing, while at a distance is the Singing and Wild Music of some Indians keeping a feast.' Perhaps he hoped these picturesque details would encourage his wife, and she must have needed encouragement, poor lady: his earlier letters, ever since he had arrived in Bombay alone to take up a position with the export firm of Higginson and Cardwell, are a litany of complaints and despondency:

Notwithstanding that I do not yet see any reason to dislike the place or the people, I must confess that I regret having engaged myself to come out here for the simple reason that it is *the most expensive place that I was ever in* . . . Houses are scarce and rents enormous – a decent place of 2 or 3 rooms only is £60 to £70 per ann. . . . From what I see and hear many Europeans must be living far beyond their means, for everything is done on an extravagant scale. I feel quite unsettled in mind and disposed at times to forfeit my Passage Money and return to Europe . . . I frequently wish for sickness to seize me and oblige me to return to you and die, in the presence of you and my dear children . . . But it is wrong I know to complain.

He was used to life abroad, he and his wife both came from British families trading in Alexandria and Malta: it is a little hard to see why he was so wretched in Bombay, but 'I have taken quite a dislike to the place in which I cannot perceive one single inducement for a European to choose it for a residence.' He had hoped to live on £100 a year himself and send £300 home to his family, but found that the style in which he would have to live and the number of servants he would have to employ would make his own outgoings nearer to £300. (It was a perennial complaint of the British in India that each class of servant had his speciality – cooking, sweeping, water-bearing, care of the horse, etc. – and that none would perform anything but his own function.) He was thinking of moving to the British Hotel for the monsoon, having reckoned that this would cost him Rs.217 or £21.14s all found per month, but shortly after that his wife seems to have announced her intention of coming out, for we find him writing: 'If you join me here we will with God's mercy continue to live in a snug quiet way and who knows that at the end of 3 years my prospects may be brighter than ever they were – cheer up again, I say.'

Mrs Terry seems in fact to have been of a more optimistic temperament than her husband. At any rate she liked the home he had provided for her. It was at Tardeo, a low-lying locality (it means 'palm god') between the more select districts of Byculla to the east and Malabar–Kamballa Hill on the west, just south of Bellasis Road and the Race Course. She writes to her eldest daughter, who had been left at boarding school in England: 'We have a sheltered walk up to the signal staff (kept by an old Irishman) at the back of our house [on Kamballa Hill] and have a view all round the Island and a fine sea breeze . . . The hill is all broken rocks and trunks of trees but the view is very pretty and I saw the races better there than one

199

day when I went in the carriage to the course.' She too complains of the cost of living: 'I wish I had laid in a stock of cheese at Malta as I meant to have done – bacon 1 shilling and 6 pence a pound, olives 2 shillings a bottle, we never get fruit or vegetables except when we have company, potatoes very dear. Rice and curry for ever, indeed I believe they currie all the old shoes.' A worse idea presently occurred to her: 'We have just had our Tiffin of Marrow bones and they were such large, clean bones that I began to fear I had been eating the Marrow out of some old Parsee's legs' – the house was not far from the Towers of Silence. However, she also noted that their cook made 'first rate jellies and pastry' with the most primitive kitchen equipment.

In the hot season water too posed problems, as the well in their garden threatened to run dry, but the coming of the monsoon in June finds her writing, 'The whole face of the country is covered with a lovely carpet of grass just like the meadows at Richmond, and I still like Bombay better than any place I was ever in. Not so yr Papa, he detests it.' A little later she reports, 'All the trees have grown so'. In their own garden they had dates, coconuts, guavas, 'Beetlenut' and mangoes. 'There are 8 or 9 different creeping plants now twining themselves from Tree to Tree, crossing up and down and across so that they form a complete jungle.' Hyenas penetrated this jungle at night, and killed some of the ducks she was trying to rear there. She had plans to plant a vegetable garden, but had difficulty in getting the seeds. A few months later she had made friends with one of the directors of the newly-established Botanical Gardens, which were on the eastern shore at Sewri, 'The Garden of Shiva', not far from Parel. (Since 1866 Shiva's Garden, with a fine assortment of exotic trees, has been the main Christian cemetery of Bombay, not unsuitably so when you consider Shiva's rôle as the Destroyer. Today it is an oasis guarded by an elderly watchman of military bearing, against the proliferating shanties that now cover the district and its once-genteel bungalows of the 1920s and 30s: the shacks even swarm up a steep hill and over the site of an eighteenth-century fort.)

Later again, when the lease of the Tardeo bungalow expired, the Terry family moved to another one which seems to have been towards the eastern side of the Island.

> At the back we look out on the Sea and the most lovely lofty
> Mountains on the other side of the water. The boats glide by
> with their Lateen Sails on the blue water, and the elegant tall
> Trees of the Coconut and Beetle bend backwards and forwards

over the wide-spreading and beautiful flowering Trees below . . . I do admire Bombay, all but the people – that is, the lazy cold proud English. No wonder they get sick when they lounge about all day with about 20 servants to wait on them.

The Terrys did not have the means to compete in the formal, ostentatious society of Bombay, and Sidney Terry probably had little desire or aptitude for socialising anyway: Mrs Terry complains several times in her letters to her daughter or to her sister, of the dullness and narrowness of her life.* But, unlike her husband, she was disposed to make the best of things, and at least managed, in the new house, to infect him with her own interest in gardens. Having nursed him through a near-fatal attack of cholera, she had convinced him of the need for outdoor exercise, the great Victorian palliative: we hear of him having the three younger children (ages then ranging from three to nine) organised into 'carrying mud and water. Yr Papa sends them over the wall to bring baskets of earth on their heads.' By February 1847 she was writing: 'Yr Papa is not yet tired of the Garden, he is always at work, such an old dirty figure, cutting and digging, and sowing and planting . . . Yr Papa is happier here . . . he has employment for his mind and is always poring over Botanical books.' Alas, less than a year later he was dead; the fortune he had come to Bombay hoping to make remained unmade. The city of gold claimed him. Like so many others before them who had staked everything on the Indian lottery and had lost, his widow and children sailed for Home, never to return.

The one consolation in this tragedy was that the children

---

* There was, however, the occasional scandal to break the monotony. One letter (not to her daughter!) contains the following: 'Sidney has reminded me that I have forgotten to tell you that your friend Mr Roussac who lives here was found asleep on the Sofa with a Mrs Leggatt. Mr Leggatt is a very respectable man; when he found them he got two Constables to seize Roussac who ran off, they chased him all round the Fort and when they caught him Mr L. gave him a good thrashing. Mr L. who has been married to his wife 15 years and has 6 children offered his wife, to whom he is devotedly attached, 2 Hundred a year to go off to England, but she will not and is living with Roussac. She had a kind husband, plenty of money, nice house, carriage and every comfort, her husband most kind and generous, yet she has forfeited all and left 6 dear children, poor Mr L. is quite broken hearted. Roussac is very poor and can hardly support himself.'

Roussac also crops up in the local Press of the period, championing a cabin boy who had been excessively flogged by a ship's captain within Bombay harbour. He seems to have been a Byronic figure.

would be reunited with their elder sister: Mrs Terry had previously written to her sister of her own distress at being parted for so long from this girl: 'She says she is quite well, and never mentions wishing to come here, but often when she writes of Mary I see where her tears have fallen on the letter. She can never feel that love for the children that they have for each other.' The smallest, Freddy, knowing his elder sister only from a picture, used to call her 'the girl behind the glass'. Exile and separation – an endlessly repeated but usually silent minor tragedy of the Anglo-Indian experience – was every bit as heart-rending in its way as the more dramatic fact of mortality. Mrs Terry had also written wistfully to her sister, who was married and settled in Egypt, wishing that she too could see their parents, then wintering in Egypt: 'Do send them on to peep at us, it is now nothing more to come to Bombay than it was to go to Ramsgate or Margate . . . except the money.' But although the great speed-up of travel in the preceding twenty years must have made this seem relatively true, she was of course exaggerating. Not for more than another hundred years would jet planes turn India into a place to which a brief trip could be envisaged.

Mrs Terry's interest in gardening and appreciation of nature and scenery in general forms part of another Bombay pattern, which stretches from da Orta and his 'delicate garden', through the mulberry trees planted in the compounds of the early-eighteenth-century houses in the Fort, to James Forbes's *Oriental Memoirs* which are illustrated with his own exquisite paintings of trees, flowers and birds, and so on onto the nineteenth century with its influx of 'botanising' visitors. In general, people with a well-developed visual sense were charmed by Bombay, even in its more backward and barbarous days, whereas those without found little compensation for the humid, insect-ridden climate. Lady West would have enjoyed Bombay more had she possessed the sketching ability of the later First Lady, Amelia Lady Falkland. Lady Falkland used to set up her easel wherever she went, to the bemused interest of native onlookers, since – 'without going far from home, there was so much to look at and admire, that I was amused with almost everything I saw'. She derived an artist's pleasure from the flowering trees and lotus-blossom-covered tank of the gardens at Parel – 'the beauty of the whole scene being enhanced by the brilliant coloured turbans worn by the native servants'. She has also left us one of the best word-pictures of the arrival of the famous late-afternoon breeze, which comes off the western (Arabian) sea even in the hottest months of the year:

Our windows [at Parel] look over what are called 'the flats' – a plain, which in the monsoon is converted into rice-fields, but is now brown, dried up and full of stubble. Beyond these flats is an extensive wood of palms [somewhere among this was hidden the Terrys' small house] which reaches as far as the seashore . . . About 5 o'clock we see the tops of those fine trees gently agitated, and we will know the breeze will not long tarry . . . At last it enters the apartment, and becoming each moment stronger, often makes the pendant drops of the chandeliers tremble . . .

The evening breeze still blows from the western sea, across Tardeo and Byculla to Parel, but today it blows over packed streets, high buildings, bazaars, mills and industrial tenements. You would seek in vain in Tardeo today for the Terrys' bungalow with its entwining creepers. The first mill in Bombay was opened near there in 1857: it is still there, somewhat altered. Many others by and by joined it, streaming up from Byculla towards Parel, changing for ever the face of the Island which so many generations of incomers had found, with all its disadvantages, so beautiful. As Indians say, 'land and houses have their own destiny'. Parel House still stands, a rare survivor of time and chance, but its surroundings are changed beyond any recognition. Some of the ancient trees survive in what remains of the garden, but their branches spread over an assortment of utilitarian twentieth-century buildings. The tank covered in lotus blossom is as distant a memory as the view across the Flats. Already, by the 1860s the house was beginning to seem ill-placed for a Governor's residence: after 1882, when Lady Fergusson died there of cholera, it was used no more. It stood empty for some years, as haunted and shunned as the Belvedere had been in an earlier generation. In 1896, during the outbreak of plague in Bombay, it became a plague-laboratory, which it remains to this day.

The year (1853) that Lady Falkland left Bombay was the year that the railway there was opened – the first ever built east of Suez. The first engine was indeed called *The Falkland*, and for the past twelve months crowds of interested Bombay inhabitants had gathered daily on the Flats to watch this new monster shunting. Lady Falkland perceived what the railway might mean in terms of great physical changes to come: 'A very handsome new temple had been commenced before the railroad was contemplated, actually contiguous to the station [at Byculla] and was on the verge of completion when the latter was opened. A railway station and a Hindu temple in juxtaposition – the work of the rulers and the ruled.' She and her husband took a trip on the train the day before its official opening: 'As we rushed along, on our return to Parell, on the occasion of the excursion . . . the palms appeared more majestic than usual, and to look down upon us with contempt and disgust, while the monster of an engine sent forth an unearthly, protracted yell as it tore over the flats of Bombay, where after sunset the jackals had for so long held undisputed sway.'

On that note, her description of the place, like her sojourn there, ends.

VIII *Engines of Change*

The 1850s brought the first cotton mill to Bombay and the first railway line, but the vast transformation that these two agents of change were to bring about did not occur in that decade. The fifties were, rather, the last period of semi-rurality in Bombay, the ending there of the pre-industrial world which had ended in England a generation or more earlier. By then, much English landscape had been transformed for ever by industry, a network of railways had superseded for ever the old, slow lines of communication and the ways that went with them, and London had welled up and spilt over in a brick-and-stucco flood that spread instant urbanisation farther and farther into the fields. But a traveller arriving in Bombay in the 1850s would have seen substantially the same kind of place as his counterpart in the 1750s: the walled town with its high wooden houses, the relatively compact harbour, the expanse of the Esplanade stretching empty to Back Bay, Mazagaon Point extending into the sea with its own separate harbour and Portuguese township. (A writer in the *Asiatic Journal* in 1830 described the latter as 'dirty, and swarming with pigs'.) The native town had crept considerably further north and west across the reclaimed Flats since the mid-eighteenth century, creating new districts at Khetwadi, Kamathipura and Dhobi Talao (the Washerman's Tank, just north of the Esplanade). The coconut and mango groves of Girgaum extending up Back Bay were heavily sprinkled with small houses, there were the new, grand houses at Byculla and four on Malabar Hill, but essentially the landscape of nature was still intact: the 'buried countryside' was not yet buried, merely tamed and populated. The numerous wooded and rocky hillocks such as

205

Narowji Hill had not yet been levelled and used to fill in the marshy hollows, the eastern shoreline had not yet been altered out of all recognition and corseted in docks. Most important of all, the Island authorities had not yet embarked on that great chapter of coastal reclamation which was to increase the area of the place by one-third between 1860 and 1950.

The Fort of the 1850s was still a complete city of the old world, rather than the specialised business-centre of a much larger metropolis which it had become a generation later. Parsi Bazaar Street and Borah Bazaar Street were still genuine bazaars, and there were several other markets including one built on purpose in the early 1800s by Governor Duncan in his ex-stable. There was a notoriously dirty and noisy slaughter house at Bori Bunder, only just outside the walls, and dyers laid their beautiful but equally stinking products to dry not far off among the wells of the Esplanade. Not till the later decades of the nineteenth century were these nuisances removed – to pollute ex-garden-suburbs further out. We have seen that most of the European population, and the wealthier native merchants, had moved their families to suburban properties, yet to describe these out-of-town quarters by that term is itself misleading, for there were as yet no paved roads there, let alone other amenities such as piped water or drains. The Fort itself had only well-water till the 1860s, when the first pure – or supposedly pure – water began to be piped thence from Vehar Lake, on the mainland. The history of Bombay's water supply, up to and including today, is the history of perpetual works undertaken to provide further supplies which by the time they arrive, never prove adequate to the perpetually increasing demand.

Both in the Fort and outside it there was no public lighting whatsoever till 1843, and ten years later there were still only fifty street lamps in the whole of the Island. There was no proper police force (police in England were introduced during the 1830's) and naturally the Esplanade and the road to the Breach were unsafe for travellers at night as the way from London to Hampstead had been unsafe a generation earlier. Sir Dinshaw Wacha, who was born into a comfortably-off Parsi family living in the Fort in 1845, could just remember the 'highwaymen . . . carrying on their nightly raids with impunity'. He recalled in his old age: 'Each house with a verandah in the Fort, in Khetwady, Chandanwady and Girgaum had a lantern with a lamp hung. The doors and windows of the ground floor of the houses were fast locked and bolted after dark and the well-to-do kept Ramosis of the old village watchman type to guard their premises at night.' Nor were native robbers the only problem. The Fort used to be the scene of regular drunken brawls between the East India Company soldiers, who were mostly Eurasians and had barracks adjoining Fort St George, sailors of all nationalities, and the Parsi liquor-sellers who stood to lose most in the disturbance.

Another trouble-spot was the neighbourhood of Sonapur, off Girgaum Road, where a cluster of taverns kept by Parsis and Portuguese attracted what Wacha refers to as 'soldiers and sailors and low-class clerks and others of the same kidney'. He adds primly that the district was 'in many ways disreputable by reason of the vulgar venuses of the locality who were there to be seen angling'. No doubt he knew better what he was talking about than Stocqueler, who, in 1854, wrote improbably: 'in our Oriental cities there are none of those lures and haunts which prove so attractive and fatal to the young Londoner . . . such scenes of debauchery as there are . . . are of the very lowest description . . .' And therefore, by implication, not attractive to a clean-limbed young English lad. Well into the twentieth century a lane in Girgaum still went under the name Bawankhani – 'Women's dwelling', i.e. prostitutes' building. In 1882 a French traveller, Louis Rousselet, recorded:

> Girgaum, the Bréda Street of Bombay, is a vast wood of coconut trees, which extend from the bazaars to Chowpatti, at the head of Back Bay. In the midst of this picturesque forest are innumerable huts, half concealed by a rich tropical vegetation, in which reside bayadières of every nation, and of all colours – the demi-monde of this immense capital . . . The refreshment rooms in the taverns are thronged with Europeans, Malays, Arabs and Chinese. Far into the night will the songs resound, and the lamps shed their light; then, when the morning is come, all will return to gloom.

But I think Rousselet's colourful information may have been out of date, for over twenty years earlier (in 1860) the *Bombay Times* could write:

> On the whole of that district lying between the sea and Girgaum Back Road, building operations have been in active progress for some years past, but have within the last two years been pushed on with unprecedented rapidity. Houses are rising in all directions, and what was some few years ago merely a coconut plantation, will, within the next half century, be as thoroughly urban as Mandvi and Khara Talao.

There is in any case documentary evidence that by the last quarter of the century, if not considerably before, Bombay's red-light district had moved to Kamathipura (Camateepoora), conveniently situated at the northern extremity of the bazaars and close, but not too close, to the polite residential area of Byculla. The Contagious Diseases Act of 1868, by making medical examination of prostitutes mandatory in an attempt to protect the British Army from the increasing ravages of venereal disease, had in effect legitimised prostitution; the move was passionately opposed by Bombay's assorted missionaries. A visiting one from England, Alfred Dyer, toured Kamathipura in 1887, and wrote an impassioned description for the London mission paper *The Sentinel* of houses with 'the ground floor open to the road, like native shops. In these lower as well as in the upper rooms were native women calling to the male passers-by of various nationalities . . . this is one of the sights of the city to natives'. (Today Kamathipura is till a sight for the same reason and is unchanged in style. It is bounded by Bellasis Road (Jehangir Boman Behram Maarg) on the north and by Grant Road on the south, and its main cross-thoroughfare is Falkland Road, a piece of town-planning of the late 1860s. I like to think that that good lady, who was once and for quite other reasons known as 'the Vice-Queen of Bombay', and who was herself the illegitimate daughter of a courtesan, would be amused rather than angry at the associations her name now carries.)

To return to the Fort of the 1850s: it was 'sleepy' in aspect compared with the way it would be ten years later during the Cotton Mania or thirty years later when Bombay had risen to the status of a great international city, but it was, compared wtih many smaller western India towns whose ancient trades were stagnating at that period, a lively place. Business was flourishing. In 1836, after the removal of all the Company's monopolies, the Bombay Chamber of Commerce had been founded by one of Bombay's many Scottish traders, John Skinner of the firm of that name: he was a cousin to the Colonel James Skinner, son of a Rajput lady, who founded Skinner's Horse. Other firms among the dozen or so founder members of the Chamber were William Nichol and Co., Ritchie Stewart (it will be remembered that the Stewarts were close friends of the Wests a decade before) and Higginson and Cardwell who were to employ the luckless Sidney Terry. Among the three original native firms was that of Dadabhoy Pestonji Wadia; more than ten years were to elapse before his fortunes went into decline following the fire at his house in Cowasji Patel Street. He himself was to die in relative poverty in 1885, in a modest house in Khetwadi, but the new house he built for himself in Cowasji Patel Street on the place of the old one was the headquarters of the Chamber of Commerce for the rest of the century. Most of the firms who founded the Chamber were relative newcomers to Bombay, and until the 1860s the 'big four' old-established houses – Forbes, Remington who occupied an old house in Marine Street next to Hornby House, Leckie and Shotton – held aloof. Their attitude may have had something to do with the fact that the Chamber openly supported Britain in her determination to continue the opium trade with China; lip-service was paid to the idea that traders should diversify into other commodities 'to prevent our commercial prosperity from being, in so large a degree, dependent on an article self-confessedly subject to greater fluctuations than ever' (i.e. it was theoretically then an illegal trade). But in practice the proportion of the trade in opium out of the total value of exports from Bombay increased in the 1840s and 50s from one-third to almost one-half.

On the credit side, the Chamber of Commerce pressed effectively for more docking facilities in place of the old Bunder boats, better pilot boats, and better charts of the harbour. They got the Sailors' Home started, as a registry for discharged seamen who were otherwise at the mercy of waterfront sharks, and finally, after much nagging, got the overland mail service to England running twice a month rather than once. (This was in the 1850s when, to send a letter across India to Calcutta, you still had to employ a *dak* – relay – of private runners as in the preceding century.) In 1844 they had all the paraphernalia of the Cotton Green, the bales, the weighing machines, the noisy cotton screws (presses) etc., moved from the Green by the Town Hall to a new Green on Colaba. Their reasoning was that the presence of the actual commodity caused a nuisance in what was becoming a modern business centre; true to nineteenth-century capitalist trends, they wanted the means of production out of sight from the windows of the counting house, and Colaba was thought to be convenient for ships. Although Skinner himself had been a leading member of the Bombay Steam Company, the railway which was, within a couple of decades, to have such far-reaching effect on the development of the cotton trade, was not yet envisaged.

John Skinner and Dadabhoy Pestonji were also two of the main promoters of the Bank of Bombay; it was set up in 1841 in spite of opposition from the Bank of Calcutta, which already began to see in Bombay a formidable rival. The scheme may have been less than popular also with local private bankers, such as Forbes and Remingtons. The chartered Mercantile Bank, the Oriental Bank and the Commercial Bank followed in the fifties; these were promoted by Indians – the Cama family were largely responsible for the Mercantile Bank – but they were run on European principles and in a European style: the days of the *babhu* clerks squatting on their haunches writing on long strips of paper, while their master sat back on floor cushions with the hookah to hand, were passing. Stone buildings were beginning to multiply in the Fort, replacing and over-topping the fretworked wooden ones: some of them looked like the semi-italianate blocks then rising in European cities, in London, Manchester, Glasgow, Paris and, for that matter, New York, but the stone most readily available in Bombay was not of the same quality as that normally used in Europe. It was Porebunder stone, brought by ship from Gujerat; it was soft and easy to carve, but it was flakey and a few years' monsoons eroded it and destroyed cornices and other decorative detail, dispersing stone particles into the already heavy city air. Because of this, twenty years later when grand neo-Gothic buildings were going up on the verge of the Esplanade and in Byculla, durable stone or terracotta dressings for these were sometimes imported from the other side of the world, thus putting the final touch to Bombay's appearance of having been brought piecemeal to India from several different European countries.

Much of the mid-nineteenth-century Fort is still intact today. As you walk round it, particularly at night when the narrow streets are empty of traffic and the large and terrible Bombay rats frisk in and out of the sewers through crumbling drain-heads, it is not hard to believe that you are actually walking round a central district of London – the City or Holborn or Seven Dials, perhaps – in the time of Dickens. Here are the handcarts stacked on the pavements, and a few dilapidated victorias parked near the Church with their drivers asleep on the leather cushions. Here are the great porticoed buildings that are the symbol of the power and prestige of money, and here the beggars and the homeless lie in wrapped sleep on the very granite steps. Here is India's present, and Britain's past.

(Sensitive Indians, embarrassed by the visible presence of such patent poverty and deprivation, in this, one of the most prosperous cities in India, often seem to imagine that the vast social and financial differences within their society are some special Third World blight or, more specifically, a function of the caste system. They might take a different and less fatalistic view of the matter if they were to realise that Indian cities just exemplify, in many respects, an industrialised society at an earlier stage of development than that of the West. It is a nineteenth-century-style poverty that Bombay suffers, and a nineteenth-century-style prosperity that benefits it, in spite of its own convictions of modernity.)

In the 1850s, the north of the Fort was still largely occupied by Parsi merchants as it had been when Burnell had described the place 150 years earlier. Their residential migration to the wooded and airy heights of Malabar Hill did not begin till the 1860s. Nearby, in Bazaargate Street (erstwhile Parsi Bazaar Street) and parallel to it in Old Mody Street, were the wealthy Hindu Banians and Bhatias such as Goculdas Tejpal; his father had come to Bombay from Kutch (Gujerat) as a pedlar earlier in the century and he was himself to make his fortune in cotton and endow a hospital on the far edge of the Esplanade. (Today the hospital, virtually bankrupt, has been demolished and part of its site has been sold to finance the construction of a new hospital.) The Tyebjee family, rich Borahs, also lived in Old Mody Street, and so did another Borah family who had done very well in the China trade, the Nooroodins. A street or two further south lived other Moslems, but, whereas the Gujerati-speaking Borahs are Shi'at Moslems, these, like the Urdu-speaking Konkanis and most of the rest of Bombay's Moslems, were Sunnis. Dinshaw Wacha remarks that these Fort Moslems, of Arab origin, were 'mostly horse dealers, but of a highly respectable and wealthy class'. Presumably they were the proprietors of the famous Arab stables in the Bhendi Bazaar in the heart of the native town. The south Fort was still mainly occupied, as ever, by European firms, with the significant addition of the Sassoons, who had houses in Military Square, near Forbes's old house, and also in Tamarind Lane.

The Sassoon family were, in several respects, the archetypal family of nineteenth-century Bombay. Arriving in 1833, the very year when immigration was finally freed of all East India Company restraints, they were able to exploit the city and the international opportunities it offered to their own advantage, and at the same time to do much for the place. Their career, and that of several other Sephardi Jewish families who arrived in Bombay or Calcutta at the same period, is analogous to that of the Parsis at a rather earlier date, but in the boom-atmosphere of nineteenth-century capitalism they rose to their peak more rapidly.

The patriarch of the Sassoons, and ancestor of all the present-day branches of the family in Europe and America, was David

Sassoon, who was born in Baghdad in 1792. He came from a long line of 'Nasis', Jewish community leaders and chief bankers to the successive rulers of Mesopotamia (modern Iraq): there had been a sizeable colony of Jews in Baghdad ever since the twelfth century. By the early nineteenth century this community were coming under pressure from the Turks, the current overlords, and were turning their eyes eastwards, attracted by accounts of the religious tolerance and trading opportunities available in British India. (This fact should not be forgotten, wherever imperialism is discussed today in contemptuous terms.) In the course of a family and political feud, David escaped to Persia with his wife, his sons and a very small proportion of the family wealth. A few years later he achieved his objective and settled in Bombay, where, a fortune-teller had told him, immense riches awaited him. There was already a handful of Sephardi Jews there, Arab-speaking merchants from Syria, who had come around the beginning of the century, and also a few other Persian-speaking Baghdadis like himself, but all were living in relative poverty and obscurity, their synagogue a makeshift shack.

David Sassoon set up his modest counting house and carpet go-down in Bombay at exactly the right moment, but it must have been his personality and his business acumen that led him so rapidly to success. He is said to have been a quiet, almost austere man to meet, who 'played his cards close to his chest'. In choosing trading commodities he tended to follow where others had already led; he was not a pioneer, but once he had decided to take up a certain line pursued it more enterprisingly than the Parsis, who were essentially middlemen. He was, in mercantile terms, an empire-builder. He bought up wharfages to ensure the smooth transit of his goods, and would finance other merchants with loans in return for their goods at preferential prices or buy up ailing businesses and revitalise them. By the end of the fifties, only twenty-five years after his arrival in Bombay, a contemporary could write: 'silver and gold, silks, gums and spices, opium and cotton, wool and wheat – whatever moves over sea or land feels the hand or bears the mark of Sassoon and Co.'. He had eight sons, by two successive wives, and as they grew up he settled them in various key trading places on the China coast and elsewhere: the use he made of these sons was, Sir Jamshetji Jeejeebhoy once remarked enviously, the chief cause of his success. (The Jeejeebhoy progeny was less wholly compliant.) But Britain was by then the world's major trading and manufacturing nation, and it was inevitable that it should act in time as a draw for some of these sons and their families. David himself was naturalised British in 1853, though he did not speak English. Contemporary photographs show him as an eastern potentate figure, complete with turban and Persian dress, but after the Bengal Uprising he allowed his sons to adopt the dress of the English gentleman. The eldest, Abdullah, liked to be called 'Albert' in later life and eventually settled in London where he became Sir Albert Sassoon, First Baronet of Kensington Gore. (He was a crony of the future Edward VII, and had named one of his sons Edward. The Sassoons, like the Rothschilds with whom they intermarried, formed natural members of the new *haute société* of money of the late nineteenth century.) He had not neglected Bombay, however. Albert's was the generation of Sassoons who established spinning and weaving mills there, and he was the Sassoon who built the first wet dock in 1875 – the Sassoon fish dock half-way down Colaba, whose distinctive smell announces its presence to this day.

The Sassoons, like their wealthy Parsi counterparts, were also charitably-minded. A synagogue in the Fort, another at Byculla (both still standing), schools, a Boys' Reformatory, a Mechanics' Institute, endowments to hospitals, a convalescent home in Poona – these were just some of the gifts that David Sassoon or his sons made to Bombay. But whereas Sir Jamshetji Jeejeebhoy seemed bent on copying right-thinking British munificence (he actually subscribed money to the relief fund set up in Lancashire at the time when Bombay was making its fortune during the Cotton Mania of the American Civil War!) the Sassoons were more conscious of their place as leaders of their own community. Perhaps their most important long-term effect on Bombay, and on the west of India generally, is that they gave a sense of corporate awareness to other Jews who, had been on the point of being swallowed by India.

There had been Jews in India when the British first came there, probably immigrants from the Babylonian diaspora, but they had all but lost sight of their own Jewishness. Accounts of them first began to filter out of India, via European travellers, in the eighteenth century. They were in two groups, the Beni Israel ('Children of Israel') who had settled in the Konkan just south of Bombay, and the 'Black Jews' of Cochin in what is now Kerala. Individuals from the two groups, each of whom had been in ignorance of the other's existence, first confronted each other at the end of the eighteenth century through immigration to Bombay, but after initial hostilities they tended to merge and absorb each other's myths of origin. Isolated in India for centuries, both groups had intermarried a good deal with their Indian hosts, and had adopted local languages,

Hindu dress and the Hindu concept of caste, but they had maintained certain dietary laws, a vestigial awareness of the major Jewish festivals and (like the Moslems) the practice of circumcision. The Beni Israels were mostly oil-pressers by trade, and were called by their neighbours the *Shanwar Telis*, 'the Saturday oil men', because their day of rest was Saturday. A number of them were recruited into the East Indian Army, and a few became officers, including Ezekiel Direkar who founded the first Bombay synagogue in 1796. Its name, the Gate of Mercy Synagogue, still survives, but the building to which it is attached in Israel Mohulla, in the heart of the bazaars, is about forty years younger. At the time that it was rebuilt, in the 1830s, a breakaway group built themselves another, more orthodox synagogue, just round the corner. Both buildings survive today, each with its own tiny, mainly elderly, congregation, Torah scrolls, phylacteries and prayer shawls, just as in Brooklyn or Golders Green.

It was the coming of the Sephardi Jews from Baghdad and elsewhere in the Middle East in the 1830s and 40s that served to raise local Jewish consciousness. The Sassoons founded schools and charities to assist their indianised brethren, and the more enterprising among these patronised brethren responded by emulating Sephardi Jewish ways and changing their Mahratti surnames to more classically Jewish ones. It was largely through the Sephardi Jews, so much more cosmopolitan than the Beni Israels and the Black Jews, that information about the early Zionist movement became disseminated in India, but whereas families like the Sassoons, the Ezras and the Judahs were, by the end of the nineteenth century, too wealthy and too well-established in a European hierarchy to want to uproot themselves and start life again in barren Palestine, the Indian Jews took to Zionism with enthusiasm. Today, because of emigration to Israel, the Jews of Cochin are a dying community, indeed almost extinguished; and though Bombay remains the last major centre of organised Jewish life in India, numbers have declined greatly there also. The Sephardis who animated it have largely disappeared, and of the Sassoons nothing remains but their name, attached to a dock and to public institutions. David Sassoon's old house, 'Sans Souci' at Byculla, is today the Massina Hospital, but it still looks like a private mansion standing in its own gardens, and inside, the double staircase in carved oak which was imported from England is still intact. It is one of the last surviving grand houses in that now densely-populated district.

In 1864, the year when David Sassoon died at his country house in Poona, the walls of Bombay were at last pulled down. People had been complaining for decades that these fortifications, ravelins, outer gates, inner gates and all, had outlived their usefulness, that it was inconvenient having to raise the gatekeeper late at night, and that the moat bred mosquitoes and 'a foul miasma'. In 1841 a letter to the *Times* scolded:

> The maintenance of the Fort of Bombay is not only useless, it has become a downright and 'most serious nuisance to the inhabitants at large. It is a source of ridiculous waste of money to Government itself: witness, the erection, not yet completed, of a gate at the cost of Rs.30,000, to block up the way to the Church. The Fort is a costly and filthy nuisance.

(The letter writer might have been less positive had he foreseen what expensive buildings the Government would eventually find itself financing on the land freed by the walls' clearance.) Not everyone took the same view, however. As late as 1859 we find Murray, author of *Handbook to India* (first edition), declaring: 'Bombay is at present weak against invasion'. He takes comfort from the fact that 'the ditch is deep at Fort George, and would therefore be a formidable obstacle to an enemy', but spends some time enumerating other points where the walls, in his view, required strengthening. One may well wonder what pike-and halberd enemy he had in mind, in an era when the railway line was already laid from a new station at Bori Bunder, to Byculla and Thana, and was on its way up the Western Ghauts to Poona, and when in any case greater Bombay was far outgrowing the old city within the walls. The answer would probably be that the Bengal Uprising had taken place two years earlier, and that its primitive barbarities were leading some British subjects to think in terms of primitive forms of defence. But in practice the Uprising itself marked the end of an era, and, in retrospect, it seems to have receded rapidly into the past, as if driven there by the network of telegraph and railway lines which, within a few years, were spreading themselves throughout India.

At all events the walls of Bombay were torn down in 1864. The Cotton Mania was at its height in the city, and all kinds of grandiose schemes were afoot, but I believe that the walls' demolition that year really had less to do with local events than with that informal, international communications-system which makes cities all over the world go in for similar transformations at the same period. In the very same year Vienna, too, lost her ancient walls, and Paris was in the throes of Haussmann redevelopment. In a more piecemeal way, British cities too were in full evolution. In London in 1863-4 turnpikes were being demolished, Charing Cross and Blackfriars stations were being built, including the bridge across Ludgate Hill, and St Pancras was being planned. The Thames Embankment was under construction, and the new museum complex in South Kensington was on the drawing-board: so were the National Gallery, the Law Courts and Holborn Viaduct. Liverpool was redeveloping; a new Gothic Assize Court opened in Manchester; a Town Hall to match was planned, and an Exchange of similar grandeur was inaugurated in Birmingham. These were the forerunners of the great piles that would go up on the Esplanade of Bombay in the 1870s, but the traffic in styles, even in the 60s, was not all one-way. Halifax acquired a new Town Hall with 'Moorish' arches, though with a French-chateau roof and spires. It is customary to attribute the works that were either planned or actually put in hand in Bombay in the years 1862-7 to a financial boom and an enterprising if extravagant Governor, Sir Bartle Frere, but I think that Bombay, given the size it had by then reached, was, rather, following an inevitable evolution that was determined by factors beyond its own immediate, local history.

No account of nineteenth-century development in India can leave out entirely the Bengal Uprising, the traumatic events of May, June and July 1857, that have been known rather inaccurately to generations of British schoolchildren as the Indian Mutiny, and even more inaccurately to present-day Indian schoolchildren as the First War of Independence. But the most significant point about the Uprising, as far as Bombay was concerned, is that it did indeed take place in Bengal, on the far side of India, and did not effectively touch Bombay at all. With historical retrospect, this hardly seems surprising. Those who trade are notoriously unmoved by nationalistic or political ideologies, and the huge native mercantile community of Bombay had nothing to gain from dislodging the British, whose interests on the whole coincided with their own. Such riots as occasionally shook the shopkeeping peace almost invariably occurred between one native faction and another – Parsis versus Moslems, or Moslems versus Hindus. During the Uprising the Parsis of Bombay sent a message of loyalty to the Government, and the Sassoon family went one better, as usual, in offering to assemble a Jewish battalion to fight Mutineers. Bombay was as different as possible from the small British military station where an isolated force of British lived alongside a relatively large number of

216

native troops, and where there were the equivocal figures of native princes to be taken into account. Indeed so different was the atmosphere of Bombay in May 1857 from that of Bengal, that the local newspapers were inclined to play down the first rumours of 'insubordination' among Sepoys in the east, and such was the slow rate of cross-country communication in those day that by the time harder news was received the whole affair was substantially over. In early August a paragraph in the *Bombay Gazette* which appears to refer to the danger of an uprising turns out to be on a far more parochial matter:

> Our worthy Deputy Commissioner of Police is always ready to 'put down' anything troublesome to the public, and we feel assured that it is only necessary to bring to his notice the annoyance met with after dusk, in the native town, from numberless herds of cows and bullocks traversing the streets in quest of fodder, to ensure the suppression of the nuisance . . .

The admiring reference to the Deputy Commissioner of Police is, however, significant, for this personage (later Commissioner of Police) was to become the key figure in a post-Mutiny myth about how Bombay was saved in the nick of time from the horrors suffered at Delhi, Lucknow and Cawnpore. He was Charles Forjett, the Eurasian whose career is briefly mentioned in Chapter V. He appears in Dinshaw Wacha's reminiscences as 'a stout, sun-burnt complexioned officer, who was always seen sitting square and tight in his saddle'. Wacha praised Forjett's 'fearless courage, unique detective faculty and wealth of resources' which is a reference to the uncovering of a supposed plot. The police force had only been re-formed on the British model three years before; few Europeans were employed in it, and Forjett was understandably keen to make his mark. With a natural taste and aptitude for detective work, and a conviction that his role was 'to crush evil in the bud', he ensured that summer, in his own words, that '*every* scoundrel in the town was closely watched and kept in a state of terror. When, on my rounds at night in disguise, I found anybody speaking of the successes of the rebels [in Bengal] in anything like a tone of exultation, I seized him on the spot. A whistle brought up three or four policemen who, too, followed in disguise, and the person or persons were at once bound and walked off to prison.' (Charles Forjett, *Our Real Danger in India*)

These brutal tactics were, not surprisingly, successful in persuading the Moslem community, who were traditionally considered the most 'unstable', to declare themselves loyal to Britain, particularly when Forjett held a special meeting to warn them that any unrest would be dealt with 'without the trammels of the law'. The *Gazetteer* of 1909 recounts in rousing terms his subsequent discovery of a Hindu plot to raise the native town during the festival of Diwali in October; though nothing had actually occurred, true to his word Forjett had the alleged ring-leaders blown from cannon on the Esplanade. 'The Diwali passed off quietly, and thus by the prescience of the Superintendent of Police, Bombay was saved from the horrors of mutiny.'

Taking a longer view, there would appear to be little evidence that a serious plot existed. The public certainly heard nothing about it all till the very afternoon in November when the grisly execution on the Esplanade was carried out. The one open riot during the preceding month involving sepoys, was triggered by nothing more significant than a drunken Christian sepoy knocking over a Hindu idol that was being carried in a procession. However, the theory that the true rôle of the British in India was that of stern (and Christian) watchdog, ever alert to prevent the natives of India from indulging their natural propensities, was one that was gaining considerable popularity in some quarters, and inevitably the Uprising encouraged it. That year the editor of the *Bombay Times*, Dr George Buist, became eloquent and obsessional in print on the subject: '. . . the ingratitude and the cruelties which horrify humanity and put the cannibal to shame are plants of oriental growth which have always flourished in the East . . . the natives of India are incapable of combination for other purposes than those of mischief; they have no truth in them and no faith in each other'. Buist was a man of many qualities, a theologian, astronomer and botanist. He loved Bombay; he had been one of the people responsible for the creation of the Botanical Gardens at Sewri, and he also ran a reform school for boys there in ramshackle premises near his own house. However, the predominately native proprietors of the *Times* could hardly be expected to tolerate him as the newly intolerant spokesman of racism, and he was dismissed from the paper.

Forjett, too, was a man of loftier ideas than his rôle in 1857 may suggest. His career in Bombay reached its peak in the 1860s, when he was made Municipal Commissioner; he was the person responsible for turning the central part of the old Green into Elphinstone Circle, thus making an elegant hub for the otherwise unplanned Fort and retaining a part of Bombay's oldest open space. He christened this pleasant classical-italianate development after

Lord Elphinstone,* the previous Governor, who had befriended and advanced him; but though he received eulogies and extra presents of money on his retirement, the other honours for which he was said to have been hoping eluded him. Brooding on the injustice of this, he lived on in England till the age of eighty. His one published work, *Our Real Danger in India,* contains an eloquent plea for the abandonment of caste and race prejudice, for 'the blending of the races' and the social acceptance of the sons of this blending – 'The Indian sun will, of course, tan their skins, but it will not impede the development of the higher virtues of courage and intellect.'

During Diwali at the beginning of November 1858, a year after the two supposed conspirators had been blown from cannon on the Esplanade, the Queen's sovereignty over a large part of the Indian sub-continent was proclaimed in Bombay from the steps of the Town Hall, facing the old Green that was shortly to be transformed. The power of the John Company had become increasingly spectral in the preceding half-century, and the last wraith of it now faded away like the grin of the Cheshire cat. In reality, the removal of trading restrictions and monopolies meant that there was less good reason now for an Empire than there had been at the beginning of the century, but that fact seems to have been lost sight of in Britain's growing conviction of her celestial destiny. The news of Victoria's elevation seems to have been well-received in Bombay, where goddesses, Great White Mothers and the like were always looked on with favour, and where the previous two decades had got the population of all communities well prepared to welcome signs of ever-increasing Progress and exciting change. The first half of the 1860s was not to disappoint them.

In 1863 the Great Indian Peninsular Railway link between Bombay and the cotton-growing areas of the Deccan plateau was at last open. Raw cotton could thus be brought down readily to the new mills that were beginning to spring up to the north of the town, and Mahratta and Konkani mill-hands imported themselves also. A year later the other main line, the Bombay, Baroda and Central India, reached Ahmedabad in Gujerat, an old-established weaving centre that already had trading links with Bombay. The self-conscious catch-phrase of the time was 'Bombay has long been the Liverpool of the East -- she is now becoming the Manchester also'. But the

* A nephew of Mountstuart Elphinstone, who was Governor 1819-27.

Liverpool aspect of the city was being enhanced too, for a network of steamers was now plying up and down the west coast of India, and the building of the Suez Canal (it was to open in 1869) made it clear that Bombay's importance could only increase.

It is from this time onwards that two contradictory yet interrelated strains appear in commentaries on Bombay, whether memoirs, guide-book descriptions or governmental papers. On the one hand there is a note of pride, of burgeoning imperialist hubris combined with innocent romanticism (*urbs prima in Indis*, The Eye of India, Queen of the Isles, etc.). But this period also marks the beginning of the persistent complaints – of Bombay's noise, dirt, overcrowding and general unmanageability – which have not ceased to this day. British metropolitanism was, in the 1860s, 70s and 80s, imported into Bombay, complete with water pipes, gas pipes, paving authorities, sewage disposal authorities, tramlines, parks, apartment blocks both grand and squalid and every other amenity of western civilisation, but imported along with them was the typically British late-Victorian idea that there was something morally or aesthetically deplorable about the whole concept of a great city.

The Good figures of the Christo-British mental landscape were pastoral: shepherds and farmers, landed gentlemen; whereas Wickedness was traditionally associated by the British with cities, to a far greater extent than on the Continent. While continental planners were building formal urban vistas, their English counterparts were exciting themselves over the possibilities of mock-rural suburbia. Those would-be Europeans, such as the Jeejeebhoys, the Tatas and the Sassoons, who built themselves country-gentleman's mansions first in Bombay's outskirts and then in such country retreats as Poona, were simply following the established British custom of making use of the city while rejecting it as a habitat. But this rejection was alien to the more faithfully Indian businessmen. In the later nineteenth century, and well into the twentieth, the area of the native town immediately north of the Esplanade, particularly that between Abdul Rehman Street and Kalba Devi where the Jumna Musjid, the Cotton Exchange and the huge covered textile market are all situated, contained the large joint-family houses of Bombay citizens every bit as wealthy as their more anglicised fellows who had taken to the leafy heights of Malabar Hill.

Because of the Victorian ambiguity of thought about city-expansion, accounts of 'improvements' tend to be somewhat contradictory, depending on whether the writer is mourning a vanished rurality (the 'Paradise Lost' view) or extolling the merits of British industry and commerce. Moreover, works which were planned and put in hand for purely commercial reasons tend to be written about subsequently as if they had been instituted uniquely from a high-minded concern for public health and decency or a nebulous 'civic pride'. Foremost among these transforming improvements were the new Bombay docks, first envisaged in the 1840s, begun in the 60s and finally constructed all up the eastern shoreline in the 70s, 80s and 90s. They were built, of course, to deal with the enormously expanded trade of this new Manchester-cum-Liverpool which Bombay was becoming. But you would never guess it from this extract from Maclean's *Guide to Bombay* of 1902 – or guess that the reclamation and embanking work in Back Bay, on the other side of the Island, had been intimately associated with the need to bring the BBCI railway line down to the Cotton Green on Colaba:

> A traveller landing at Apollo Bundar thirty years ago would (with the single exception of a few thousand feet frontage at the Dockyard, Custom House and Castle) have found a foul and hideous foreshore from the Fort to Sewri on the east; from Apollo Bundar round Colaba and Back Bay to the west. All round the Island of Bombay was one foul cesspool, sewers discharging on the sands, rocks used only for the purposes of nature. To ride home to Malabar Hill along the sands of Back Bay was to encounter sights and odours too horrible to describe – to leap four several sewers, whose gaping mouths discharged deep black streams across your path – to be impeded as you neared Chowpatty by boats and nets and stacks of firewood, and to be choked by the fumes from the burning Ghaut and many an ancient and fishlike smell. To travel by rail from Boree Bunder to Byculla, or to go into Mody Bay, was to see in the foreshore the latrine of the whole population of the native town.

The general prosperity of Bombay by 1860 was such that it was inevitable that extensive municipal improvements should be taken in hand. The volume of her trade had increased very greatly in the last half-dozen years alone. For this reason, I think that too much emphasis should not be placed on the Cotton Mania (or Cotton Boom or Shares Mania as it is also called) of the early sixties as the prime 'cause' of Bombay's growth and change. Certainly this boom had a precipitating effect on changes (such as the demolition of the

221

old town walls) that were already coming, and certainly many developments were planned in that brief, heady time – though in most cases they did not come about till many years later. But to imagine, as some commentators appear to, that the outbreak of the American Civil War in 1861 is *the* reason for the creation of the High Victorian townscape of Bombay, is to ignore many other more general factors in the change and growth of cities. It would almost be true to say that if the American War had not provided Bombay with a cotton boom at that precise time, Bombay would have invented another reason for a financial bonanza. Indeed the essentially unstable and ultimately disastrous nature of the wave of speculation that engulfed the city during 1862-5 suggests that it *was* to some extent invented.

Briefly, what occurred was this. Before the American Civil War, Britain got only about 20 per cent of her raw cotton from India. American cotton had a longer staple, it was felt to be superior because it did not break so easily in the spinning, and anyway British mill-machinery was adapted to it. However, at an early stage in the Civil War the Northerners blockaded the Confederacy ports of the South, and cotton exports from America virtually ceased; Manchester began to discuss with excitement the possibility of Indian cotton replacing it entirely. Nearly all this cotton would have to pass through Bombay. In consequence, the price for which cotton sold in Bombay began steadily to climb, reaching its peak at the end of 1863 and the beginning of 1864 but remaining infinitely higher than the pre-war price, regardless of quality, and thus earning for Bombay over five years an estimated extra £70 million sterling or more. In March 1865, when unexpected news of the decisive Northern victory over Lee's army reached Bombay, prices began to fall, and during the next few months crisis succeeded crisis with brief rallies in between. By April the following year, with Britain importing American cotton again – 'treachery' they called it in Bombay – the whole boom was over.

But it was, of course, more than a cotton boom: it followed the classic form of the financial 'bubble', in which profitable speculation in a solid commodity inflates the supposed value of other, more notional commodities, chiefly land. Shares in land and property companies then reach unprecedented heights, holding companies are set up, and in the end the speculator is speculating in nothing more than money itself – or rather in bits of paper which, when the slump comes, are discovered to have nothing to back them. In Bombay all sorts of land usage and dock-construction schemes were floated during 1862-5, with other even less firmly based enterprises: by January 1865 there were in Bombay no less than 31 banks, 16 financial associations, 8 land companies, 16 press companies (i.e. cotton processing companies), 10 shipping companies, 20 insurance companies, and 62 joint stock companies. It was an exciting time – while it lasted. Looking back on it from the 1890s, Arthur Crawford, a later Municipal Commissioner of Bombay, wrote:

> How many alive still remember those silver times? When reclamation schemes turned everybody's brain – when 'Back Bays' fluctuated between twenty and forty-five thousand rupees premium – when 'Mazagons' and 'Colabas' followed suit – when there was a new Bank or a new 'Financial' almost every day – when it was a common thing, in strolling from your office to the dear old Indian Navy Club, to stop a moment in the seething Share Market and ask your broker, 'Well, Mr B. or Bomanji! What's doing?' 'Oh Sir! So-and-So Financials are rising – they say Premchand is buying.' 'Ah well, just buy me fifty or a hundred shares' (as your inclination prompted you). You went to your 'tiffin' or luncheon, at that memorable long table; you ordered a pint of champagne – no one ever drank anything but champagne in those days . . . [The afternoon was pleasantly passed in manoeuvring for lucrative 'allotments' in new schemes.] Four o'clock saw you on your way back to the office, and you stopped to ask your broker how your 'financials' stood. 'Rising slowly, sir!' would be the answer; with a calm acceptance you said, 'Then please sell mine,' and the morrow brought you a cheque for fifty or a hundred or two hundred rupees as the case might be.

Champagne was not the only sign of decadence. Some people gave up steady employment to spend their days buying and selling. European 'loafers' were numerous in Bombay, curiously analogous to the hippie parasites who found their way to Bombay in another time of affluence, the 1960s and early 70s. They were said to be 'not unintelligent'; a few managed to get supervisory jobs on the numerous Reclamation works, while others 'wandered the suburbs, pretending to be gardeners', or in the country side sponging off villagers.

One of the few inhabitants of Bombay said to be quite unimpressed by the boom was Dr Wilson, who was by then old. He was forced to leave his small house at Ambroli, for with the general inflation in property values* the owner wanted Rs.300 a month for it, but he was given another cottage by an admirer, on Malabar Hill. He said in 1863 that the boom would collapse, and his plain-living-

and-high-thinking suspicion of greed and usury turned out correct. Rather interestingly, the native fortune-tellers had been persistently saying the same thing, but apparently no one listened to them either.

The Premchand referred to in Crawford's memoir is Premchand Roychand, the most famous of all the Hindu brokers and bankers of the period. Wacha refers to him as 'the King of that Speculation, the idol of multitudes, and the Great God of Gold, at whose shrine European and Indian alike paid puja'. Wacha was one of the accountants employed to go through Roychand's books when the God of Gold met his defeat, and elsewhere he describes him less flamboyantly as a quiet, courteous, quick-moving, modest man of few words whose manner remained the same whatever his fortunes. 'He was devoid of worldly ambition . . . his pleasure was in the race run, not the prize.' He made a fortune in the cotton speculation by sending out 'country boats' (small craft) to waylay the mail ships at the lighthouses and collect messages from the captains about the recent London price before the ships docked in Bombay. Reading between the lines, Roychand seems, for all his flair, a somewhat childlike personality; his air of caution surely concealed a basic irresponsibility, but it was an air that certainly encouraged others to trust him. He was a promoter and shareholder in both the Commercial and the Mercantile banks, and, by the boom, had become a major shareholder of the Bank of Bombay and thus its effective controller. The other shareholders and directors allowed him to withdraw vast amounts of money from the Bank to finance his multitudinous schemes – directly and indirectly 1.38 crore rupees (well over £1 million sterling) which, as Wacha remarks, was 'a colossal and unheard of advance . . . It may be enquired whether in the financial history of the various countries of Europe and America, during the whole of the nineteenth century, it has been recorded that a single individual had had at his nod and beck the coffers of seventy monetary and other institutions from which he was able to draw for himself and his friends any amount of funds that he wished.' When the collapse came, fully 40 per cent of the advances from the Bank of Bombay had to be written off as irrecoverable. The Bank crashed.

Sir George Birdwood, the new editor of the *Bombay Times* (which was to become the *Times of India*), was a friend of

---

* In fact the price of everything inflated, including that of the commonest household commodities, so that those, like civil servants, who were prohibited from joining in the speculative bonanza, were 'pinched for food'.

Roychand's. He wrote of the 'Black Day' when the whole jerry-built edifice of speculation began to collapse:

> I was at a business meeting in the Fort, at the offices of one of the leading European 'Houses', and representatives of most of the great Firms were present; and some of the philanthropic movements then in progress in Bombay. In the midst of the consideration of schemes before them, a clerk presently brought in the telegram announcing the surrender of Lee's Army. For a moment dead silence filled the room, which also seemed lighted up with a strangely unnatural light . . . In another moment or two someone said: 'Well, it's a good thing to be made to sit up to your business once again'; while Premchand Roychand on my leaving the room said: 'This, Birdwood, means beginning my life over again'; and he began his life over again that night.

He was in fact almost ruined, but he continued as a broker in a more modest way, and was able to make charitable bequests. The clock-tower of Bombay University, with its bells that played British tunes, was a gift from him. Not all those who failed in the crash were able to rehabilitate themselves so well. Two of the Cama family failed, and Dadabhoy Pestonji Wadia's fortunes received a further blow. Two of the Jeejeebhoy family failed, one permanently, and so to some extent did Goculdas Tejpal and the Readymoney family: Cowasji Jehangir, after whom Forjett was to name his large house in Buckinghamshire, was a Readymoney, an ex-Director of the Bank of Bombay who had tried, while he was in charge, to keep Roychand's borrowing in check. European firms suffered too. Nichol and Co. was crippled; it struggled on till 1878 when the failure of the Glasgow Bank finished it off – bank failure was a commoner feature of life in the nineteenth century both in Britain and abroad than it is today: the failure of the Overend Gurney Bank in London in 1866 was partly related to the Bombay crash and, in turn, brought further bankruptcies in India. Ritchie Stewart and Co. also collapsed: Roychand had long been their chief broker, they had a large sum in the Bank of Bombay and they were the main promoters of the Back Bay Reclamation Company, whose shares for the time being worth next to nothing. For a number of years the unfinished works were to remain derelict, and eventually it was public, not private, money that was to revive them.

Jamshetji Nusserwanji Tata was badly caught, because he had the misfortune to be *en route* between Bombay and London when the bubble broke and the price of cotton, in which he was trading, came down with a rush. The scrip he had on him was near worthless by the time the ship docked in London. By his personality alone he had to convince his bankers and creditors that he would be able to salvage sufficient from the disaster to cover his debts. He did so, returning to Bombay and retrenching. His official (though rather inaccurate) biography remarks: 'The crisis through which he had passed left an indelible mark upon Mr Tata's character, and confirmed in him that need for caution which formed his guiding line in after life.' In fact his subsequent and highly successful career suggests enterprise and opportunism rather than caution. Three years after the crash he was able to rehabilitate his fortunes by provisioning the British Army for an expedition to Abyssinia. He lived to build mills in Bombay and the Deccan, a hydro-electric works at Lake Wawhan on the mainland south of Bombay, a steel works in Jamshedpur, iron-ore mines in central India, a shipping line, the opulent house by the Bombay Gymkhana, a block of flats nearby for 'the European man of attenuated means' (a most considerate thought, that!) and also his most celebrated memorial, the Taj Hotel on Apollo Bunder (see Chapter I). He was an enthusiastic purchaser of land in adjacent mainland areas such as Salsette, all of which is worth infinitely more today than when he bought it. He professed a particular liking for Salsette, claiming to an English friend that it reminded him 'of Scotland and the Lake District': a theoretical admiration, à la Queen Victoria, for all things Scottish seems to have been one of the many upper-class British habits adopted by Parsis of his generation. He was not in fact particularly anglophile, and never got a knighthood, though by a quirk of fate he is buried in England. He died while on a European trip, and since Europe unfortunately can offer neither Towers of Silence nor vultures, his family had to content themselves with Brookwood Cemetery in Surrey. The name of Tata still wields enormous power in Bombay, and indeed throughout India, where the company is popularly regarded as 'owning' a number of national assets, including Air India. The airline did in fact start life as a Tata enterprise.

Dramatic and final as the crash of 1865 seemed at the time, many firms and individuals did in fact recover from it, and, with setbacks in the late 1860s, Bombay regained her prosperity. Trade continued to increase, factories multiplied. But land wealth had tended to pass into the hands of a few enormously wealthy families such as the Sassoons, who had kept clear of trouble, the Tatas, and 'Maharajah' Goculdas, who had made a complete recovery. More cautious European methods of stockbroking came in. Within a few years, with the telegraph established, Premchand Roychand's secret boat-trips would seem a quaint memory of another time, as would his habit of conducting shareholders' meetings either under fig trees in Rampart Row or on the verandah of the Mercantile Bank. In 1875 a stock-exchange building on the European model was opened in Dalal Street, the first in India: brokers can be seen on the floor there gesticulating and shouting to this day, although a new concrete tower of inflexible Manhattan design awaits them nearby. After the crash, according to Dinshaw Wacha, the old word-of-mouth way of settling money-bargains changed:

> The one permanent evil consequence of the era was that commercial integrity of the old and puritan type was swept away. Liquidations and bankruptcies led to fraudulent practices . . . When liquidation came to a close and Bombay breathed afresh it was found that the old commercial honesty had disappeared. The refined civilisation of the West, with its refined way of transacting business, came into vogue.

IX *Palaces and Drains*

In 1672 Aungier laid his fine, but mostly unrealised plans, for 'the city, which by God's assistance is intended to be built'. Almost exactly two hundred years later, in a world transformed by the steamship, the railway engine, the telegraph and, most of all, by the effects of the industrial revolution, Sir Bartle Frere, in his valedictory speech as Governor of Bombay, declared that his aim had been 'to make good the omissions and neglect of former ages . . . I look forward with the utmost confidence to the time when we shall hear that Bombay has taken her place among cities, owing as much to art as she does to nature and position'. He went on to remark that Bombay had by then (1867) twice the population of Glasgow. True or not – and population estimates for the 1850s and 60s vary remarkably – the comparison indicates the *way* in which Bombay was being viewed, and was particularly well-chosen when you consider the substantial hand expatriate Scots had had in setting up her commerce and her educational institutions. (Frere himself was a Scot, and one of the new generation of middle-class administrators who had 'come up' via Haileybury, through the colonial ranks. He was celebrated in Bombay for having reviewed troops wearing a frock coat and a panama hat rather than a ceremonial uniform.) Bombay was henceforth to be considered a town which, by the assistance of some doubtless Nonconformist God, *had* been built, and it only remained to beautify and grandify it. The same approach lay behind a comment made a few years later in the Report of Dr Gilham Hewlett, the Municipal Commissioner, when he complained that 'the apologies for sewers' in the southern part of the Fort 'would disgrace the streets of a third-rate French

228

sea-port town'. To get the full flavour of this remark, you have to realise the degree of scorn and mistrust in which the British bourgeoisie of the nineteenth century held all things French, but in any case the message is clear: the days when Bombay might herself have been considered a third-rate sea-port town were definitely over.

The building of docks, either in fact or in plan, preoccupied Bombay for the whole of the second half of the nineteenth century, just as it had London in the first half of the century. The Elphinstone Land and Press Company (no direct connection with either Governor of that name) was launched by Nichol and Co. in 1858, with the object of creating docks along the foreshore between the existing harbours which were in Mody Bay beneath the Castle walls and at Mazagaon town. With the Cotton Mania the scheme expanded, psychologically and materially, and the promoters made an agreement with the Government in 1862 to provide 100 acres for the new GIP railway terminus at Bori Bunder in return for the right to claim 250 acres from the sea. In other words they had acquired, by this deal, a monopoly of the best potential dockland on the Island. However, the Elphinstone Company suffered during the crash; just fulfilling their agreement with the Government expended all their remaining available capital, and they could not complete their further schemes. It was felt in any case by then that it was undesirable that works of such magnitude and such significance for the future of the city should be in the hands of a private company: the era of municipalisation and public ownership was dawning; in London the Metropolitan Board of Works (the forerunner of the LCC and hence of the modern system of county council responsibility) was founded in 1868. At about the same time in Bombay negotiations were started for the Government of Bombay to buy out the Elphinstone Company, and in 1873, when Bombay got the first elected municipal council in India, the Port Trust was formed as a Government subsidiary: henceforth all dock developments were under the aegis of this body.

By the mid-1880s the map of Bombay shows the eastern foreshore from Apollo Bunder up to Mazagaon heavily reclaimed (Narowji Hill and a large part of the hill where the Belvedere had stood had been demolished and thrown into the sea in this cause): it also shows this 'new' land sprinkled with wet docks, both potential and actual. (The Port Trust also acquired the Sassoon Dock on Colaba in 1889.) By 1900 the new land between long, straight Frere Road and the docks was lattice-worked with new streets, and dockland was spreading further north still, towards the semi-rural wilderness of Sewri where the Cotton Green was finally to be re-located in 1928. In 1915 the Harbour Railway was completed; its branches run like a nervous system through the dockland, and link the area with the main lines via substantial goods sidings just below the remnant of Mazagaon Hill, at the spot where Eliza Draper once embarked down a rope into a small boat and the arms of her incidental lover.

The Back Bay reclamation scheme, on the western side of the Island, had a more chequered history. There was no question of building docks in those shallow waters, but the Bombay, Baroda and Central India Railway, which was being built between Bombay and Gujerat c.1860, had its eye on a lucrative line down to the Cotton Green at Colaba, where it might hope to take much of the cotton transporting business away from the port. For this, a major creek would have to be filled in at Colaba and several minor ones up the foreshore of Back Bay, which would have to be generally cleared and strengthened to take the tracks. ('To ride home to Malabar Hill along the sands of Back Bay was to encounter sights and odours too horrible to describe', as the Guidebook pusillanimously put it a generation later.) During the boom year of 1863, therefore, a company was formed with the grandiose object of reclaiming 1,500 acres from the sea, in a broadening swathe down Back Bay from Chowpatti beach at its northern end to the very tip of Colaba peninsula, which would be more than doubled in width. Out of this new-found land they promised the Government of Bombay 300 acres, in return for which the Government was to purchase a block of 400 shares in the Company at their face value of Rs.5,000 each. Subsequently the Secretary of State for India raised objections to the Government holding shares in a private company, but this did not seem to matter at the time as Bombay was feeling so financially buoyant. Although there were those, even then, who were convinced that 'throwing earth into the sea is just throwing gold into the sea', the speculation caught the public imagination. The idea that land, which by then equalled money, could be created just like that, exactly matched the spirit of the times, and the shares rose to Rs.30,000 each. Premchand Roychand was one of the scheme's promoters. The BB&CI railway happily undertook to transport the material the company needed to begin its filling operations, and chunks of Kamballa Hill were taken away for this purpose. But before 300 acres along Back Bay had been reclaimed the Bank of Bombay crashed, and the company crashed with it.

A few years later the seashore railway line at least was continued, in spite of the protests of those who pointed out that this would deprive Bombay of 'a promenade which any seaside place in the world might well have envied': after all, the railway company argued, the line had been the reason for the land-reclamation in the first place. (Not till well into the twentieth century was the 'promenade' achieved by a further extension of land west of the railway in the shape of glamorous Marine Drive, leaving the Edwardian blocks in Queens Road, that were hopefully called names like 'Sea View', bereft of that attribute.) There was a row about Charni Road Station: it was originally to be sited in the heart of the old Sonapur district, opposite a Parsi fire temple, but the Parsis felt that the presence of fire so near at hand and put to mundane use in a steam engine was offensive, and in deference to their sensibilities it was built further north. It took the best part of another decade for the line to get as far as Churchgate, in the mid 1870s – the name perpetuating the memory of the demolished Fort ramparts. There it stayed for a while, in a countrified little station variously described as reminding one of 'a cosy Swiss chalet' or 'a pretty collection of dovecotes'. (It is said to have been designed in deliberate contrast to, and perhaps in implicit criticism of, Victoria Terminus, which the rival GIP railway was then planning at Bori Bunder at a cost of £300,000. Later, however, the BB&CI were to build their own rival grandiose pile – the company's offices next to Churchgate – and the pretty little station was hideously remodelled in 1928.) At Churchgate the line stuck again, while abortive schemes for the further reclamation of Back Bay came and went and the site of the old workings remained derelict, battered by the waves of successive monsoons.

There was a theory for a while that the line might be put underground as far as Colaba; however, this came to nothing, and it finally made its way to the Cotton Green in 1893, where a modestly Gothic terminus was built. It had come too late, really: a generation later the cotton bales were all evacuated to Sewri, and the line which had caused such controversy was cut back to Churchgate again. The Colaba Station has been demolished now, but the stabling that was attached to it and part of an overbridge still stand, by the junction of Wodehouse Road and Cuffe Parade: grass-grown and apparently disused, these relics harbour a busy night life all their own.

Cuffe Parade itself, with its rococo bungalows, was part of a new, grand scheme for Back Bay and Colaba that was put forward by the Bombay Improvement Trust (founded in 1899). They reclaimed about 900 square yards before giving up in the face of expense and further public opposition. Later, private schemes followed, most of them too ambitious to find either finance or general acceptance. In 1920 a huge Government loan was floated, to back a scheme for reclaiming over 1,000 acres behind a retaining sea wall, mostly at the Colaba end of the Bay. Marine Drive ('Ocean Way' as it was originally designated) was first conceived at this time, and was supposedly to run down the whole sweep of the new western foreshore. Maps of the period show the infill as if it already existed, but in fact only a fraction of it was achieved and much remains undone to this day – part of Cuffe Parade still retains, if perilously, its sea view. A fringe of playing fields and the like were wrested from the beach on the seaward side of the railway line, opposite the old cemeteries, but Marine Drive was not completed till the 1940s; it was the last gift of the British to Bombay, and still peters out in an unfinished sea wall at about the level of the bandstand.

Other grand plans of the 1920s, such as putting the shoreline railway underground (again) and building 'a shopping mall' over it have never come to pass, and are hardly likely to. Indeed if every town planning scheme for the southern section of Bombay put forward since 1863 had actually been built, the whole of the old Esplanade (today's *maidans*) would have disappeared under large stone blocks, and a positive Haussmannville of august urban vistas would have extended Bombay far out into Back Bay. (One particularly far-fetched scheme envisaged turning into solid land the entire Bay from Colaba Point to Malabar Point!) But, as it is, the only substantial area of planned townscape in Bombay lies on the unfinished Colaba Reclamation Scheme south of Churchgate. It includes various Babar-King-of-the-Elephants Governmental buildings, and a more recent huddle of glass skyscrapers where the reclamation arbitrarily ends at what has become known as 'Narriman Point'. It is not currently considered a very well conceived development: it lacks the dramatic style of Manhattan or Chicago at which it was presumably aiming, and certainly has not fulfilled the hopes of those who, more than fifty years ago, first began to design it. 'When the reorganisation contemplated under this part of the scheme has taken place,' a Government booklet of that period remarked optimistically, 'Bombay will become one of the most orderly cities in the world' – surely a prime contender in the improbable prediction stakes! There was even the belief that, in some way never quite explained, the creation of a new prestige grand-public-buildings area to the south-west of the old Fort would bring about an easing of pressures on land and buildings elsewhere – 'As the supply catches up with the demand and, in the course of time, overtakes it, it is hoped rents will fall automatically.'

In fact the kind of development with which this new land-from-the-sea is covered has had no effect on the rest of Bombay, nor was it ever likely to: its rationale is not sensible use of valuable land but municipal, federal or national hubris. In any case this has all happened before. The post-Independence designers who finally got the buildings up were behaving in essentially the same way as the British themselves had behaved when, under Bartle Frere, they planned the impressive phalanx of buildings just outside the Fort, fringeing the Esplanade. The only substantial difference was that the modern development occupies virgin territory, whereas Bartle Frere's 'New Town on the Esplanade' followed the line of pre-existing development. When they were built these great monuments to British rule – the Secretariat, the University, the Law Courts, the Municipal Building, the old Post Office, etc. – had a clear view out to the sea. Seventy-five years later, when the building of Queens Road along the railway line and then Marine Drive had robbed them of their commanding aspect, the seaside palaces of Narriman Point had to be conceived. And if any future great scheme does remove the shallow waters of Back Bay yet further from their original beach, no doubt Narriman Point will, in turn, be abandoned for some new sea view.

The Gothic Revival buildings that began to edge the Esplanade once the old Fort walls had been pulled down, changing the whole aspect of the city, are now generally agreed to be successful of their kind. A modern expert (Gavin Stamp) has written: 'In India . . . architects could fully indulge in open stair-cases and galleries, balconies and verandahs, and know they were suited to a hot climate . . . The most elaborate and picturesque Victorian buildings usually do not seem out of place in India.' In Bombay the buildings were mainly in buff or blue stone from Kurla, on the nearby mainland, with detail in Porebunder sandstone or red sandstone from Bassein. In Calcutta, where building materials were scant and of poor quality, Gothic Revival buildings were much less successful.

In their heyday, Bombay's buildings were much appreciated. A turn-of-the-century visitor from England, G. W. Stevens (no relation, I think, to the Stevens who built several of them) sounds dazzled with their pleasure and variety:

First comes the Venetian Secretariat, then the Gothic University Library and the French University Hall, between them the great Clock Tower, which peals forth hymn-tunes on Sunday, and on weekdays 'God Save the Queen!' and 'Home sweet Home'. The white-pinnacled Law Courts follow in Early English, then the Post and Telegraph Offices in Miscellaneous Gothic. But the jewel of Bombay is the Victoria Railway Station, a vast domed mass of stone fretted with point and column statuary . . . A proud and comely city, you say, the Briton feels himself a greater man for his first sight of Bombay.

But fashions in architecture change still more quickly than fashions in imperialism. By 1926 Aldous Huxley, one of a generation whose rejection of 'Victorianism' was profound and heartfelt, could write that Bombay was 'one of the most appalling cities of either hemisphere. It had the misfortune to develop during what was, perhaps, the darkest period of all architectural history.' The opinionated and eccentric traveller Robert Byron writing in the *Architectural Review* a few years later, went even further, considering Bombay 'an architectural Sodom' and that the ugliness of its buildings was 'positive, daemonic'. One can only be thankful, with hindsight, that Bombay in the 1920s and 30s was, like all industrial cities, affected by the world recession and did not feel itself in a position to indulge in any extensive rebuilding. Had it done so, Bartle Frere's magisterial 'New Bombay'* would almost certainly have been reduced to rubble. Indeed this might well have happened had Bombay felt sufficiently prosperous in the 1950s and 60s: it happened to Victorian Birmingham and Bradford and to some extent in Manchester and Liverpool. It is fortunate that, by the 1970s when Bombay was enjoying a boom, the idea that 'these quaint old buildings' were after all to be admired as works of art rather than despised as symbols of imperialism, was beginning to filter through from the West to informed Indian circles. It may be said that those who, in London, failed to save the Euston Arch and the Coal Exchange but subsequently managed to preserve St Pancras Station and many other Victorian creations, were indirectly responsible for saving Bombay's heritage also, though most of them were probably unaware that it existed.

The curious thing is that those admired Bombay building were

---

* Not to be confused with the 'New Bombay' currently planned for the mainland. (See Chapter I).

not, in the main, built by internationally distinguished architects. Almost the only exception is the Venetian-style University, with its openwork spiral staircases, which was built to designs sent out from England by the prolific George Gilbert Scott, who does not actually seem to have visited the site. F. W. Stevens, who was responsible for the delights of Victoria Terminus and the Municipal Building, as well as several others, was a local man. He trained in England and first went out to Bombay in 1867 as an assistant engineer in the newly-formed Public Works Department. Similarly, Frere's first project, the Secretariat (now in turn become the *old* Secretariat, as the still older one in the Fort is forgotten and a newer one stands to the south-west on reclaimed land) was designed by a Colonel H. St Clair Wilkins of the Royal Engineers. A plaque on it records appreciatively that whereas the estimated cost was Rs. 1,280,731, the actual cost was only Rs. 1,260,844.

The Bombay Builder, a publication which existed only for a few years in the late 1860s, is interminably scathing about such architects as Wilkins and Stevens: 'Bombay has at the present moment a chance of becoming at least in part a splendid city, a second Indian City of Palaces . . . Who is there in the Public Works Department who has the smallest artistic power? Or who even knows anything at all about architecture?' A captain of the Royal Engineers, first class, only earned, it was pointed out, a little over Rs. 1,000 a year; clearly this was regarded as an insufficient income to support artistic power. The Public Works Department was using the wrong materials, it was claimed – the Kurla stone parts of Elphinstone College and the Mechanics Institute were flaking – and some PWD bungalows for officers in Marine Lines had cost far more than they were worth. Also, 'How is it that the Architectural Executive Engineer does not know how to turn a pointed arch? . . . He would do well, I think, to take a lesson in brick arches from the Catholic priest who built the schools in Nesbit Lane. In the Secretariat there is not a single arch turned correctly . . . ' In addition to the continual moans about poor quality the *Builder* also frequently castigated Bombay Government servants for extravagance, including Crawford the Municipal Commissioner, Frere himself and Hewlett the Public Health Officer – though one might agree with Hewlett that the comprehensive system of drainage which he was trying to impose on the place was *the* first requirement of any City of Palaces that came up to nineteenth-century standards.

Little or nothing seems to have satisfied *The Bombay Builder.*

It despised the older Georgian or neo-Georgian buildings – the Town Hall reminded it of 'a decayed old beau of the last century, whose wig sits awry and whose false teeth are falling out', the Scotch church was 'designed in the spirit of the coldest classicism' and the Bank of Bombay in the same idiom was 'a gruesome pile'. Such strictures were commonplace by the 1860s (Ruskin himself had considered classical Gower Street 'the ugliest street in London'). Two more generations were to pass before twentieth-century viewers such as Aldous Huxley were to regard the Town Hall as almost the *only* tolerable building – 'in Bombay, it seems the Parthenon'. But the romantic exuberance of style then in fashion did not particularly please the exigent *Builder* either. At any rate it could not resist digs at Watson's Hotel, Crawford's covered market ('altogether unsuited to a Bombay climate') or the new plans for John Lockwood Kipling's School of Art – 'Thirteenth century French Gothic, which style it appears Mr Burgess considers the most suited to our modern wants'. (In fact, Burgess's design was not built.) As for the new churches of varied denominations then going up around Bombay, they 'might have been imported in a batch from home, nay, it would almost seem that they all came together'. The last stricture is true, as a matter of fact – but what, exactly, did the *Builder* want? It hardly seems surprising that the publication did not attract sufficient readership to survive.

A number of building commodities, apart from designs, were imported from England at that period. All iron railway bridges had to be, since there was as yet no foundry in India capable of manufacturing them. (The Byculla Iron Works was started in 1857 and is there and flourishing under the names of its founders to this day, but its early development was slow and difficult.) For his galleried hotel Watson shipped out not only iron but also bricks, from Webster's Manufactury in Burham; and Portland stone and cement too were brought from the other side of the world to build Bombay's mills. At Victoria Gardens, the horticultural park then being laid out at Byculla to replace that at Sewri, a triumphal arch and clock tower were being built complete with terracotta ornamental panels all the way from Blashfield's factory at Stamford, Lincs. These, and the Minton floor tiles, are there to this day, and so is the turnstile at the entrance to the gardens, still bearing in brightly polished brass the information that it was manufactured in Bear Lane, Southwark. The wrought iron for the interior structure of the small museum in the gardens presumably came from England also, likewise the iron structure for the new markets not far away in

Erskine Road in the heart of the bazaars. The floor of these markets was covered with stone flags all the way from Yorkshire. How far off seem the days, not really so very long distant, when all Bombay buildings were held up by *chunam*, a local lime made by grinding and burning sea-shells, and when the European inhabitants of the Island waited eagerly for the slow arrival of such relatively light objects as French ribbon or Stilton cheeses.

Another covered market, the Crawford Market at the bazaar end of the *maidans*, is today perhaps one of the most widely known and durably useful of all the buildings conceived at this period. It was the brain-child of Sir Arthur Crawford; he nursed several other projects, including a 'Crawford Crescent' to be built on the Esplanade, which it is perhaps as well never materialised. Described in some guides as 'Flemish-Moorish', the Market (with stone flooring from Caithness) is in fact vaguely Norman in style, and why the *Builder* was so rude about its suitability for the climate is hard to see. True, the covered permanent *souk* was a Middle Eastern phenomenon which had not developed spontaneously in India, but this had less to do with the weather than with the essentially itinerant, even nomadic life of the traditional Indian traders: to them in the past a market had never been a fixed location, business had to be portable. But this attitude, in itself, was the product of centuries of local unrest and danger, and in Bombay this risk was largely removed. Today, Crawford Market still houses coolly and comfortably huge meat, fish and vegetable markets. It was designed the same year that Baroness Burdett Coutts's less successful Columbia Market was designed for London's East End, and seems to exude something of the same spirit of visionary philanthropy; perhaps this spirit was actually better suited to the social conditions in Bombay, with its big floating ex-peasant population, than to the industrial proletariat of London. The stone reliefs set high on the exterior of the building evince a monolithic idealism – a William Morris concept of the dignity and beauty of the Life Agricultural complete with Noble Peasants, attended by man's friend the dog, standing upright amid stone wheat gazing soulfully into a splendid co-operative future – but one must admit that this ideal seems oddly at variance with the life of competitive and passionate expedience actually being carried on at their feet. These carvings remind one of nothing so much as official Soviet statuary, but they represent such an India as Kipling's father dreamed of, for they are his designs.

This was unusual. Most of the carving on the buildings of this period was left to native stone-masons. Like the medieval masons of

European cathedrals (whom in life-style these hereditary craftsmen resembled) they were given a fairly free hand. Thus the pillar-cornices within the Venetian-style galleries of the High Court, a splendid Gothic pile in blue basalt designed by an otherwise obscure General Fuller of the Royal Engineers, are ornamented with apes at play. Here and there a half-blind ape holds a scales of justice, a fox wears a barrister's bands, a pig and a tiger fight, and birds cavort knowingly among entwining leaves. Round these galleries, which have to be screened with bamboo curtains when the monsoon rains blast in from the western sea, hurry lawyers in the white bands, black gowns and striped trousers of a culture now at several removes from present-day India. Only the wigs of the Strand Law Courts (built at the same period) have been discarded. The ushers, who move rather more slowly, are dressed in red gowns that appear to be made of wool, and round padded hats, like extras in a Shakespearean production.

All this was the public face of Bombay, the new 'European' city that delighted chauvinistic travellers or reassured timid ones on their arrival at Apollo Pier: it was the Mysterious East made acceptable and civilised. But there was another, less salubrious side to Bombay that was developing just as rapidly. The two aspects of the city are generally presented in contemporary sources as a contrast to one another, but they were really two inextricably linked aspects of the same phenomenon: economic growth.

This growth can to some extent be measured in terms of people coming to the city. During the Cotton Mania unofficial estimates of the town's population put the figure at over 800,000, though this included a large floating population of traders and labourers of all kinds who left the place again when prosperity temporarily slumped. By 1872, the year of the first proper Government Census, the figure was 644,405, over two-thirds of whom had not been born in Bombay. The establishment of the 'fire carriage' was now encouraging more of them who came to the city in search of work to bring their whole families with them. Nine year later the figure was 773,195, and by 1891 it had continued to rise at the same steady pace to 821,764. At that period Bombay had outstripped Calcutta, and was the largest city in the East after Tokyo. Population had slumped again slightly by the next Census in 1901, which followed several years of plague on the Island that had frightened people away, but by 1911 it was close on a million. It has been rising ever since, and the rate of rise has increased also.

What this growth in population indicates is the increase in Bombay's factories, pre-eminently in textile mills. In the mid-1860s 10 mills employed some 6–7,000 workers. By 1872 there were 12, and 17 by 1875. By 1879 there were 30, and more opening each year. By the early 1880s 30,000 workers, mostly male, were employed by the textile industry, and by the end of the century 82 mills were employing nearly 73,000 workers, or almost one in ten of the whole population. And this was all in the one industry; numerous other incomers to Bombay worked in other trades, in Tata's oil-pressing plant at Chinchpoglie ('the tamarind grove'), or in the new iron works that were springing up, or on the docks. In addition, and in apparent contradiction to a well-established twentieth-century myth about industrialisation driving out older skills, hand-crafts also received a boost from Bombay's general prosperity. An illustrated commercial directory of the period, a piece of informative and lavish PR put out by the *Times of India*, mentions this flourishing free-lance sector: silk was being woven on hand looms in the quarter near the Gaol, Jain craftsmen-jewellers were establishing themselves in the Zaveri Bazaar off Kalba Devi, where gold and silver thread for ornamenting saris was also spun, and copper and brass-smiths were occupied nearby at Mumba Devi. They, and the jewellers, are still there today. Leatherwork was also thriving: traditionally an 'untouchable' trade, it is one at which it is possible to make a lot of money; today Bombay has at least one very wealthy family of hereditary shoe-makers. Carriages were made at Byculla, ivory, sandal-wood and tortoise-shell were worked there and in Mazagaon: at Mazagaon too there had long been saw-mills. Today Victoria Road (Sant Savata Maarg), which runs eastwards from Byculla towards the dockland, is still the main supply-point for Bombay's furniture-making industry; stacks of wood and ox carts wait beneath its shady trees in a pleasant and countrified aroma of wood-shavings.

Between the traditional caste-tied skilled workers and the new, mobile masses of ex-peasant mill-hands and labourers, were many other levels of society and contrivances for living. It seems probable, for instance, that it was the incoming Moslems, particularly the Borahs, who filled one important service function; from having been peddlers, many established themselves in the food business, selling the meat, fish and vegetables that caste-Hindus would not deal in and no-caste Hindus must not touch. The *Gazetteer* of 1909 mentions a more ingenious and specific shift: 'The import of kerosine oil has given rise to a new industry. Bohras buy empty tins for about 2 annas each and fashion them into lanterns, boxes, trunks, oil-pots and other cheap articles.'

One of the best descriptions of Bombay at a slightly earlier stage in its commercial and manufacturing evolution is to be found in *Macleans Guide* for 1877, the year in which Queen Victoria was proclaimed Empress of India and a statue of her was erected outside the Central Telegraph Office gazing out across the *maidans*. (The statue is banished now, a grumpy fallen goddess, to the Victoria Gardens.) J. M. Maclean was editor of the *Bombay Gazette,* and lived for many years at chambers in the Byculla Club, which were much sought-after at a cost of Rs.350 a month all-in. (Daily fare featured prawn curries, a shoulder of mutton, and the 'Byculla soufflé' full of liqueurs.) Maclean wrote:

> We would recommend anyone who wishes to find out the bad as well as the good points of Bombay to turn off the Parell Road at the Elphinstone College and drive across the Flats by the Clerk Road to Mahalaxmi.* The whole of the ground he will traverse was not many years ago a dismal swamp for the greater part of the year, and much of it is not much better now. Building is, however, constantly going on; and already there are numerous cotton mills, with their surroundings of labourers' houses, stretching across the Flats from Tardeo all the way to Parell. Before the end of this century there will be as many tall chimneys in this region as in any equal space of ground in Lancashire. The visitor will be horrified to find that an open main drain,† carrying away the sewage of Bombay, still runs across the Flats to windward of Byculla. Any worse nuisance, in a tropical climate, it is impossible to conceive, and the Municipal authorities, who have already begun reclamation of the Flats with town sweepings – a method of doubtful sanitary advantage – should make it an urgent duty to get the money for thoroughly draining this part of Bombay.

On the Byculla Club itself he remarked: 'The view of the Race Course is now so much interrupted by the lofty buildings in the neighbourhood that the stewards have determined to hold the

---

* The Elphinstone College building at Byculla still exists, but is no longer in the same use. Clerk Road was, when Maclean was writing, a new east-west cross-route. The Mahalaxmi temple was reinstated at the Breach by a wealthy Hindu in the 1830s, and after that its name began to supplant 'the Breach' as a way of indicating that stretch of shore.

† This, later encased in a pipe, gave its name to the bazaar through which it ran and which is known as the Nul Bazaar to this day (*nala* = drain).

race meeting for 1878 on the Flats, where a clear course can be obtained.' The Byculla area had been 'Flats' itself before the Hornby Vellard had reduced the area of land liable to flood. The Club had been contemplating the move for some time: a full thirteen years earlier, at the height of the Cotton Mania, the *Bombay Saturday Review* had predicted: 'What with the railways and the Foras Road across the flats, and the building that is going on all round, Byculla will soon become (if it is not already) quite unsuited for the purpose of horse-racing; and it would be prudent to consider in time whether a move further out of town ought not to be made as soon as possible.' In 1878, as noted by Maclean, the races were held for the first time on the present-day site, north of Clerk Road and nearer the sea; for a few years yet the stewards dickered between the two courses but finally, in the 1890s, they settled on the new one.

The Club's failure to move itself, and its consequent decline, provides an instructive illustration of urban change. Various schemes for moving the Club were mooted in these years: it was suggested it might go to Chowpatti, to Queens Road, to Marine Lines or to Malabar Hill – the tide of fashion and European occupation was moving inexorably westwards, following the sea-breezes which now no longer reached the central bowl of Bombay so easily. Arthur Crawford had an ambitious scheme that a tunnel should be made through Malabar Hill, and the excavated material used to reclaim part of the foreshore there in two tiers with a new Club premises occupying one of them. It was a pity for the Club that this ingenious idea was never carried out, for Malabar hill remains today the most exclusive area of Bombay, while Byculla is a densely populated, lower-middle-class Moslem area. By the end of the century the Club was in obvious decline; the Bombay Club (first in the Fort and later at Chowpatti) had long usurped its prestige, and in 1898 the new Yacht Club Chambers at Apollo Bunder usurped its only remaining function. There was a feeble attempt to pretend, in the 1900s, that the coming of electric power to the mills that now blocked the Club's view to the north would render them innocuous as neighbours, but this deceived no one. By 1905 a visitor could say that the Club 'now stands an almost solitary landmark among cotton-mill chimneys and teeming native tenements'. It finished its days as a military hospital during the First World War, and the site was sold for redevelopment during the 1920s, making a lot of welcome if undeserved money for the current surviving members. Today the main state transport depot occupies the site of the Club-house itself: I believe a large tree by the gate is the only specific survival of former days. There is, however, a general trace of the Club's existence and importance in the fact that the land immediately to the north of it, on the far side of where the race course once lay (later used for a cricket ground and garden), was developed in the 1890s and 1900s with rather grand houses, many of which are still there. It is still, today, an enclave of surprisingly peaceful and spacious tree-lined streets surrounded by much poorer, noisier districts.

Maclean also remarked in 1877 that the bazaars themselves were becoming more conventionally urban, in that many substantial stone buildings were by then going up in them, particularly in the triangle bounded by Kalba Devi, Sheik Memon Street and the *maidan* to the south, where the rich Hindu Banians and Mawaris lived; for the first time shop-signs in European lettering were also appearing there. Girgaum Road too was getting larger buildings and was losing its coconut trees and its rural nature. At its southern end, in the area known as Dhobi Talao, a colony of the poorer Parsis lived 'for the most part in immense houses . . . like regular rabbit warrens'. It was they who objected to the BB&CI's intention to build a station opposite a fire-temple. The district had been the scene of important Parsi–Moslem riots in 1874, when the Parsis had become alarmed at the size of a Moslem funeral procession wending its way to the cemetery at Sonapur, and threw stones, one of which killed an old man. There are many contemporary accounts of this, but Maclean's revealing comment is: 'there would, however, have been no disturbance at all if the Government had taken proper precautions to keep the peace. Unfortuanately Sir Phillip Wodehouse [the Governor, remembered in Wodehouse Road, Colaba] left the people to protect themselves; forgetting that, if the people in India could protect themselves from violence and rapine, they would not want the English to rule them.'

This view was then a very widely held one. The gradual removal of the trading justification for an Empire, in an era of buoyant free trade, had left a rational vacuum which had to be filled by a mythology – of Britain as the spiritual and moral leader of the world, who had been invited to be a sort of super-parent to India's brown children. This bizarre situation was neatly analysed by H. G. Wells after the turn of the century as 'a sort of magic inconclusiveness . . . We make nothing happen, at the most we prevent things happening . . . Our flag is spread over the peninsula without plans, without intention – a vast preventative!' It was not even as if the British Government played a very active role in India's industrial development, except insofar as it provided the conditions (i.e. the peace and communications systems) that helped the development along. Until after the First World War, it was private enterprise, almost entirely, that built the industries of Bombay and the Deccan. But to determinedly patriotic British eyes, any and every aspect of Indian success was, as to a fond parent, a subject for self-congratulation. These were people who 'secure under a British administration, have embarked their capital in factories instead of hoarding it in secret places, and are now competing with the mills of Lancashire in producing cotton goods' (*The Fortnightly Review*, 1882).

Bombay's general transformation into a nineteenth-century urban metropolis proceeded apace. In 1865 there were still only 220 gas lamps in all the Island, but twenty years later there were 2,500. The slaughter-houses were removed from the edge of the Fort to Bandra, a suburb on Salsette, the tanneries were sent to Mahim, the dyers were chased from the Esplanade to the old Portuguese suburb of Dadar beyond Parel; attempts were made to get the cows who supplied Bombay's milk out of the smelly cow-houses and into more salubrious and distant accommodation. Exactly the same improvements were being made at the same time in London. In the 1870s the first horse-drawn tramway network was opened in Bombay, just as it had been in recent years in European cities. Not only were the horsedrawn trams – forerunners of the present-day red double-decker buses – shipped from England; the horses were sent out too, complete with straw hats to protect their English brows from the tropical sun. Roads and footpaths were widened to accommodate the increased traffic and several new roads were constructed to service and suburbanise the new bungalows on Kamballa and Malabar Hill, which had previously had only rough tracks. Another guide-book of the period remarks: 'The drive from Malabar Hill to Chowpatty along the foot of the cliffs is very pretty. The steep banks are covered with foliage . . . among the basaltic masses of rock above the road is domesticated a colony of coolies, who, having few wants, are quite happy in their miserable huts.' Today that, at least, has not changed. There is still a shanty-town there, clinging tenaciously to some of the most valuable land in the world, and there is no reason to suppose that they are any more or less unhappy than most of Bombay's overcrowded and skimpily-lodged eight milion.

The theme of overcrowding, and the associated themes of lack of adequate building regulations and adequate drains, become constant ones in the last three decades of the century. It is possible that the growing municipal super-structure, replete with Departments and Reports that had been unknown in the days when Bombay was run by a bench of local JPs, was revealing horrors that till then had been hidden from the eye of authority; it is also undoubted that, as European standards of public health improved, those in charge looked more askance on dirty cow-sheds and open dung-heaps than they would have done in the early part of the century. It must, however, have been true as well, in Bombay as in London and Manchester, that *laissez-faire* urbanisation brought with it a range of new evils and dangers and a dinginess and grimness which had been unknown in the primitive, semi-rural conditions. Today, a European traveller visiting Bombay or Calcutta tends to see the shaky public health provisions as evidence of a kind of cultural struggle – eastern squalor versus western amenity. But it was not always so. The problems the municipality of Bombay was trying to combat a hundred years ago were essentially the *same* as the problems that the Metropolitan Board of Works in London was then facing, and the new squalor and dirt of the expanding city was, in origin, largely a western phenomenon. London too at that time had its typhoid and cholera epidemics (the last bad cholera outbreak was in 1866) and its undrained, ill-built houses pullulating with stunted human life. Indeed there was even a period in the late 1860s when the death rate in Bombay was below that of London.

The indefatigable Dr Hewlett, Public Health Officer under Frere and later Municipal Commissioner, published long reports full of complaints and suggestions, followed by further complaints that these were ignored and that funds were not forthcoming for all that needed doing. He had a particular hatred for what was left of Narowji Hill, the old Sett property where the fort of Dongri had stood in the eighteenth century. Now it had become 'the great labour quarter' of Bombay, and was much depleted by quarrying. There were landslips there and waterholes in which people were occasionally drowned, and 'the owner lets out plots of land to persons to build on as they please, without any definite plan to ensure breadth of streets and ventilation of houses'. But he was equally rude about

> the dirty, irregular labyrinth of Cavel . . . Vehicles can only pass a very short distance into it, and one of the principal thoroughfares to it is through a liquor shop in the Girgaum Road . . . Khetwaree [Khetwadi], formerly fields, is now rapidly becoming built over . . . If only there were an Act to

244

enable us to regulate the construction and ventilation of *new* houses, we could in a few years effect a very decided change in the health of this and other districts . . . A portion of Khetwaree was some years ago, in spite of my remonstrances, reclaimed by town-sweepings. Chawls are beginning to be built over a portion so reclaimed, but we have no power to prevent them . . . I much wish that a factory Act was introduced, and one that would not only regulate the ages of the young hands and their hours of labour etc. but would insist on the owners of each mill providing sufficient house accommodation for their employés. (1872 *Bombay Public Consultations*)

Dr Hewlett also suggested the building of a 'model village' at Tardeo to house its 5,000 factory workers: 'village' was a moral word in Progressive, late-Victorian terminology, carrying as it did overtones of pastoral decency and a lost innocence, but he seems to have known that the idea would not really work. The by-then well-established British stereotype of the wicked mill-owner failing to provide proper accommodation for his work-force was, however true in part, inadequate as a total explanation for overcrowding in a city like Bombay: it was not only the poor who lived in overcrowded houses jammed into narrow lanes. Hewlett worked out that over a third of the population lived on only 3·5 per cent of the Island's surface:* 'What has been said of Scotland may with equal truth be applied to Bombay, that families instead of living on the earth in the pure air with the sky over their dwellings, in many instances prefer laying stratum over stratum in flats opening onto a common staircase, a "continuation of the street" as it has been called, which receives the organic emanations of the families on each floor.' To want to live in the centre of the city if you were not actually forced to by your humble station in life was, to the English way of thinking, perverse. (This was the era when, in London, suburban railways with special cheap fares for working men were being developed in an attempt to encourage the respectable working and lower middle classes into low-density villa accommodation – the beginning of the great British suburban sprawl.) Particularly incomprehensible, to the British authorities, were the Jain merchants from Gujerat, who came to Bombay in large numbers during the 1870s and 80s. This community was not a poor one and was noted for its attention to ritual hygiene and

* Fifty years later 70 per cent of the households in Bombay lived in one-room tenements. Today, the figure is slightly higher.

vegetarianism, but its members were given by tradition to crowding defensively together in already overcrowded and old houses right in the bazaars, as near as possible to their businesses. As a result the mortality rate among the Jains was relatively high* – far higher than that of the Brahmins whose life-style was in other respects similar. It was also higher than that of Parsis, Hindus of intermediary castes, Eurasians, native Christians and Jews, but on the same level as that of the Bhatias, who also tended to live in congested districts. (The highest death-rate of all was found, not surprisingly, among the Hindu Untouchables – and the next highest among the Europeans. Clearly even the best living conditions on the Island could not necessarily protect those who arrived from England with no immunity against the Indian sicknesses.)

In 1864-5, just to depress everyone further when the financial bubble burst, there was a bad outbreak of cholera; it was the last one, for after this, although general mortality figures fluctuated, going through good and bad periods, cholera itself declined markedly: Lady Fergusson's death from it in 1882 was untypical, and probably tells one something about the water supply at Parel House. Dr Hewlett, writing as early as 1872, believed cholera's sudden decline was due to the fact that the wells and tanks that had previously supplied the city's drinking water had been supplanted, during the 1860s, by connection to the Lake Vehar Water Main (opened 1859). After that no more acute water famines occurred, with desperate poor families scooping muddy slime from the bottoms of tanks, but within a few years Vehar proved insufficient to the needs of the expanding city and had to be supplemented – never quite adequately – by other mainland reservoirs. As early as 1871 over 10,000 houses had piped water, which also supplied 51 new public wells and 51 drinking fountains. These were supposed to replace such older amenities as the well in the Scottish graveyard in Marine Lines, described in the Report of 1872 as 'recently closed by the authorities, its waters upon analysis affording nitrates which were considered the result of animal decomposition'. Closed in theory it may have been, but it is there and in use to this day.

All the wells in the Sonapur district were looked on askance, for obvious reasons, and indeed Hewlett and his Department made strenuous attempts to get the cemeteries there closed and the dead

---

* It has also been suggested to me that their ideological refusal to kill any vermin, including rats and flies, was a factor in their proneness to disease.

sent to some more discreetly remote spot. The Christian community proved fairly amenable, and this was when the botanical gardens at Sewri were made over to the dead, but the authorities made no headway with the Moslems, whose religion dictates that they carry their dead on foot to their resting place. Hewlett found them 'inaccessible to arguments drawn from sanitary science', and the different sects disagreed among themselves anyway. Nor did he have any success in persuading the Hindus to abandon their traditional burning ground: these were horrified at the Municipality's bright new idea that the dead could be carried by a special train to a new site right beyond the Island. Perhaps they objected to the fact that the very same method had recently been adopted as a solution to Bombay's garbage disposal problem.

Garbage disposal, the 'sweepings problem' or, more precisely, the disposal of human excrement, is indeed the dominant theme of the Health Department's successive Reports. Traditionally, and from time immemorial, the ordinary people of Bombay had used the shoreline that surrounded them for the purposes of nature ('the latrine of the entire native town'), but the reclamation and dock-building of the 1860s and 70s forced them to change their habits. Some commentators believed that the decline in cholera must be due to just that, adducing as evidence that it used to be extremely prevalent amongst sailors on ships in the old harbour but was no longer. However, Dr Hewlett was in a position to know that the nuisance had merely been displaced; it was not removed: 'Government has taken away the whole of the eastern foreshore from the inhabitants. Where are the poor people to go to? The houseless and wanderers, the vast numbers who have no fixed place of residence – what are they to do? Nature must be obeyed, in spite of the Police, and the result is that the by-lanes in the City are fouled every night.' In any case, where conveniently accessible beaches still existed, all round Colaba or at Mahalaxmi by the Breach, it was not only the product of the poor that ended up there. Private sweepers employed in residential bungalows to clean the usual offices 'are supposed to take it down to low water mark and throw it into the sea, but too often they simply deposit it behind any convenient rock'. The water closet appears to have been unknown in India at that period – houses in the bazaars and in Girgaum simply had their communal latrines set over ancient cess-pits, as in medieval London, or over primitive gullies that might or might not soak away into the open northbound Town Drain which caused such offence when it passed the Byculla Club on its way out of town.

Although the water closet was coming in rapidly in England at that period its value was still disputed. Some people believed that any general system of water-borne drainage would inevitably contaminate the drinking water supply, and advocated instead a disposal system based on a scientific updating of the earth closet. Ironically, although the water-borne system has become general the world over, the fears of the Jeremiahs have, in some places, proved founded, and Bombay is one of them. The system laid down by the British in Bombay in the 1870s and 80s today co-exists in a confused way with water pipes from more recently constructed lake reservoirs. As everything has to come and go down the same route, from the north, water pipes have been laid alongside old sewers, with results that can be imagined. The situation is worsened by the fact that the insatiable demand for water in modern Bombay empties the mains at certain times of day, and impurities are all the more easily sucked in.

To read the Health Reports of the period when the system of sweepers and defecation on the beach was giving way to more modern practices, is to have a vision of Bombay being progressively submerged in an inexhaustible tide of human faeces. It is clear that Dr Hewlett had something of the same vision. He reported that in 1867 the night-soil collectors had collected a nightly average of 106.3 tons, some in wooden carts and some in 43 lb baskets carried on the head. (An unenviable lot, that of the night-soil collector even if the Hindu system does encourage acceptance of one's place in the scheme of things.) In 1872 the nightly average was 153.8 tons, still some in head-loads but mostly in iron carts sent from England for the purpose. But with a population of 644,405 this was not enough. By Dr Hewlett's reckoning the sweepers 'ought' to be collecting 2½ oz of faeces per person per day plus 40 oz of urine: clearly what was in fact being laboriously collected, taken by special train to Sion and Kurla, mixed with ash and vegetable matter and dumped into salt marshes, was not nearly enough. Hewlett was dubious in any case about the wisdom of the dumping method, particularly as the 'sweepings' were often dumped into holes much nearer to the centre of town: they were, as he said, used in reclamation on Colaba peninsula and on the Flats and in Khetwadi – anywhere in fact, where the sea showed its old habit of creeping in under sea-walls, creating swamps. He advocated a comprehensive system of drainage throughout the Island, as did his successor, Dr Weirs, who wrote in 1876:

The European inhabitants of Bombay can scarcely form any
adequate idea of the sufferings the people in the town endure
from the Halalcore [sweeper] system, and of the disgusting
nuisances that are nakedly exposed to their view every
day . . . Picture to yourself the life of a Hindu gentleman in the
heart of the city. Disturbed in the early morning, long before
sunrise, by the sweepers at work, he gets up and goes to the
verandah in front of his house to breathe the cool and refreshing
air of the morning; but even that comfort – and how dear it is
to all India! – is denied him, for he is driven from the verandah
by the sweepers passing to and fro in front of his dwelling, and
the horrid odours that taint the morning breeze . . . That a city
which advances pretentions to be the first in India should have
so long submitted to such intolerable and loathsome nuisance is
incredible.

In fact Hindu gentlemen – not to mention European
ones – had been submitting calmly to the system for centuries, but
Victorian society was engaged in raising the sanitary consciousness
of its subjects. What was really significant to Bombay was that
Calcutta already had a water and drainage system.

Two years and numerous arguments later – would water-
borne sewage affect the wet docks being planned? Was the sea the
right place for sewage at all? – work started on a pumping station
and outfall at the prettily named Love Grove at Worli, and there
much of Bombay's sewage is disposed of to this day. If it is treated at
all, that treatment is inadequate: no one in his senses would swim in
those waters today, in spite of the tale of the drowned lovers and the
picturesque Hadji Ali mosque on the little islet in the bay.

The swampy parts of the Flats were eventually reclaimed, with
sweepings or with more resistant matter, or at any rate covered over,
to create what is now the northern-central part of Bombay. After
complaints that the district degenerated into 'a squalid Venice' each
time the rains came, storm drains were laid to carry off the excess
water; but the area is so low-lying that the drop from the drains into
the sea is minimal and the water only runs away slowly, like the
contents of a ground-floor bath-tub. If a monsoon downpour
coincides with a high tide the water still builds up to a depth of a foot
or so in some of the main streets, like a ghostly reminder of the
broad creek that once ran there between the rocky islands. Double-
decker buses, bullock carts and pedestrians plough determinedly
through the flood, other traffic stalls and jams. The Municipality
have considered putting in pumps, but have decided that the huge

expense would not be justified for such occasional use. Bombay has not quite conquered the sea after all.

And so, as the nineteenth century neared its end, Bombay continued to grow, northwards and ever northwards, in an *ad hoc*, unplanned and apparently unplannable way. The Bombay Improvement Trust, when it was called into being at the turn of the century, did a certain amount, but it did it for the most part in a rather unimaginative and rigid way – a road cut through here, a block of industrial dwellings there, a couple of new roundabouts – and was no match for the city's basic urge towards expansion. There was still a lot of land to be devoured on the Island itself, though planned railway suburbs on the mainland of Salsette and Thana were one of the favourite projects of successive municipal leaders. Describing north Bombay in 1896 – the year that the plague first reappeared in the city in spite of all the 'improvements' of the previous thirty or forty years – an Indian physician has written:

> Extensive areas like Dadar, Matunga, Sewri, Worli etc. were devoid of any house or roads, being fields or low-lying waste land, with rural conditions prevailing. Even the Parel district, apart from the Parel village, the mills and the two railway workshops, consisted of thick clumps of toddy palms with pathways zigzagging amongst them. As each new mill was built, those date palms had to be cut down to make room for it . . . (P. A. Dalal, in an article in *The Indian Practitioner*, 1959)

Another observer (Sir Edwin Arnold) writing of the same period described a journey through these districts by train – the same ride that Lady Falkland had taken almost fifty years earlier when the railway was first opened. Then, the Flats had been lonely and empty. Now, 'Leaving Byculla station, the traveller threads through the thoroughly "Hindu" suburbs of Parel, Dadur and Chichpoogly, his train flying through groves of date and coconut palms, amid temples, mosques, synagogues and churches; dyeing grounds spread with acres of new-dipped brilliant silks and calicoes; by burning-ghauts and burying places; by mills, stone-yards, and fish-drying sheds, through herds . . . '

Among such continual change, nothing, in essence, changes. The track-side landscape on the ride out of Bombay is still like that today – it has merely been displaced further out, out across the big creeks to the mainland areas of the reservoir lakes and Bassein where Bombay's ex-urban hinterland now lies. There the bright-coloured cloths still lie drying on the stones beside the tracks, there the famous, stinking dried fish of Bombay still hangs in open sheds beneath great trees, there the gaff-rigged country boats that catch the fish still sail the creeks as they did in the time of the Moghuls; the cow-yards and salt-pans that have decorated, in turn, Byculla, Parel, Matunga and Sion, now extend themselves across the marshy spaces of yet further unplanned territories. At one suburban station on the GIP line up to Poona, a brightly painted temple and a countrified railway station, looking as if it should be serving some village in Buckinghamshire or Sussex, stand 'in juxtaposition' among the palm trees as in the Byculla of Lady Falkland's day. But the juxtaposition no longer strikes the eye as incongruous. The railway system, Britain's great gift to India, has become naturalised; today India, the archetypal land of journeys, where people are always travelling for something at any hour of the day or night, or just travelling for its own sake, is far more the land of the train than Britain herself.

As the train finally passes out into open countryside, and the mountains of the Deccan rise up clear and near, small groups of palm-roofed houses appear in the distance, identical to those which, three centuries ago, greeted the traveller standing on the deck of his sailing ship in the sheltered, natural harbour of Bombay.

Epilogue: 'A Real Indian Town'

By the end of the nineteenth century Bombay had taken on the essential form and character that it retains today. Eighty more years have produced considerable further growth, but most of it in the same direction – both literally and metaphorically. By the Edwardian era it was considered a 'world city' and that it remains. Today India, in spite of its much-publicised poverty, is one of the world's largest manufacturing nations, and the Bombay–Poona district is the biggest industrial complex on mainland Asia.

And yet there remains a contradiction in the heart of Bombay, an inbuilt paradox not only in the contrasts of wealth and poverty to be found there but in the bizarre amalgam of eastern and western influences. You might suppose – indeed the pronouncements of the late-Victorian municipality would lead one to suppose – that the more Bombay grew in industry, wealth and importance the more it shed its specifically 'Indian' characteristics. But Bombay was never an 'Indian' town to start with, and in practice its growth has all along been accompanied by a growth in non-European influences: every mill that has been built has created mud-shanties somewhere near to hand; every block of flats that has been built, from the ponderous 'Hindustan Chambers' or 'Dharbanga Mansions' of the high Edwardian era to the glass towers of the present, has attracted into the city yet more up-country people with country standards and country ways. Moreover, many of these people do not become entirely or permanently urbanised. Early this century an observer perspicaciously remarked that whereas the migrants into Leeds or London had, within a generation, virtually forgotten their rural origins and had formed a new urban proletariat, the same was far less

252

true of their counterparts in Bombay – 'the mill-workers are thinking constantly of their native village, and when times in Bombay are bad they return to it'. This is still true today.

People who are more familiar with the smaller, old Moghul towns of Gujerat, or with old Delhi, or who know only the southern, business district of Bombay, consider Bombay a 'westernised' city, but there is little that is specifically western about great stretches of mid and up-town Bombay. Indeed the paradox is that had prosperity deserted Bombay for some reason after 1900, the place would probably appear today much more of a tidy model British town than it does. The *Times of India* in 1904 invoked pious hopes that Bombay would not only 'grow more beautiful' (all those smelly bazaars replaced by covered markets, perhaps, and the shanty-dwellers removed to Model Industrial Chawls?)but that she would in some general way come to resemble more closely 'that parent land which, like herself, is encompassed by the ocean inviolate'. But the commercial pressures on Bombay, and the subsequent general history of India, have made such a hope seem an absurdity. Even at the time, indeed, it was an unrealistically bland view of the place, and more acute observers saw this:

> The Island City is unique – a *diluvies gentium*, a well into which the races of Asia have poured themselves, or perhaps one should say a reservoir out of which they pass as fast as they flow in. It is full of the wealth of the East and the wealth of the West, and of the poverty and vice of both. It has its palaces fit for a prince, and its human kennels unfit for a dog. The hand of Vishnu the Preserver, and of Shiva the Destroyer, are felt in their might daily . . . It is the city of the Parsi millionaire. It is the city of the Plague . . . (Sidney Low, *A Vision of India*, 1906)

Sure enough, as if to remind the Empire builders, the enthusiastic successors to Frere and Crawford, that Bombay was *not* London, Manchester or Liverpool, plague had reappeared in the late 1890s. Some of Bombay's more innocently patriotic citizens believed it was a just retribution for the fact that Queen Victoria's statue had been daubed with paint during the Diamond Jubilee of 1897, but the generally accepted view was that, like the Plague of London two centuries earlier, it was rat-borne. Already the previous year dead rats had been seen in the grain go-downs of the Mandvi district near the docks; and the coolies who worked in those go-downs had been the first human casualties, followed by the grain merchants. The disease spread, and at its height in 1899 over 2,800

253

people a week were dying, and an estimated half of the population of the city had fled back to the countryside where its roots lay, jamming the roads and the railway stations in their atavistic fear.

It was ten years before the Plague really receded, but long before that the population got used to the idea of it and gradually, though people still died of it, life returned to normal. The Improvement Trust was brought into being, some slums were cleared – or at any rate the inhabitants dispersed to create other slums elsewhere – more swampy ground was drained, more rice-paddies were turned into streets, more houses were built, more blocks of flats, more chawls, more villas with names like 'Sunny Home' and 'Anand Mahal', more houses, more houses, more *houses* . . . But the Plague was remembered. It is still remembered. Never again would any municipal government feel sure that the oriental nature of Bombay was quite under control, or that the past could not return. And indeed why should they?

Already, in what is now considered nostalgically the Edwardian heyday of the Empire, the ideas that had called it into being were passing. When George V and his Queen visited India in 1911 for the Delhi Durbar that was in fact the ending of an era. And when the Gateway to India was belatedly (in 1927) erected on Apollo Bunder to commemorate their visit, what the Government was unbeknown erecting for itself was not a triumphal entry-arch but a place of exit: the very last British troops to leave India at Independence marched through the Gateway to their launches and thence to their ship home a mere twenty years later.

It has sometimes been said that nothing about the British conduct of their Empire became them like the leaving of it. Certainly, in the case of Bombay, the British did not leave an orphaned place, an illegitimate child that could not fend for itself. Bombay, at any rate, could flourish without them, she no longer needed them: perhaps for a long time she had not really needed them. And even at the time of George V's visit this fact was, to a discerning visitor, already apparent. The Editor of the *Westminster Gazette*, visiting India in the Durbar press party, wrote:

> In spite of the alien rule, Bombay strikes you as eminently belonging to itself, as being in fact a real Indian town; and as remote as possible from a British colony. This, perhaps, is the greatest tribute that can be paid to the English who made it, or at least made it possible.

Select bibliography

Arnold, Edwin, *India Revisited*, London, 1886.

Aurther, T.C. [Arthur Crawford] *Reminiscences of an Indian Police Official*, London, 1894.

Ballhatchet, Kenneth, *Race, Sex and Class Under the Raj*, Weidenfeld & Nicolson, 1980.

Bellasis, M., *Houourable Company*, Hollis and Carter, 1952.

Bence, Mark, *Palaces of the Raj*, Allen and Unwin, 1973.

Boman-Behram, B.K. and Confectioner, A.N., *The Decline of Bombay*, Bombay, 1969.

Brown, Hilton (ed.), *The Sahibs*, Hodge, 1948.

Buckland, *Dictionary of Indian Biography*, Swan Sonnerschein & Co., 1906.

Burford, R., *Decription of a view of the island and harbour of Bombay*, London, 1831.

Burnell, J., *Bombay in the days of Queen Anne*, Hakluyt Society Series II, Vol. lxxii, London 1933.

Burnett-Hurst, A.R., *Labour and Housing in Bombay*, King & Son, 1925.

Chaudhuri, Nirad, *A Passage to England*, Macmillan, 1959.

Chittar, S.D., *The Port of Bombay: a Brief History*, privately published, Bombay, 1973.

Claridge, G., *Old and New Bombay*, Bombay, 1911.

Cox, H.E., *The Story of St Thomas's Cathedral*, Bombay, 1947.

Cross, Wilbur (ed.), *The Journal to Eliza and Various Letters by Laurence Sterne and Eliza Draper*, Taylor & Co, New York, 1904.

Dalal, P.A. *Bombay in 1896*, in *The Indian Practitioner*, 1959.

David, M.D., *History of Bombay 1661-1708*, University of Bombay Press, 1973.

David, M.D., *John Wilson and his Institution*, John Wilson Education Society, 1975.

Deshmukh, Cynthia, *Bombay Cottons On-A Case Study of the Economic Revolution in Bombay . . . 1850-1914*, Heras Institute publication, undated.

Dobbin, Christine, *Urban Leadership in Western India: politics and communities in Bombay City 1840-85'* Oxford University Press, 1972.

Douglas, James, *Bombay and Western India*, Sampson Low, Marston & Co., 1893.

Drewitt, F. Dawtrey (ed.), *Bombay in the Days of George IV: Memoirs of Sir Edward West*, Longmans Green, 1907.

Dyos, H.J. and Wolff, Michael, *The Victorian City, Images and Realities*, Routledge & Kegan Paul, 1973.

Dyson, K.K., *A Various Universe*, Oxford University Press, 1978.

Edwardes, S.M., *The Rise of Bombay*, Times of India Press, 1902.

Edwards, Michael, *Bound to Exile: the Victorians in India*, Sidgwick &

Jackson, 1969.

Edwards, Michael, *East-West Passage, the travel of ideas, arts and inventions between Asia and the Western world*, Cassell, 1971.

Epstein, William H., *John Cleland: Images of a Life*, Columbia University Press, 1974.

Falkland, Amelia Lady, *Chow Chow*, Hurst and Blackett, 1848.

Forbes, James, *Oriental Memoirs*, Whiter Cochrane, 1813 (revised edition, Bentley, 1834).

Forjett, Charles, *Our Real Danger in India*, Cassell, 1878.

Fryer, John, *A New Account of East India and Persia, being nine years' travel 1672-81*, London, 1698.

Gardner, Brian, *The East India Company*, Hart Davies, 1971.

Graham, Maria, *Journal of a Residence in Western India, 1810*, edited and published by Constable, 1912.

Grose, John Henry, *A Voyage to the East Indies, with Observations on various parts there*, London, Hopper and Morlay, 1757.

Haris, Frank, *Jamsetji Nusserwanji Tata: a Chronicle of his Life*, Blackie and Sons, India, 1958.

Harris, Nigel, *Economic Development, Cities and Planning: the case of Bombay*, Oxford University Press, Bombay, 1978.

Jackson, Stanley, *The Sassoons*, Heinemann, 1968.

Jacobs, Jane, *The Economy of Cities'* Cape 1970.

Karkaria, R.P (ed.), *The Charm of Bombay: an anthology of writings in praise of the first city in India*, Taraporevala, Bombay, 1915.

Kulke, Eckehard, *The Parsees in India: a Minority as an Agent of Social Change*, Vikas, India, 1978.

le Faye, Deirdre, article on Jane Austen's relatives in *Review of English Studies*, New Series, Vol. *XXX*, No. 17 (Feb. 1977).

Leith, A.M. *Report on the Sanitary State of the Island of Bombay*, Bombay, 1864.

Lethbridge, Roger, *The Golden Book of India*, Macmillan, 1893.

Maclean, J.M., *Guide to Bombay* editions of 1875-7, 1879-80, 1886-90 and 1902, Bombay Gazette Steam Press.

Masani, R.P., *N.M. Wadia and His Foundation*, Popular Books, Bombay, 1961.

Manshardt, Clifford, *Bombay Today and Tomorrow*, Taraporevala, Bombay, 1930.

Mason, Phillip, *Skinner of Skinner's Horse, a fictional portrait*, Deutsch, 1979.

Masselos, J.C. *Towards Nationalism: group affiliation and the politics of public associations in nineteenth century western India*, Popular Books, Bombay, 1974.

Masselos, J.C. *Bombay in the 1870's* article in *The Journal of South Asian Studies*, No.I, University of Western Australia Press,

Mitter, Partha, *Much Maligned Monsters*, Oxford University Press, 1977.

Moorhouse, Geoffrey, *Calcutta* , Weidenfeld & Nicolson, 1971.

SELECT BIBLIOGRAPHY

Morris, James, *Pax Britannica: the Climax of an Empire*, Faber, 1968.

Mottram, R.H., *Traders' Dream: the Romance of the British East India Company* Appleton Century, New York 1939.

Mudford, Peter, *Birds of a Different Plumage*, Collins, 1974.

Murray, John, *Handbook for India*, Murray, editions of 1859, 1880, 1887.

Nightingale, Pamela, *Trade and Empire in Western India 1784-1806*, Cambridge University Press, 1970.

Noorani, A.G. Bombay, article in *Imprint*, August 1977, published Bombay.

Ovington, J., *A Voyage to Surat in the Year 1689*, edited by H.G. Rawlinson, Oxford University Press, 1929.

Postans, Mrs Marianne, *Western India in 1838*, Saunders & Otley, 1839.

Pulsaker, A.D. and Dighe, V.G., *Bombay: story of the island city*, Bombay, 1949.

Roberts, Emma, *Overland Journey to Bombay*, London 1845.

Sheppard, Samuel T., *The Byculla Club*, privately printed in Bombay, 1916.

Sheppard, Samuel T., *Bombay Place-Names and Street Names*, Times of India Press, 1917.

Sherwood, Mrs Henry, *Autobiography*, London, 1854.

Singh, Nihal, *The Development of Bombay*, published by the Development Dept.,? 1925.

Sinha, Pradip, *Calcutta in Urban History*, Calcutta, 1978.

Smith, George, *The Life of John Wilson*, Murray, 1878.

Spear, Percival, *The Nabobs*, Oxford University Press, 1932.

Stevens, G.W., *In India*, Blackwood & Sons, 1905.

Stocqueler, J.H., *The Handbook of British India*, W.H. Allen, 1854.

Strizower, Schifra, *The Children of Israel: the Bene Israel of Bombay*, Oxford University Press (India) 1971.

Sullivan, Raymond J.F., *One Hundred Years of Bombay: the history of the Bombay Chamber of Commerce, 1836-1936*, Times of India Press, 1937.

Trevelyan, G.O., *The Competition Wallah*, Macmillan, 1864.

Wacha, Sir D.E., *Rise and Growth of Bombay Municipal Government* Madras, 1913.

Wacha, Sir D.E., *Premchand Roychand*, Times Of India Press, 1913.

Wacha, Sir D.E., *Shells from the Sands of Bombay-My Recollections and Reminiscences 1860-75*, Bombay, 1920.

Wadia, Ruttonjee Ardeshir, *Scions of Lowjee Wadia*, Bombay, 1964.

Wilbur, Marguerite Eyer, *The East India Company and the British Empire in the Far East*, Richard R. Smith, New York, 1945.

Wilkinson, Theon, *Two Monsoons*, Duckworth, 1976.

Unpublished theses

Pramar, V.S., *Wooden Architecture of Gujerat*, D. Phil. & Arch. submitted to the MS University of Baroda 1980 (available in the Library of the Museum of Mankind, London).

Vicziany, A.M., *The Cotton Trade and the Commercial Development of Bombay 1855-75*, Ph.D submitted to London University, 1975.

Anonymous works

Life in Bombay and the neighbouring out-stations, Bentley, London, 1852.

Bombay Ilustrated: Her Resources, Industries and Commerce, Times of India, 1940.

Indian Railways, One Hundred Years, Government of India, 1953.

Regional Plan for Bombay Metropolitan Region 1970-91, Bombay Metropolitan Regional Planning Board, 1974.

The main source are the Government of Bombay publications, viz. the Gazeteers, especially the *Gazeteer of the Bombay Presidency: compendium of Information*, in 28 vols, published in Bombay 1882-4, and the *Gazeteer of Bombay City and Island*, in 3 vols, published in Bombay 1909-10, and largely compiled by S.M. Edwardes. See also: *Bombay Presidency: Selections from the Letters, despatches and other state papers preserved in the Bombay Secretariat: Home Series*, 2 vols, 1887.

In addition to the above printed works, use had also been made of certain MS sources held by the India Office Library, London, viz: *Bombay Public Consultions*, esp. for the years 1864-6 *Bombay Municipal Report*, 1827-6. *Bombay List of Tombs and Monuments*, 1901, revised 1912.

The archives of the Heras Institute, St Xavier's College, Bombay, contain a collection of mostly undated and sometimes untitled pamphlets, privately printed, written by J.R.B. Jeejeebhoy. I have made use of: 'The Parsees of Bombay', 'Rash Driving in Bombay', 'Bombay Green', 'The Duke of Wellington', 'A Short History of Mahim' and 'Social Activities of the Bombay Government House' (1932) among others. I have also been privileged to read and quote from an extensive collection of MS notes and cuttings, mostly unattributed, compiled by J.R.B. Jeejeebhoy at the same period, and currently in the possession of Mr Jamshed Jeejeebhoy.

In the archives of the Centre for South Asian Studies in Cambridge, I have consulted and made use of: The Forbes papers, the Terry letters, the Stewart papers, the Kenyon papers and the Jameson papers ('Journal of a Voyage to Bombay, 1820').

I have also made use of newspaper archive material, in particular the *Bombay Gazette* and *Bombay Times* (India Office Newspaper Library, Bush House, London) and the *Bombay Builder*, July 1865–April 1869 (Patent Office Library, British Library).

Index

INDEX

INDEX

INDEX

INDEX

INDEX

Lightning Source UK Ltd.
Milton Keynes UK
UKOW05f2336240117
292822UK00008B/226/P